The
Human Resources
Software Handbook

The Human Resources Software Handbook

Evaluating Technology Solutions for Your Organization

James G. Meade

Pfeiffer
A Wiley Imprint
www.pfeiffer.com

Published by Jossey-Bass/Pfeiffer
A Wiley Imprint
989 Market Street, San Francisco, CA 94103-1741 www.pfeiffer.com

Acquiring Editor: Josh Blatter
Director of Development: Kathleen Dolan Davies
Developmental Editor: Susan Rachmeler
Editor: Rebecca Taff
Senior Production Editor: Dawn Kilgore
Manufacturing Supervisor: Becky Carreño
Cover Design: Bruce Lundquist

ISBN 978-1-118-33633-5

Library of Congress Cataloging-in-Publication Data

Meade, James G.
    The human resources software handbook : evaluating technology
solutions for your organization / James G. Meade.
        p. cm.
Includes index.
    ISBN 0-7879-6251-1 (alk. paper)
    1. Personnel management—Software—Handbooks, manuals, etc. 2.
Personnel management—Computer network resources—Handbooks, manuals,
etc. I. Title.
    HF5549.A27 M43 2003
    658.3'00285'53—dc21   2002008890

Printing 10 9 8 7 6

In memory of Margaret Byrd Rawson, 1899–2001
Friend, Mentor, Collaborator
Dyslexia luminary and passionate developer
of "human resources"

Contents

List of Figures, Tables, and Exhibits

CD-ROM Contents

Documents

Sample Needs Assessment Report [Exhibit 5.1]

Sample Vendor-Suggested Needs Analysis [Chapter 5]

Project Planning Sheet [Chapter 5]

Vendor Supplied RFP Questions, Example 1 [Chapter 6]

Vendor Supplied RFP Questions, Example 2 [Chapter 6]

Sample RFP [Chapter 6]

Sample Standardized RFP Response [Chapter 6]

HRIS Product Demonstration Script [Exhibit 7.2]

Sample Selection Checklist [Exhibit 9.1]

Sample Selection Questionnaire [Exhibit 9.2]

Sample Selection Table [Exhibit 9.3]

ROI Report [Chapter 11]

Sample Implementation Plan [Chapter 12]

Software Demos

Abra—HRIS. This is the traditional low-end market leader. Check it out to see the most common features in an entry-level HRIS.

Employease. Click the link to see the leader in web-based "rental-only" solutions for the low-end and mid-market.

Genesys. Known for taking on tough problems, Genesys does both payroll and HRIS.

HR Microsystems—HRIS. This PowerPoint view will give you a flavor of a long-standing mid-market HRIS with a loyal customer base.

HR Office. Take a trial run with this thirty-day version of a low-end and mid-market product strong in handling benefits, attendance, and more.

iVantage. Try out this longstanding mid-market product in this pure Web version.

MyHRIS. Here's a link to a mid-market player with powerful features besides the standard HRIS capabilities.

People-Trak—HRIS. One of the "big three" in the low end, this product is moving solidly into the mid-market as well. Strong on both capabilities and pricing.

Perfect Software—HRIS. Try out this familiar, strong player in the HR mid-market.

RMS Software—HRIS. Try a nice, low-cost HRIS for the low end. The trial version includes all of the features of the full version of HRmgr, except that it restricts the number of employee records to five.

SkillView. You need some background before you try out an actual hands-on demo. This PowerPoint presentation can help you understand this specialty product for skills management. When you're ready, the vendor will set you up with a demo.

!Trak-It HR. Try out a popular low-end HRIS product.

!Trak-It Applicant. Try out this low-end applicant tracking package.

Visual 360. See what it's like to automate performance management.

Acknowledgments

A book of this scale is never the work of one person but of many. I would like to thank as many as possible of those people directly and tip my hat as well to all who have helped me over the years by providing demos, interviews, and "scuttlebutt" about the HR software marketplace.

Thanks to Lori Woehrle, who originally asked me to prepare the book, and to Carol Bowie, who guided me in an early stage. Thanks to Maureen Sullivan of DBM for assistance in choosing the best publisher. Above all, I want to express appreciation to the publishing team at Jossey-Bass/Pfeiffer—acquisitions editor Josh Blatter, director of development Kathleen Dolan Davies, developmental editor Susan Rachmeler, assistant editor Samya Sattar, and all those who design, produce, and distribute this book.

As always, my gratitude to Nina, my guiding light, and to Molly, Ben, and Josh.

The
Human Resources
Software Handbook

Introduction

"Scuttlebutt." It may seem a strange word to describe human resources (HR) software selection, but, in one sense, selecting HR software is all about scuttlebutt. "What is the *real* story about this software?" you want to know as you plunge into the process of purchasing HR software. What is the word on the street? Vendors make their claims about themselves, and those claims are informative to some degree. But vendors, as the name suggests, are salespeople. They do not give the whole story.

But when you decide on software to which you plan to make a major commitment, you want to know the whole story. "Does the software solve real problems?" you want to know. "Does it have hidden costs?" "Are those who have purchased it happy with the result?" "Is the company sound, or is it facing rocky times?" To some extent, at least, you want to know the scuttlebutt—not what the company wants you to believe but what you actually should believe. You want to be able to balance your potential vendor's perspective with the opinions of competing vendors and to evaluate all the information systematically—a process defined for you in this book.

This book is for HR folks taking the plunge into HR software or the plunge into new versions of software already in place. Often people want to select software themselves, but they need a few pointers about how to start. This book provides those pointers. People want to know the methodology other companies are using. This book provides that methodology. People want to be up-to-speed quickly, as if they have been searching for HR software for some time (even though they may be just beginning). This book acquaints people with the latest "buzz" and the substance behind it.

This single volume is the first of its kind in helping people feel comfortable, in fact quite at home, in the diversified and rather dizzying world of HR software. So many products compete for your attention. So many companies come and go. So many methodologies offer themselves as essential steps in the process. People want to know enough about the marketplace to feel confident in venturing into it themselves. This book provides that confidence, and it provides the tools for stepping through the marketplace and reaching a reliable decision.

Not only do you want to know the truth, but you want the truth *for you.* Truth varies from user company to user company. That is, the right product for someone else is not always the right product for you. A human resource information system (HRIS) that is ideal for a pharmaceutical manufacturer may not work at all for a small, nonprofit legal firm. One company's needs differ dramatically from those of another company.

"Scuttlebutt" may not tell you what is right *for you,* but it may help. You can find out what is going on in the marketplace and what needs show up at other companies. You can find out the needs that software tends to address, then compare those needs with your own. One year, for instance, the scuttlebutt has everyone looking for Internet products, and companies realize they have a need for Internet-ready software. Another year a backlash has set in, and people arc looking for in-house, client/server software. You may choose to follow the current trend or not to follow it. But it is helpful to know the trend in either case.

Scuttlebutt can be most helpful, too, for answering perhaps the most difficult question of all in selecting HR software. Purchasing companies simply do not know where to start. Not only do purchasers want to know which are the best suppliers of, say, software for tracking benefits. They want to know which companies are suppliers at all. They want to know the names of companies to start with (that is, they want the word on the street). Given a few names of companies that are lively and competitive at the moment, users can often follow through on the rest of the selection process themselves.

Buying HR software, after all, is not that different from buying a kitchen stove, a PC, or a car. You find out what is popular at the moment. You check a few references to see if there is a good reason for the popularity. You listen to sales pitches, do a few comparisons, negotiate, get approval from whoever controls the purse strings, and make a purchase.

In many respects, then, the scuttlebutt is all you need to launch you as you select your own HR software. This book is not a gossip book about the marketplace, at least not primarily. It is a compendium of the latest "word on the street" about how to go through the selection process and which products to look at as you do so. It is a practical guide to "getting real" in selecting HR software . . . to going past the hype to what matters most to you as you make your selection.

WHO SHOULD READ THIS BOOK

The book is for HR folks planning to purchase software. People in HR, although knowing a great deal about HR, generally do not know that much about HR software. HR, after all, is not information technology (IT). Human resources is about people, not machines; and you can spend a long career in HR without spending much time at all finding out about HR technology. Many companies perform their HR activities without using the latest technology. They use the telephone. They use manila folders. They meet people in person. And they track information on Excel worksheets, in word processing files, or in their own memories.

However, HR technology has been with us for fifteen or more years and has become amazingly streamlined and valuable. For example, you can certainly find candidates by advertising in the Sunday paper and collecting paper resumes. But can you find them just as fast by advertising on a Web job board and having people respond directly to your website? Can you move a candidate through the selection process as quickly and efficiently without applicant tracking software as you can with it?

This book begins with the market for smaller, less-expensive software and works its way up . . . rather than working in the other direction, from the large companies down. A company of any size can benefit from this book. However, the largest companies—Fortune 50 companies—tend to have committees and processes and purchasing departments in place for the kind of activity described in this book. Those companies can pick up a good deal of "scuttlebutt" from this book and should refer to it. But smaller and mid-sized companies (from one hundred to ten thousand employees) are most likely to find in this book the guidance they need but may not have been able to find anywhere else. Small and mid-sized companies may not have standing departments for conducting software searches. They may not have procedures in place for the search. Yet they want the results, and they do not want to leave out an important step simply because they have not been through the process before. This book targets, especially, those small and mid-sized companies and departments or divisions of large companies looking toward the purchase of their own software.

WHY I WROTE THIS BOOK

The surge in human resources software has happened rather quietly. Fifteen years ago, HR software was rare except at the largest companies. One or two providers seemed to control the marketplace. Now the marketplace is bulging with more than two thousand HR software packages. Human resources software is so quiet, though, that the news about market size might come as a shock. Unless you did a bit of research, you might think there were just three or four HR software providers—giant PeopleSoft and one or two others. The surge has come about quietly while HR has been diligently going about its business of counseling folks and providing regular reports. The software has come into being, but no roadmap has been there to help people navigate among all the possibilities . . . or even to recognize that the possibilities are there.

This book has come about in response to the need for just such a guidebook. People face these risks:

- They can miss out on the many possibilities and simply make a quick decision, which might well be a wrong decision;

- On the other end of the spectrum, they can be so overwhelmed by the possibilities out there that they can be virtually paralyzed . . . and again may make a quick decision rather than a considered decision;

- People can fall victim to a number of "gotchas" in the marketplace and become overwhelmed by sales pitches and never get a clear view of the market;

- They can fail to plan properly for implementation . . . and find themselves spending two or three times what they expected during implementation.

The gotchas exist. The book helps identify them.

The HR marketplace is made up of sophisticated business people. Human resources folks can be sophisticated buyers. But they have lacked basic tools and guidelines to help them be sophisticated purchasers of HR technology. This book addresses that need.

WHAT IS IN THIS BOOK

You will find essentially three useful kinds of information in this book:

- *How-to information.* A more-or-less formal process has evolved for evaluating and selecting HR software. As consultants and purchasing departments have purchased such software over the years, they have learned steps that work particularly well and others that may sound good but may not work so well. This book recounts the present state of the art for selecting HR software. A needs analysis, for instance, works quite well. A formal Request for Proposal (RFP) does not work so well. This book shows how to conduct a software analysis, from beginning to end.

- *Specific information about products and companies.* Like many other fields such as basketball or the opera, HR software has a collection of commonly known information (what I have referred to in this introduction as "scuttlebutt"). In the world of basketball, for instance, people know that a team with Michael Jordan on it is likely to be a competitive team. In HR software, certain products are major players. You almost have to consider them. Others are aspirants. Others may not even belong on the court, although this book does not generally contain such judgments.

  This book does provide a head-on look at a number of specific products in a number of major categories. You can find out specific information about specific products, and about strengths and weaknesses of those products. You may read, for instance, that "this product is good for companies committed to Microsoft" or "this product is particularly good for companies in the health and service sectors." As you look into real information about real companies, you begin to discover your own preferences and re-evaluate your own needs. Specific information is gold in the search for HR software, and you will find it here.

- *Analysis of the information.* Vendors provide information about themselves, and you will find that information here. Analyzing such information is a separate challenge altogether. Consultants, competing vendors, and users do analyze HR software products, and this book passes along conclusions from them. "This product is excellent if you are looking for outsourcing," they may conclude about one product, or "this product is technically rich but not very well-known" or "this product is strong but is available for purchase only, not for rental." You not only receive information but are allowed to look behind the information. Such analysis is useful for specific products but also useful for culturing the habit of thinking analytically as you go into the marketplace.

HOW THIS BOOK IS ORGANIZED

The organization of the book is as simple as I could make it. The book is meant to guide you through the chronological process of evaluating and selecting HR software. Here is a description of the parts.

Part One will help you warm up and give you an overall feel for the HR marketplace. That marketplace can be overwhelming in its size, dizzying in its choices, and bewildering as to the simple question of "What is it?" In this part you will become familiar with the marketplace, the players, and the software features and functions you will be examining. You gain the confidence to launch into your own software search knowing that you have "the lay of the land."

Part Two provides you with a step-by-step guide through the latest process for evaluating actual software. You will see how to define your needs (a much overlooked step), how to gather the right information from vendors, how to script a meaningful demo, and how to check references to best advantage.

Part Three introduces you to best practice in what is generally considered the "crunch time" of software selection. You will find out how to "pull the trigger" on your choice of software, how to negotiate in ways that benefit you without damaging the deal, how best to get management on your side, and how to prepare for an implementation that will live up to your expectations.

In Part Four you plunge right into a look at vendors of HRIS systems for smaller companies. We introduce the players, show product strengths, and provide some gentle caveats. The section is helpful both for its information on specific vendors and for the way it allows you to become acquainted with specific criteria you can use with any vendor.

Part Five continues the process that began in Part Four, this time with an introduction to vendors for mid-sized companies and larger companies, as well as specialty vendors and those in the once explosive e-recruiting sector.

An appendix lists the software vendors from the book, their products, and information on how to reach them.

A CD-ROM has working versions of selected HR software programs. The products are restricted in one way or another. Usually, they expire after thirty days, but they allow you to try out the real products to begin to see what they can do for you. Also on the CD-ROM are useful tools such as sample RFPs, questions you might ask vendors during the selection process, and a sample report showing return on investment (ROI) for purchasing an HR software system.

HOW TO USE THIS BOOK

This book provides the information you need in more-or-less chronological sequence, but I invite you to use it in the way that suits you best. The book is a reference tool. You do not have to read it end-to-end. Looking for tips on mid-market HRIS software? Just read the chapters dealing with that subject. Want to know about conducting an RFP (request for proposal)? Check out the section on RFPs. Plan to bone up on trends in the marketplace? Read the chapter on that topic.

If you are looking for an overall briefing, though, you can begin at the beginning of the book and move on through to the end. Even if you read sequentially, you do not have to read everything. If you are looking for highlights, you'll find plenty of bulleted lists, figures, tables, and other materials to help you summarize information quickly. As you read through the book, you will find yourself gaining an awareness of the marketplace and growing in sophistication as a buyer. You may find precisely the product you need or just the tip you were looking for. On the other hand, you may simply acquire a kind of savvy about the marketplace overall.

Do not feel confined to any one fixed way to read the book, just as you cannot expect a single, fixed answer to the question, "What software should I select?" What you read depends on where you are in the selection process. You will find that this book will support you whatever approach you are taking—whether a "guerrilla warfare" approach to the marketplace—where you grab information here and there as you need it—or a systematic approach—where you gather all your materials and proceed methodically.

A NOTE FROM THE AUTHOR

I have been writing HR-related software reviews for over ten years and am not affiliated with any vendor. As a consultant and writer in the HR marketplace, I occasionally prepare written materials for vendors or—as the situation may demand—advise or consult in other capacities. Such in-depth work with client companies sharpens my knowledge of companies and of the HR marketplace as a whole. Companies have not paid to appear in this book; I have selected them on the basis of my opinion of their merit and their potential value to you, the reader.

Many may think of the search for HR software as a dry, businesslike process. To me, however, it is an adventure and quite a bit of fun. The software promises to transform your business, and the search itself takes place with an air of expectation around it. The technical community has invested billions in creating this software, and it is rich. As you sort through the software, you are likely to find yourself enjoying the search almost as much as you will later enjoy the fruits of that search. As you search, you need guidelines. You need hard information. You need as much scuttlebutt as you can find, because the word on the street tends to have a special value of its own. You need systematic processes to go beyond the scuttlebutt. And you need a companion to cheer you and guide you through the entire process. This book meets those needs.

Getting Started

"Where do I start?" is a natural question for anyone addressing the need for HR software. In this part, you will find answers to that tough question. You find out the right questions to ask as you begin your software search, trends in the industry that you may want to follow, key features and functions to look for in HR software, who some of the vendors are, and guidelines on using consultants—what they can do for you and whether you need them.

A Few Key Questions

Selecting HR software. Do you really want to do this? Chances are you may not, in some respect. You've been doing your HR in some way until now. Perhaps you've already automated with technology and worry that you're out-of-date. A surprising number of HR folks, though, haven't automated at all. Estimates vary. Recent research by one company showed that up to 90 percent of smaller companies did not use HR software. They just kept track of things with slips of paper . . . well, OK, with file folders and maybe some spread-sheets. Paper piles up for you, and it may take weeks to put together a report on something like "How many employees do we have?" If you can handle that one, maybe you run up against a wall with, "How much are we spending on compensating each of our different types of employees?" You've heard about HR software, and it seems like a great idea—if it's all selected already, and running, and being used, and getting results. However, the idea of going from here to there—from no software to smooth-running, powered up automation—is a somewhat ominous prospect . . . one of those "put-offable" things that you have been putting off now for a decade or two and can just as well put off for another decade or two until you retire.

But maybe the whole process doesn't have to be quite as daunting as the experts make it out to be. In this chapter I look at some of those nagging questions that are probably in your mind before you even start. And I attempt to lay some of your doubts to rest. You can do this.

DO I EVEN NEED HR TECHNOLOGY?

In all likelihood, yes, you need it. If you're small enough, you don't really need it, but small here means really small—perhaps ten people or fewer. Most experts I know put the cutoff point at fifty or even one hundred. That is, when your company hits those numbers, you can't do it all with spreadsheets any more. Even the small companies, however, can benefit from software that saves time, keeps employees happy, avoids mistakes, saves money, avoids lawsuits, and provides a competitive business edge.

The International Association for Human Resource Management (IHRIM) recently summarized the reasons why a company might turn to HR software for tracking benefits. In my estimation, many of the criteria apply pretty well no matter what category of HR software you may be considering. Here are some of the IHRIM points, from a "An IHRIM Go-to-Guide (G2G)," published in 2001.

You should power up, according to the guide, under these conditions:

- When HR is bogged down in administrivia;
- When your HR staff spends 60 to 70 percent of its time on employee questions;
- When you want your HR professionals to concentrate on strategic work;
- When you want employees to take charge of their own HR management;
- When employee productivity is a major concern;
- When your enterprise lacks a competitive advantage;
- When your company is struggling to recruit and retain employees;
- When HR administration is not considered a core competency but should be;
- When you want to transform HR and take leadership;
- When HR seeks a leadership role in knowledge management;
- When your company is extremely cost-conscious;
- When you want to replace legacy systems with new millennium technology;

- When you are not using Internet tools to integrate and streamline applications; and

- When lack of company experience or expertise suggests outsourcing.

"In other words," according to the white paper, "e-benefits is an appropriate solution at almost any time, for almost any organization." I would say the same for almost any form of HR automation—for tracking employee data, training, performance, salary, or you name it.

WHERE DO I START?

If you have taken even a glimpse at HR software selections—at a trade show, in talking with vendors, or even in talking with HR folks—you have probably had a chance to reach the standard condition for someone seeking HR software. That is, you're probably bewildered. How could you not be? First of all, think about how many software packages there are to consider. You'll be amazed. Human resources, after all, is a straightforward function. There ought to be three or four packages to choose from, right? Wrong.

Comprehensive software for the complete HR function—complete HRIS software—is one category. In *The 2000 Personnel Software Census, Volume 2—HR Information Systems,* editor Richard B. Frantzreb catalogs more than 150 such systems, from AIM Technology, Inc., through JAMLogic to the inevitable Zebra Software, Inc. One hundred fifty comprehensive HRIS packages. That is a considerable number.

As for specialized products, the list has grown "like Topsy." Whereas Frantzreb's initial catalog in 1984 contained about two hundred products, by 1999 Frantzreb was describing twenty-five hundred HR software products, and he didn't even claim to have found them all. "The real universe is closer to 3,000 products, from about 1,700 vendors," he said at that time, and the number has been growing. Expanding. Mushrooming. Barely dimmed by occasional economic downturns. As an indication of how much specialized software is available, here is a list of main headings in the Contents of Frantzreb's *The 1999 Personnel Software Census:*

- Employment Management

- Relocation Management

- Equal Employment Opportunity

- Training Management
- Instructional Design
- Conference/Meeting Management
- Career Development
- Performance Management
- Skills Management
- Human Resource Planning
- Organizational Development
- Organization Planning
- Personnel Policy
- Survey Processing
- Employee Communications
- Labor Relations
- Safety
- Health
- Employee Scheduling
- Attendance/Timekeeping
- Payroll
- Misc. Personnel Software

If you are not bewildered when you start the process of selecting HR software, you become that way quite quickly. Often people don't even know about the Frantzreb volume. They dive in thinking they will get to the core quite quickly. Instead, they dive into a pool that has no bottom. It's definitely on the overwhelming side. However, with a few guidelines like those in this book, you can dive into the process of selecting HR software and come out unscathed. In fact, you can come out holding software products that enrich your job and make you more effective besides.

DO I HAVE TO GO THROUGH A "PROCESS" HERE?

You don't need an MBA to buy a car, do you? But people have long felt that they have to have one to purchase HR software. For large companies, an elaborate process makes a good deal of sense. You form committees. You include people from the appropriate departments—someone from IT, someone from top management, someone from finance, someone from HR, someone from payroll. You hammer out selection criteria. You prepare forms to express those criteria, and you receive information in return. You meet to evaluate the returned information. On and on. You get the idea.

"Extensive and elaborate evaluation and selection processes were developed by consultants and were widely employed to assist companies in the needs analysis and in the evaluation process," explains Jim Spoor in a white paper titled "Fresh Perspectives on Evaluating and Selecting an HR System for Small and Mid-Sized Organizations." Spoor, president and CEO of SPECTRUM Human Resource Systems Corporation, continues, "These early stage evaluation and selection processes included elaborate in-depth interviews with senior executive staff, studies of corporate needs and expectations, analysis of the requirements of existing and/or changed business processes, a review of the information and process requirements of strategic corporate and HR initiatives, and detailed analysis of desired areas of change. Getting through this highly structured process required the broadly based involvement of not only high priced consultants but also large numbers of internal company staff from many sectors of the organization."

That was then. According to Spoor, "What it is important to recognize today is that the HR systems industry has matured substantially. It is no longer a nascent, early stage industry. Systems from all of the well-established and longer term vendors have now reached a mature state and content is no longer a major differentiating factor."

Spoor is, of course, a vendor himself, but it's difficult to see a major flaw in the argument. You just don't have to go through the painstaking evaluation process you needed ten years ago. In other words, you don't have to suffer the "evaluation shock" that has no doubt kept many small and mid-sized companies from entering the arena at all.

You still do have to be systematic in certain respects. You should indeed follow a process—a logical, chronological process with clear criteria and clear results. You probably should not completely "shoot from the hip" in selecting your HR software. But you don't have to look upon the process as so detailed and so tedious that you just would never do it. The simple steps in this book are enough.

Following are the standard steps to follow in software selection:

- Do some up-front research on HRIS systems (orient yourself);
- Obtain generic buy-in from management that you should be pursuing selection of an HRIS;

- Develop a needs analysis;

- Develop an RFP (optional);

- Develop a demo script;

- Schedule demos with a small number of vendors;

- Develop a selection matrix to compare the vendors;

- Make a selection;

- Negotiate an agreement;

- Obtain buy-in/approval from all involved, especially management;

- Develop an implementation project plan; and

- Go to it.

HOW MUCH IS THE PROCESS GOING TO COST?

In the old days, the process probably cost more than the software. People's time is valuable, and at that time you would have had to include many others in the process. You needed HR's participation, obviously, and you may have needed the time of multiple people from the HR department. You needed to involve top management. Talk about expensive time. Every hour a top manager spends in a software selection meeting represents a significant dollar investment. You had to meet at each stage of the process—to define needs, to set criteria, to sit through a demo and another demo and more, to evaluate the information from each product demonstration, to do a comparative analysis of all the demonstrations. You had to meet to set negotiating criteria, and you had to meet to evaluate the responses to the criteria.

The process, with such a business model, could cost you a good bit more than you wanted to spend. However, in the mature market for HR software, you can shortcut the process in a number of ways. You can fairly quickly arrive at a viable list of providers, such as those suggested in the later stages of this book. (You can always be on the lookout for the aggressive new provider on the block, and you can still find such folks, of course.)

You can minimize the time of many of the key players. For example, IT can verify that the software provided matches with the systems you have in place. Such input needn't require hours and hours of time, though. Top management can take the "management by exception" approach and simply respond to major difficulties that arise. In most cases, top management won't need to be convinced that HR software is a viable consideration but simply that it is viable for your company.

In today's marketplace, you still have to invest some employee time—but a good deal less time than you did five years ago. The time involved is affordable. Besides, during selection, people become informed about the products and begin to become skilled at using them. It is time well-spent.

HOW DO I DEAL WITH VENDORS?

Vendors are all the same. It's all "me, me, me." If they weren't like that, they wouldn't be vendors. An HR trade show, particularly one with many providers of HR software, can sometimes seem like an open-air bazaar where merchants hawk their wares and "let the buyer beware." Vendors often pass along rumors that such and such other vendor is about to go bankrupt or is about to be acquired or has suffered a major management shakeout. Vendors will seek any edge.

By following even a rudimentary process, you protect yourself from being overwhelmed by vendors. Let them know that you are gathering material from multiple sources, that you go through an approval process internally, and that the "quick close" is not likely. Gather material systematically, and don't be shy about placing restrictions on the vendors. For instance, you can spell out exactly what you want the vendors to demonstrate for you. They'll deviate from your script, but the script allows you to say, "Come back to this point."

In the mature marketplace that HR has become, you can be reasonably certain that you are dealing with viable providers—vendors who are not just marketing a concept and some preliminary code but a market-tested product. Check references. Review a company's reputation. Involve IT if you plan to go with a new provider without the standard credentials. But proceed with confidence. The HR marketplace now has a large number of understanding, civilized vendors who will compete based on the quality of their products and not through tricks or other devious means.

HOW LONG IS ALL THIS GOING TO TAKE?

Don't think of HR software selection as a two- or three-year process. It used to be that, in the time when the vendors themselves were figuring out what to provide and the software purchasers had little clue about where to begin.

Larger companies are probably well-advised to take some time for the process. The investment for them is a major commitment, possibly of millions of dollars. Whoever makes the decision has to be accountable and has to be able to demonstrate the basis for the decision.

Smaller and even mid-sized companies, though, can decide in a matter of months, not years . . . perhaps even three months or so. Most of the products will meet common basic needs. Only a few will meet a particular specialized need you may have (such as that the product be completely Web native, or that it be 100 percent Microsoft, or some other strong criterion). You can narrow the search quickly and often reach a decision and obtain approval just as quickly.

"BUT I DON'T KNOW ANYTHING ABOUT TECHNOLOGY"

Human resources has always previously been the "people place." Human resources has been considered the workplace for people who deal with "softer" matters, such as employees who are getting married or having babies. Human resources leaves the numbers to accounting and IT. "How can an HR person decide about technology?" people used to wonder.

Times have changed. First of all, HR is rarely as "all thumbs" about technology as it used to be. Most people use a personal computer and do things on the Internet. Many have become reasonably sophisticated and can sort items on a spreadsheet, send mail to multiple recipients, do an advanced search on the Internet, and prepare a PowerPoint presentation. Human resources is no longer as computerphobic as it once was. On the other side, too, things are better. As HR has become more sophisticated, technology has become easier and easier to use. If you can point and click with a mouse, you can probably find out for top management who its top performers are, how much the company spent on benefits last month, and who has unused vacation time for last year.

Despite the large number of products, the wide variety of HR software products doesn't constitute the "Tower of Babel." In the initial days, companies tended to have to define their own "look and feel." Increasingly, the look and feel have become standardized. "Microsoft owns the desktop," Spoor notes. If you have been using Microsoft Word or another Microsoft desktop product, you probably need no instruction in using the menus, keystrokes, and shortcuts of many of the HR software products. Those that may still have a proprietary look and feel of their own generally have plans to move into a "Windows" look and feel before long.

Even those in HR who for some reason may not yet know Microsoft's Office products probably are familiar with their own Web browser, and often that is all the technology they need to be able to use to enjoy the capabilities of their HR software.

On the back end—the computers and networks that HR software runs on—the complex connectivity problems have begun to go away as well. Increasingly, larger companies use client/server networks based on Microsoft SQL or Oracle databases. Other products tend to be at least compliant with one of the familiar ones. If a company is using some other operating environment, generally connectivity is available to allow an HR system to share data with the company's operating environment.

WHAT SHOULD I DO FIRST?

Often these days the quest for HR software begins with an e-mail sent down from top management: "Shouldn't we have something like this for our company?" Top management recognizes that it can control head count with effective HR software. It can increase employee satisfaction with tools like employee self-service that let employees sit down at any time, even in the middle of the night, and manage their 401(k)s or make decisions about benefits. Top management can bring HR onto the management team by empowering it to answer key questions such as, "With the kind of personnel we have on hand, what makes sense for our company as a strategic direction in the new economy?"

If you have top management's buyoff, you have taken the right first step in your process of selecting software. Without such buyoff, the whole process can go for naught. Top management certainly has a few doubters, even in this day and age, and it is the job of top management to insist on being convinced: "Do we need this, and why?"

A good place to start would be to find out top management's stance at your own company on the question of "Do we need HR software?" If you have buyoff, you're off to the races and can do everything else recommended in this book. If you don't have buyoff, the process of software selection, for you, becomes primarily a process of "management convincing." You have to put together the right information and the right suggestions to convince top management to support you. (Or you have to be able to start on using such software within your current departmental budget, with no top management approval required.)

CONCLUSION

If you're thinking about HR software selection at all, then you're probably grappling with some of the kinds of questions set forth in this chapter. The bad news is that, yes, such questions do exist. The good news is that things have grown better and better. The software marketplace has become standardized in many respects, so that you don't have to worry as much about being able to find what you need. At the same time, multiple vendors assure that you can still play providers off against one another and enjoy all the benefits of competition and free enterprise.

The reasons for *not* starting the search for the right HR software used to outweigh the reasons for starting. People just put off that move to power up their people processes. Today, the reasons for starting significantly outweigh any reasons for not starting. You just may be amazed at how much it can do for your company, for the people you support, and—incidentally—for your own career. The technology can save you time, and acquiring the software doesn't have to be the headache that it used to be. As a matter of fact, contemplating the possibilities and powering up your people processes can be fun.

First, you may want to take a look at some of the trends around the HR industry so that you can feel up-to-speed with the industry. The next chapter describes some of the trends affecting HR software and tells why you may find them important.

Knowing the Trends

A s someone wanting to select HR software, why would you care about trends, right? You have some needs, and you want to fill them. You're a realist, not someone who is fashion conscious. Well, there are a few reasons you probably would care:

- Trends, particularly technology trends, often point in the direction of genuine breakthroughs that lead to competitive advantage. Years ago, many argued that nobody needed Microsoft Windows, that MS-DOS was enough. But Windows was a coming trend that won out. Following the trend was not a bad idea.

- Those who ignore trends can find themselves antiquated in ways that may matter. They may have difficulty connecting with other new technologies. Upgrades may be difficult. Networked personal computers made mainframes, to some degree at least, outdated (though not entirely obsolete). Internet-based software had a similar effect on client/server (networked) computers, although client/server networks continued to perform in the background.

- Trends can indicate where you can save money and be more competitive on the business side. In some companies, HR is beginning to show companies where to excel in such matters as "time to hire" or in performing a quality, well-designed restructuring. Companies that ignore such trends may suffer in plain, old bottom-line efficiency.

- Trends are lots of fun. There is a buzz about them. Starry-eyed new vendors raise venture capital and come in, waving their hands and saying, "This is going to change the world." Listening to the pitch from such people is inspiring, and sometimes they are right. At a minimum, their arguments are informative.

With such practical business reasons in mind for viewing trends while selecting software, I hereby share with you a few of the trends I have observed in recent years in HR:

- Social and economic trends;
- Outsourcing the HR function;
- HR as a "strategic partner";
- From "human resources" to "human capital management";
- HR becoming more technically savvy; and
- The Internet becoming an everyday tool.

Note that such trends inevitably turn on their heads. The specific trends are outdated almost as soon as you name them. The underlying patterns continue, though. By reviewing trends, you inevitably become familiar with market currents you will want to swim in effectively as the times change. The following sections explain the trends, all of which influence how HR thinks about technology and what it selects as it implements technology.

SOCIAL AND ECONOMIC TRENDS

First of all, social and economic trends have immeasurable effect on the HR marketplace. You never know what is going to happen next, and whatever happens can change everything. For years, during the upward economic swing of the 1990s, expansion was everything. Of course, before that expansion, and sometimes during it, terms like "downsizing" defined the mood of the world and of the HR marketplace. Both trends—boom and bust, upward and downward, expansion and contraction—seem to have an ever-present influence on HR. Whenever one is the trend, the other is always lurking as a countertrend.

September 11 created whole new patterns in HR. Security, always a concern, became an utmost priority. Previously, background checking has been a narrow niche of HR software, an earnest voice crying out to be heard from companies like HireRight and Avert.

An economic downturn in 2001 and afterward similarly reawakened thoughts of "downsizing" and "restructuring" in the world of HR. Human resources tools that had been vehicles for recruiting in a competitive hiring place were redesigned as powerful mechanisms for re-deploying the existing salesforce and for intelligently and legally laying off some of the workforce.

One company, for instance, is competing for qualified IT people, who, at times, are in short supply. The company's competitiveness, even its very survival at those times, depends on the success of its staffing efforts. Under pressure itself, the company cannot help but put pressure on its HR people. "We're being measured on time-to-hire, cost-per-hire, quality of the hire, and a lot more," an HR person at the company relates. Software, of course, is key to performing such measurements in a timely, effective manner. Software also is the key to being able to live up to the standards of such measurements. The company has adopted software with enthusiasm and a spokesperson admits, "They call me the 'automation queen.'" But she has adopted software not just because she is attracted to it. She sees little choice. Says this HR manager of other HR departments attempting to become automated, "If they don't get there, they will be outsourced. They have to do it. There isn't a choice."

OUTSOURCING THE HR FUNCTION

Human resources often has to wear the label of being "overhead." Human resources is not a direct profit center. It doesn't sell products. It doesn't develop products that others can sell. It keeps the salespeople and developers running smoothly, but companies often see the HR function as too far removed from the front lines. Its functions are essential, but often companies are willing to pass those functions along to an outside company rather than keep them in-house.

Outsourcing offers all kinds of advantages. Larry Morgan, a senior manager with Grant Thornton LLP in Appleton, Wisconsin, for instance, in a slide presentation lists these reasons to outsource:

1. Extensive regulations [for HR to track];

2. [HR is now] technically complex, difficult to keep current;

3. [HR] requires expertise generally not found in smaller organizations;

4. Companies don't want to staff up to the level required;

5. [HR is] too labor-intensive, not value-added enough; and/or

6. Outsourcing does it better, faster, cheaper.

Let's briefly consider each of the reasons. First, federal and state regulations such as Equal Employment Opportunity legislation and Occupational Safety and Health Administration are becoming so complex that you almost have to be an attorney to administer them well. The consequences for failing to follow them can be disastrous in penalties to the government for noncompliance or, possibly, in sums paid out for litigation.

Second, as a field that is evolving technically, HR is now taking on new dimensions faster than before. For example, recruiting alone can require both business and Internet expertise and a good bit more than that. In addition, HR takes on new responsibilities frequently, such as adopting new methods for reviewing performance or moving into the role of assessing skills and managing skills for the entire workplace.

Third, especially in smaller organizations, the HR person has come up through the ranks without having specific, professional training in human resources. Such a person can handle day-to-day administration and help employees with ordinary requests such as, "How much sick time do I have available?" But as those companies face the challenges of Internet hiring or the intricacies of selecting HR software, they may want to move beyond their internal "non-specialist" HR person. The choices would be to train the HR person, hire additional people with the needed skills, or to outsource. Often outsourcing seems the fastest, easiest, and least expensive choice.

Fourth, outsourcing avoids the entire question of staffing up internally to meet rising HR needs. Yes, your company must pay up-front and pay on an ongoing basis for the outsourced services, but the outsourcing company already has the needed staff available, or at least the outsourcing company can do the worrying about where to find such qualified staff.

Internal HR departments do offer a number of advantages. Internal HR people know their own company and its unique culture. Internal HR is directly accountable to company management and therefore often more responsive to that management. Internal HR is closer to the company's own employees, often helping maintain morale (and thereby lowering turnover).

Because outsourcers can afford to keep the latest technology and know the latest management techniques, they receive a quick payback in greater profits for their business efficiency. They can be lean, mean human resource machines. Rather than attempt to be as lean and mean internally, companies often simply choose to outsource.

Observes consultant John Hagerty, research director of enterprise applications with AMR Research in Boston, "A lot of day-to-day [HR] tasks will disappear even more so than now. They will be put into the hands of the person who can do them effectively." The old "personnel" activities of handing out forms, collecting completed forms, and passing out routine information such as benefits available will in many cases simply become the responsibility of outsourcing agencies or, as I discuss later in this chapter, of the employees and managers themselves.

HR AS A "STRATEGIC PARTNER"

Pressures on HR, then, are in some cases even sending HR functions outside the walls of the company. The pressure is also transforming the nature of the HR department that continues inside the company. "Advances in enterprise resource planning (ERP) systems, an array of human resources management systems (HRMS), workflow, self-service, computer instruction, and Internet-based training are drastically changing the structure and role of the HR department. They're transforming human resources professionals into internal consultants and analysts who must understand technology and what it can do for the business," says Samuel Greengard (1999).

For example, Moore (1999) talked about intranets and employee self-service. In the article, Ed Lawler, director of the Center for Effective Organizations at the University of Southern California, is quoted as saying: "If HR manages this well, it will allow them to become more of a business partner. However, if HR isn't up to the task of giving expert advice, it will essentially go away."

Morgan of Grant Thornton sees an overall evolution in the nature of the HR function, from the old personnel function to a corporate cop role that might help avert litigation to the emerging role as a "strategic resource." Human resources is no longer just a record keeper but an intelligent, contributing member of the management team.

In his IHRIM visioning article, Spoor (2000) sees HR moving into what he calls a "workforce management function." He says, "The newly framed workforce management function will still be responsible for assuring that many of the traditional HR needs are met but, more importantly, it will be much more involved in the strategic business planning processes."

Says Spoor in an interview, HR will take a "much stronger role in assisting line managers in optimizing all aspects of the workforce." What will HR do? Noting that the workplace is critically short of skills, Spoor says, "Until the labor market has an adequate supply of those skills, HR has to be very innovative in identifying and recruiting those skills. Also, [HR has to be innovative] in developing internal staff, and doing that in ways that allow the company to achieve a return on its investment. HR now needs to be much more strategically involved in identifying what are the needs, how do we meet those needs, and then how do we retain those people so that they can provide a return on our investment."

Even standard reporting on HR information takes on strategic value as HR provides the information to decision makers. Morgan (1998), for instance, notes some of the HR reports management often needs as the basis of sound, strategic decisions:

> "Fortunately, human resource software is available to help you answer questions such as:
>
> - "What is my current headcount?
> - "What is my payroll or benefit cost?
> - "How long does it take me to hire a new employee?
> - "When is Susan's next performance appraisal?
> - "Do I have any employees who can speak Portuguese?
> - "What is our rate of employee turnover?
> - "What was the average merit increase given to salaried employees last year?"

By seeing in black and white the answer to the question "How long does it take to hire a new employee?" for example, management has the basis for finding ways to shorten the time and, thereby, can help the company compete for skilled workers in today's marketplace. Information from HR can also help point to causes of the problem if the time to hire is too long. Does it take too long to have requisitions approved? Does it take too long to locate qualified applicants? How effective is classified advertising?

Human resources, too, can identify solutions, such as more effective advertising, a streamlined requisition process, internal training programs that can fill positions from within, and other solutions. With effective reporting, HR becomes a strategic partner that presents information in useful ways instead of simply a department that passively collects information.

FROM HUMAN RESOURCES TO HUMAN CAPITAL MANAGEMENT

Human resources is currently showing signs of a trend to becoming "HC" or "HCM" (human capital management). Spoor suggests one of the typical questions HR is now being expected to answer: "Based on what we know about our people and their performance, what are the best indicators and predictors of individual performance?"

PeopleSoft Fellow Row Henson, in an interview with the author, suggests another question HR is now becoming equipped to answer: "Does our workforce makeup fit our business strategy?"

Eric Lane, vice president and chief talent strategist with Icarian of Sunnyvale, California, suggests yet another question that the new, analytical HR ought to be able to answer: "Do we really lack talent, or are we not doing a good job of defining what we need?"

A question from the world of recruiting might be this one, suggested by Mark Lange, vice president of marketing and business development with BrassRing Systems in San Mateo, California: "How many people are we losing in blown first interviews, and why?"

Benchmarking, once a specialized undertaking for advanced MBAs, is now becoming mainstream for the "human capital management" professional. According to benchmarking pioneer Dr. Jack Fitz-enz, founder of the Saratoga Institute of Santa Clara, California, benchmarking allows companies to ask not just "What is our cost to hire?" but "How does our cost-to-hire compare with other companies in our region or in our industry?"

Another HCM term enjoying widespread popularity is "balanced scorecard." Identified with Robert S. Kaplan and David P. Norton of the Harvard Business School, the approach is a complete, analytical tool for the organization. Says Doug Reed, vice president of human capital management at SAP America, Inc., of

Cincinnati, "[The approach] sets up strategies and goals for the organization for all levels, from the overall organization down to the team and the individual. It sets up 'management by objective' and ties rewards to measurable results."

HR BECOMING MORE TECHNICALLY SAVVY

How does a once-clerical function become a strategic function? Instead of just collecting information, as mentioned, it collects meaningful information, analyzes that information, engages in planning, and presents valuable approaches ("strategies") to the rest of the management team.

Whereas in the late 1980s HR people may have been in many cases the classic "computer-phobics," they have in the ensuing years become increasingly technical. One HR manager interviewed by this author has been using software to offload some of the mundane tasks HR previously used to address. What is the department doing with its newfound time? "We don't have any extra time," she notes. "The staff we have added has a different skill set [from previous HR employees]. We added a very strong technology person. We added a person strong in Web-based recruitment. We have looked to see how we could be more efficient and effective by utilizing technology."

Previously, HR departments turned to the IT department for hand-holding in technical matters. Although IT continues to be an advisor to HR in technical matters, HR is taking more and more responsibility for its own human resource software, and even the underlying hardware. Existing HR personnel are becoming more computer savvy, and HR departments are hiring people with more technical know-how. The result is increasingly technical HR departments.

Bill Roberts (1999) quotes Steve Hitzeman, a former HRIS practitioner and now senior consultant at Watson Wyatt Worldwide, a Bethesda, Maryland-based benefits, human capital, and HR technology consulting firm: "HR systems support HR; they don't support IT. HR is the driver for the system. They should be the ones who are developing priorities for functionality and enhancements, how it will be used, who gets to use it, and what data will be kept there."

Concurring that HR is now quite capable of manning its own systems, Jim Witschger, president of Technical Differences, Inc., in Bonsall, California, makers of People-Trak HRIS software, has put out a paper titled "HRMS Software—Myths and Reality." One myth he addresses is the common understanding that "HR software requires constant IS involvement." Says Witschger, "Some HRMS software may require constant IS involvement, but a well-designed and well-implemented product should not. If you are not getting constant IS involvement with your system now (manual or automated), you should not need it with a new automated system, unless of course, the software is poorly designed, poorly conceived, and/or poorly implemented."

Spoor, too, sees HR becoming more self-sufficient technically. "The real issue," says Spoor (2001) boils down to an operational issue of 'To what extent does HR want to be dependent on other resources that are also serving other departments?' "

When HR is dependent on another department, such as IT, often HR is not the first priority for that IT department. Truthfully, HR is likely to be the lowest priority. Reports that might take a few minutes if HR could do them may take days or may not be done at all if HR has to wait for IT to do them. It makes sense for HR to become technically self-sufficient, and it is beginning to move in that direction.

THE INTERNET BECOMING AN EVERYDAY TOOL

The Internet has burst on the HR technology scene like a tidal wave. Its influence is impossible to minimize, even in a world that is seeing a considerable backlash against the initial "dot-com" rage.

The Internet, first of all, means that everyone in the company around the world can access the same software, readily, using a standard interface (the browser) that everybody knows. Besides standardizing the browser interface, the Internet solves problems of the "back end" as well. End users do not have to know what kinds of contortions a service provider may be going through to make information available on the Internet or an intranet. The end user simply uses a browser and accesses the information. Increasingly popular are application service providers (ASPs), who offer their services over the Internet for a fee. When using an ASP, HR users don't even have to face the problems of setting up their own hardware systems or making their HR software work with an existing system. They simply use their browser and work over the Internet. The service provider solves all technical problems and keeps the software current.

Whether offering software through an ASP or through other licensing and pricing arrangements, the Internet is revolutionizing HR software. "I see almost a frenzy on the part of software vendors to either web-enable existing products or create native Internet or intranet applications. It's the biggie. Everything pales in comparison to that," says Frantzreb in an interview with the author.

The Internet, as mentioned, makes software easy to use. Also, because people can use their familiar Web browsers, training costs for Internet software are often less than for non-Internet products. Internet software can be much cheaper to end users than software they purchase themselves, and often users can avoid or minimize costs for software maintenance, software support, and purchasing new versions. Internet software in a special form, as a company intranet, has other special advantages for HR. Security is much tighter than on the Internet, allowing HR to post and distribute information within the company that it may not want to share with the outside world (such as information on areas where the company is falling short of expectations).

The Internet is opening an entire world of e-cruiting and e-commerce that goes well beyond the "simple" world of installing and using software. In the world of recruiting, job boards like monster.com are far faster and more powerful than classified ads for locating qualified candidates. Electronic searches on the Internet help companies wend their way through applications much more successfully than before. Internet "portals" provide a whole range of services beyond simply supplying resumes by collecting in one place a number of related websites for recruiting activities. Beyond portals are newly emerging hiring management systems, which not only help you find useful sites but in fact walk you through the complete hiring process.

On the Internet and intranets, employee self-service and manager self-service have gone from being buzzwords used by a few companies to being commonplace. With employee self-service, employees can enroll in benefits over the Web, instead of requiring the HR person to conduct the enrollment for them. Employee self-service doesn't just save administrative time. It improves the quality of service to employees. "The biggest change I notice," says an HR manager, "is that [employee self-service] enables employees to have the necessary information regarding the various benefits plans, to enable them to make informed decisions about their changes [when they enroll]."

With manager self-service, managers can themselves do such tasks as managing new hires, changing employee salaries, or planning compensation without having to involve the HR professional. The result, again, can be better service to both the managers and employees and higher productivity and morale at the company.

Yet, every trend has its countertrend. While companies continue to develop Internet products, vendors continue to have success with products that are not Internet-based. The ASP model, for all its benefits, means that you are renting and not buying. You don't control the central technology or, at least, you share control with someone who is providing it. Some people prefer to purchase their own software and use it in-house rather than rent it and use it over the Internet.

CONCLUSION

As noted at the beginning of this chapter, those who adopt the new technologies find new power and stature available to them. Those who ignore them risk being outsourced before too long. Some, in smaller companies and less fast-paced industries, may continue to be effective using manual methods. Certainly many continue to do so.

As Grant Thornton's Morgan put it at the end of one of his presentations, "Those who fail to keep up with the new technology need only ask one question: 'Do you want paper or plastic with that ma'am?'"—because they will find themselves unqualified for professional work in HR. Things aren't so bad most of the time, of course. In any case, HR software is there as an easily mastered tool to power up HR and turn it into whatever the trends of time should require it to be.

Knowing the trends in HR and in HR software help prepare you for selecting HR software. Such trends as the move to strategic planning in HR, the move to the Internet, and the increasing popularity of analytics might well influence your choice of software. The real process of software selection begins when you start to look at actual software. The next chapter helps you start looking at actual features and functions in HR software.

Previewing HR Software

You'll often hear advisers in HR selection say, "You have to do a thorough needs analysis before you can select the right software for yourself." What many in the HR industry have observed, though, is that people like to do a little window shopping even before they do the needs analysis. By seeing what's out there, they accomplish two key steps:

1. A little pre-shopping creates a realistic picture of what to look for. If you're shopping for an oven, and you need one that does microwaving for the first hour, then switches to standard baking, you're out of luck if nobody makes such a thing. If you feel that an amphibious vehicle would best suit your needs when buying a car (perhaps your office is on an island), you have a problem if the only place to purchase such a thing is from your nation's armed forces. If you start out by defining totally unrealistic needs, you create headaches for yourself and for the vendors.

2. On the other hand, and perhaps even more important, seeing what's out there may well help give you a good idea of what to look for, even as you define your own needs. After all, companies and vendors have evolved the products on the market over years, even decades, of "survival of the fittest" in the marketplace. You may not have thought about the need for an Internet-based product, for instance. When you see that the Internet is

arguably the best way for a company with multiple locations to meet its needs, you may decide that, yes, an Internet product is what you need. Or you may never have thought about allowing employees to review their own insurance and investment options at any time. When you see that many vendors provide such a thing, you may see its advantages for your own company and quickly set it up as a need.

A little bit of window shopping before you buy orients you to the marketplace. It warms you up, educates you, and even inspires you. In this chapter, you first glimpse a few HRIS products from the low-cost sector of the market. Here, ideally, you can gain a view of the possibilities in a simple enough form for you to have a feel for the marketplace. Then I enrich the mixture a bit by showing you the offerings from several mid-market players. You also should get a feel for specialty players, and here you can see what is available from a few of them.

Human resources data, ultimately, is for HR reporting. The number of possible reports is literally infinite. And the one that your manager wants is almost always one from that extended set of possibilities you do not yet have on hand. Nevertheless, a quick survey of the reports from one program gives you an idea of what you can accomplish with HR reporting. Finally, I'll offer some ways to find software vendors.

CHECKING OUT FEATURES OF LOW-END PRODUCTS

In my opinion, the best way to orient oneself to the various HRIS products without getting "feature shock" right away is to sit down with a product or two or three and just play with them. If you haven't been using an HRIS at all, then such time will be well-spent. The world of HR automation will open up, and you'll begin to see what all the fuss is about. "You mean, I can have all this at my fingertips?" you are likely to find yourself asking. Fortunately, a number of vendors are more than willing to make it easy for you to go on a test drive. In fact, in the age of the Internet, quite a few products are available for testing.

Here's a tip from my point of view: Whenever you can, do a real test drive yourself, and don't just settle for a PowerPoint presentation or a Flash (Web) demo. Programs are interactive, and you get the best feel for them when you, too, interact. Makers of the smaller products will often let you try out a time-locked version of the product, generally for thirty days. Makers of the products for the mid-market often let you sign up online for a temporary demo password.

A nice, simple product that allows you to orient quickly is Abra Suite from Best Software (a division of Sage). Abra long had the reputation of being the leading seller in software for smaller companies, and it earned the reputation at least in part because of its ability to keep a finger on the pulse of the marketplace. Abra is a good place to look for what might be typical in the HR marketplace. It also has an attractive interface that you can readily see and understand. Figure 3.1 shows a picture of the main screen.

Notice that the main areas of activity in tracking HR data are these:

- Human Resources
- Payroll
- Attendance
- Applicant
- Training Management

Figure 3.1. Abra Suite Opening Menu

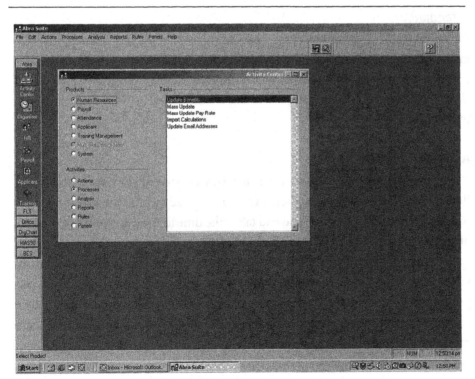

- System

- Employee Self-Service

As you're about to see in the world of HR software, if you haven't seen it already, the possibilities for data are almost unlimited. Human resources, after all, is information about your people. You could track employee shoe sizes, if you wanted. You could track psychological profiles (as complex as those might be). The bulleted items in the above list, though, represent more or less a mainstream of the key kinds of information you are likely to track in an HRIS system. Here's a brief explanation of some of the modules.

Human Resources

This section is the heart of any HR software system except a specialty product (such as one for planning succession or analyzing compensation or any of a multitude of other activities). Here you track an employee's personal information (name, address, job title, cubicle number, EEO classification, favorite movie from the 70s, whatever).

Attendance

Almost no subject, other than pay, seems to interest employees more than "How much vacation time do I have, and when can I take it?" Here you track that information. Attendance isn't always a main module in HRIS programs, and it isn't always available. Abra is probably reflecting the marketplace nicely by including it, though.

Applicant

Applicant tracking may well be the roller-coaster ride of the new millennium. Before just a few years ago, applicant tracking tended to be something of a lesser priority. Generally, by the time you had taken the time to track an applicant's history of applying for the job, he or she had already found a job (often with someone else).

The Internet transformed the whole category of hiring into a highly stream-lined, often Web-based affair. HRIS providers like Abra found themselves hard-pressed to include applicant tracking or else fall behind the competition. When economic times slowed, though, so did interest in the now indispensable applicant module for all general HRIS programs.

Training Management

Training management, like attendance, is not always a firm requirement at all companies looking for HRIS software. But most products offer it. With the training management module, you can track the training programs an employee has attended, programs that ought to be attended, and overall programs available. Sophisticated programs may analyze employee skills or competencies, identify gaps in those competencies, and specify training programs to lead employees on an upward career path to specific objectives (such as vice president of accounting).

System

Generally called "system administration," such a module is a necessary evil for every HR program or, for that matter, just about every software program. Some program has to offer the ability for someone to go into the inner workings of a program, fix things that break, change things such as the offerings available on certain menus, and generally fine-tune and maintain the program. The HR person is not always the one to use such a menu option, although often at least one person in the HR department becomes proficient at maintaining the system.

Another product you could install and play with on your own is People-Trak from Technical Difference, Inc. Figure 3.2 shows the main screen for the program, with its main modules displayed.

Note that the modules are similar to those from Abra, although not identical. The modules are these:

- Personnel
- Applicants
- Requisitions
- Job Profiles
- Contacts

If you open the Personnel module, you see a screen that more or less reflects the guts of any HRIS program. (See Figure 3.3.) The program lists data fields you can use to create a multitude of reports. In fact, if you look at the choices across the top, you see that the second menu item is "Reporting."

As you become more and more familiar with a product like People-Trak, you find that you can gather more and more information in often surprising ways. Not

Figure 3.2. People-Trak Main Screen

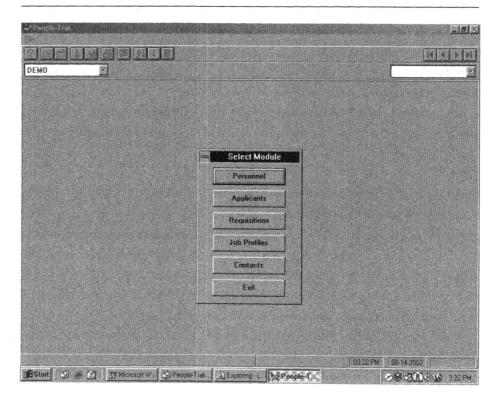

only can you send out letters, for instance, to job applicants, but you can also trace the history of information you might want, such as a history of the previous positions a person has held.

Pure Internet-based products are another group of low-end products. One such product, Employease Network from Employease in Atlanta, is available on a rental-only basis. Figure 3.4 shows its main screen. Graphic tabs along the top guide you into your main HR activities—benefits, HR, employee, reports, and others such as employee and manager self-service.

SEEING WHAT MID-MARKET PRODUCTS OFFER

When you move into the mid-market, you find products that may still work in the same categories as the more introductory products. But these advanced products offer much more information and allow you to retrieve it in more powerful ways than the low-cost products. At least the intent is that the more expensive

Figure 3.3. People-Trak Personnel Module

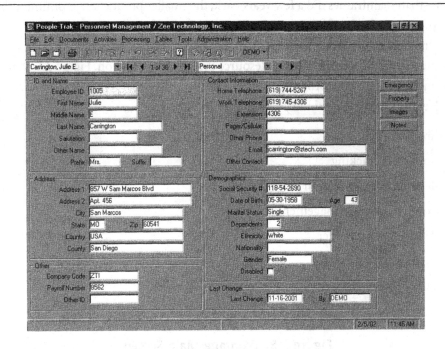

Figure 3.4. Employease Main Screen

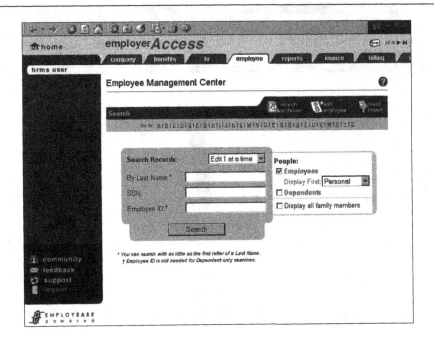

products provide more power. As in the world of PC hardware, where PCs now do more than mainframes did a few years back, the smaller products are continuously nipping at the heels of the larger products in terms of product capability.

One nice mid-market package that can give you a feel for what is available is iVantage from Spectrum Human Resource Systems Corporation. Figure 3.5 shows the main screen of the program.

Here is a list of the primary capabilities in iVantage:

- Absence Tracking

- Applicant Tracking

- Benefits Administration

- Compensation Management

- Person Record Finder

- Qualification Tracking

- Salary Planning

Figure 3.5. iVantage Main Screen

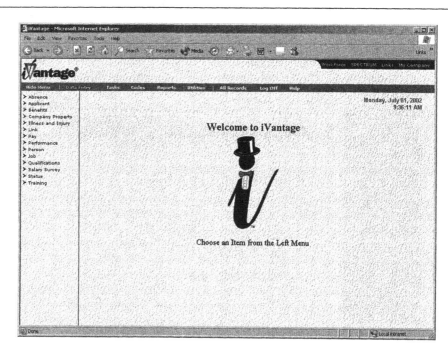

- Training History
- Governmental Compliance
- Query Tools
- Security Roles
- Unlimited History

A number of other companies vie for leadership in the mid-market, such as Ultimate Software, hrWindows, Best Software, and NuView Systems. Figure 3.6 shows the menu for the Personnel Module of NuView's MyHRIS.

Choices in the module include the following:

- Basic Info
- Pay
- Payroll
- Background

Figure 3.6. MyHRIS Personnel Module Menu

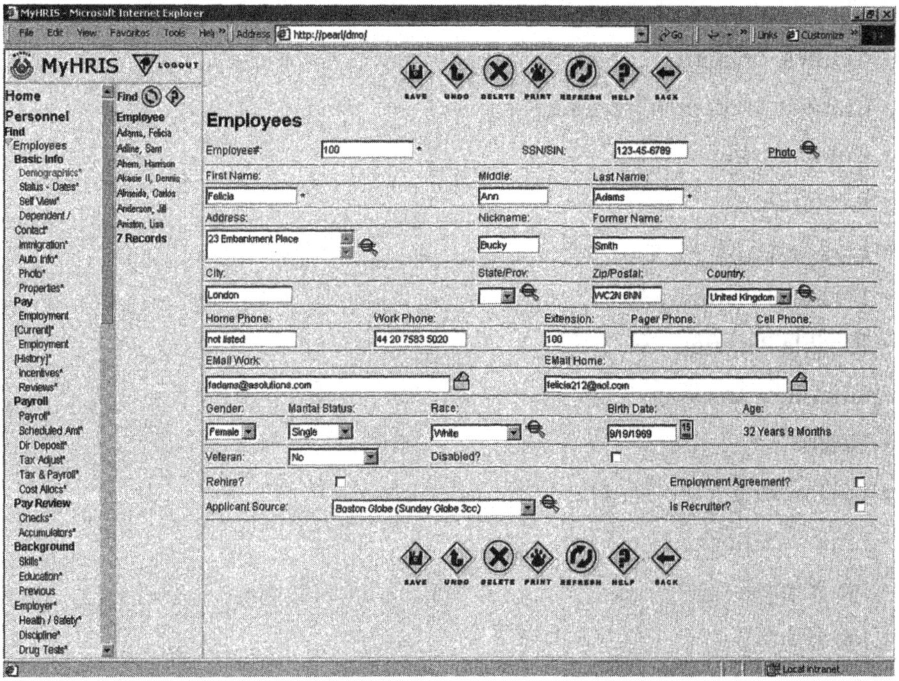

- Benefits
- Time/Attendance
- Investments
- Training
- Development
- Termination

Although the basic categories tend to parallel those in the introductory Abra module, there are more categories, and the amount of detail available is greater. As you begin to use the product, you discover such things as skills-based analysis of an employee, used in succession planning and in training administration.

Another mid-market product, hrWindows from PerfectSoftware, offers the following quick summary of the areas of interest for which its product stores data:

- Applicant Management
- Benefit Statements
- Benefits Administration
- Cafeteria Benefits
- Client/Server
- COBRA Tracking
- Company Property Tracking
- Compensation
- Education
- EEO and AAP
- Financial Planning
- Flexible Benefits
- Grievance Tracking
- Health
- I-9 Tracking
- Import/Export
- Job Analysis
- Job History

- Life/Accident Insurance
- Medical Insurance
- Multiple Job/Cost Centers
- Organizational Development
- Payroll Interface
- Position Control
- Review Forms
- Safety
- Salary Administration
- Salary Analysis
- Salary History
- Site Replication
- Skills Tracking
- Terminations
- Training
- Vacation Accruals
- Wellness
- Workers' Compensation
- Other

The listing from hrWindows is more detailed than those I've provided from other mid-market vendors, but the chances are that any of them would provide all of the information listed here. The general conclusion is simply that mid-market HRIS providers supply a great deal of information having to do with almost anything to do with the professional life of your company's employees.

WHAT TO EXPECT FROM A SPECIALTY PRODUCT

HRIS products are comprehensive products that just may meet all of your needs. Specialty products are focused on a single area. In general, such products have the advantage that all specialists have. They are focused, and that focus is more in-depth into a particular business activity than a general product is. Again, as in the question of small versus larger HRIS providers, vendors in the field dispute the claim that the specialty products can outdo the general products. You have to reach your own conclusions after evaluating competing products. Following are examples of three specialty products.

HR Tools Applicant Tracking Software from Archer Software, shown in Figure 3.7, is a highly affordable program with a simple mission—to help you track applicants.

The program is a simple illustration of what all HR software is about, ultimately. It helps you keep track of information. "You put the data down electronically, and you can refer back to it later," company founder, president, and one-man band Ed Carson says of the product. For instance, you may simply want to find out the desired salary for an applicant. Or you may want to find out his or her education or previous work experience. If you have put the information into your applicant tracking system, you can readily pull it out.

Figure 3.7. HR Tools Applicant Tracking Software

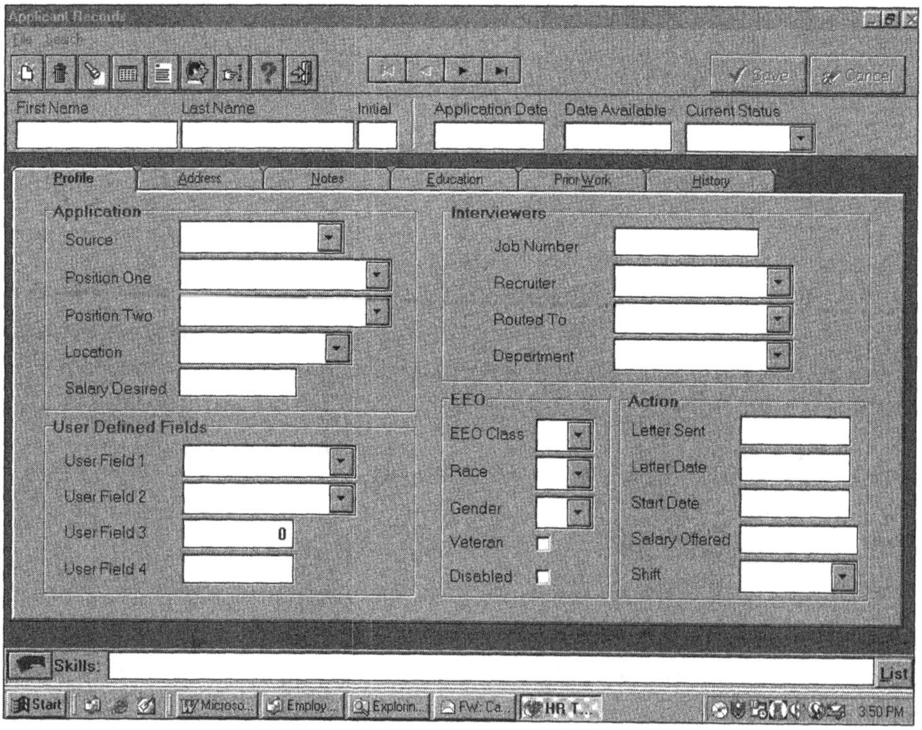

Figure 3.8 shows another specialized HR product, Kronos Time and Attendance Tracking. Sure, almost all the programs may offer something in the time and attendance category. But how many of them show you "missed punches" when an employee forgets to clock in or out. This product does that and such other functions as calculating real-time vacation time built up for all employees in the system, or giving detailed reports on how well your company is meeting requirements of FMLA (the Family and Medical Leave Act).

In another example of a specialized product, Kadiri TotalComp from Kadiri Inc. does a whole lot more for your salary planning than simply telling you who makes what in your company. You can play with each employee's planned salary, see the effect of potential increases on the person's annual salary, and look at a running tally for your overall budget at the same time. It's a great tool for "what if" scenarios. Figure 3.9 shows the main screen for Kadiri TotalComp, where you analyze salaries for the company.

Figure 3.8. Kronos Time and Attendance Tracking

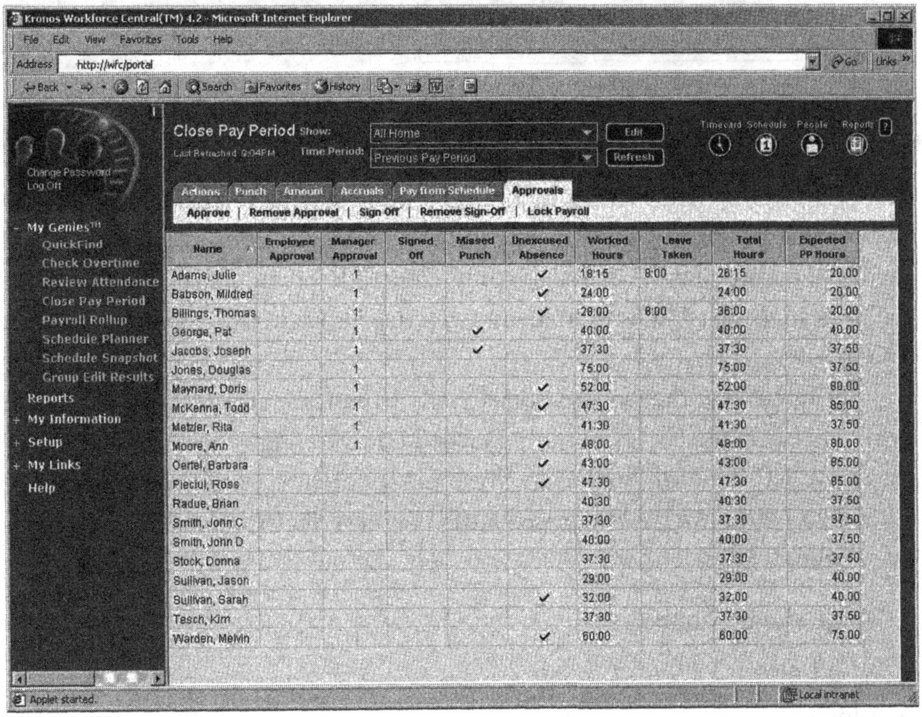

Figure 3.9. Kadiri TotalComp

Figure 3.9. Kadiri TotalComp

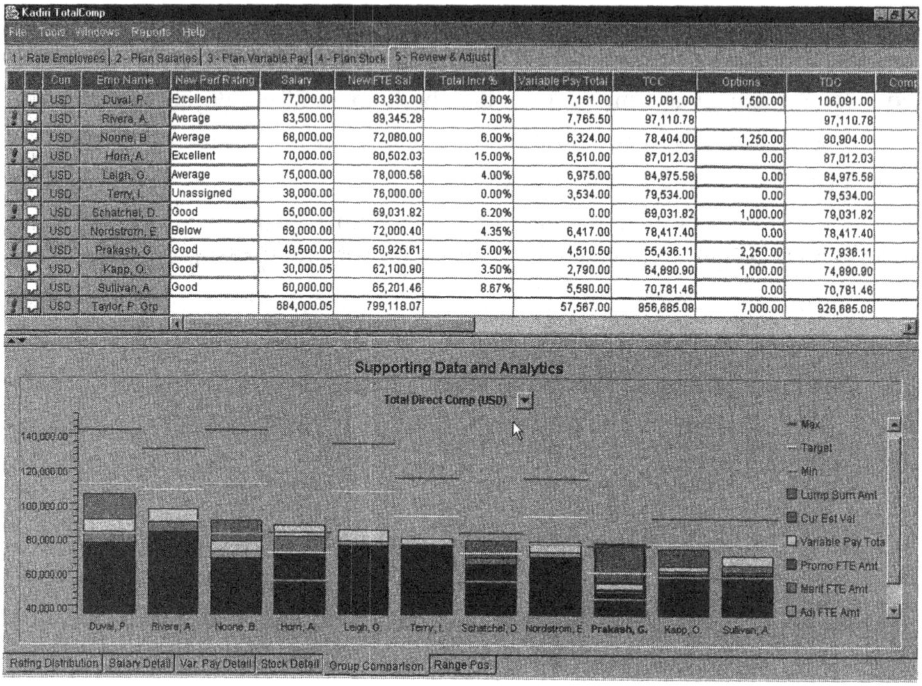

LOOKING OVER STANDARD DATA FIELDS

By looking at the main screens of a number of products, you can gain a general idea of what HR software may accomplish. It's difficult, from such a view, to get an idea of the amount of detail these programs track for you (detail that otherwise you track in manila folders or in memory . . . detail that, in fact, you otherwise just tend to lose).

"One document that we use occasionally to educate prospects on what data items can be tracked is Commonly Tracked HR Data Items.doc," says company president Jeff Moe of Auxillium West in Cupertino, California, makers of HRSource. HRSource is a low-priced HRIS that nevertheless offers the many fields listed below:

- Home Phone Number
- Birth Date
- Address

- City
- State
- Zip Code
- Ethnic Code
- Gender
- Employee ID, badge number, or payroll number (could use Social Security number)
- First Name
- Last Name
- FLSA Code
- Hire Date
- Department
- Job Code/Title
- Next Review Date
- Salary
- Pay Rate Type
- Rate Effective Date
- Rehire Date as Applicable
- Social Security Number
- Status
- Termination Date
- Termination Reason
- Office Information (e.g. extension, phone, fax, e-mail, etc.)
- Emergency Contact
- Specific Leave Information (family leave, unpaid leave, etc.)
- Category—Full-Time/Part-Time, etc.
- Contract Employees
- Disability

- Veteran Status
- Visa Expiration Date
- Manager
- Division/Location
- Education
- Skill Code
- Performance Ratings
- Past Employment
- Time-Off Accruals
- Benefits
- Training/Certification
- Work-Related Illnesses and Injuries
- Bonuses
- Company Property

CONSIDERING REPORTS

The reason to compile information is, of course, to be able to find that information later. That is, you gather the data so you can report on it. Almost every program comes with a list of pre-designed reports. You can simply click on the report name in a listing, perhaps click on one or two other variables, and receive a copy of a report on anything from your company's compliance with Equal Employment Opportunity (EEO) requirements to performance review tracking (Whose reports are due? Whose are late?) to hiring effectiveness (as shown, for instance, in the oft-mentioned "time to hire" report).

An interesting point about reports is that the one you want is almost never available in the list . . . no matter how many preprogrammed reports a company provides you. Generally, you have to have the ability to create your own ad hoc reports. At a minimum, you have to be able to customize the existing reports to fit your own purposes.

Of course, in a perennial game of catch up, vendors are always hearing about widely requested reports and building those reports into their programs. Perhaps a day will come when the existing reports already match the requirements of management. However, the creativity of management always seems to outstrip the ability of technology to anticipate what will be needed. So you are well-advised to look for the ability to generate fresh reports with your program and not simply get a comfortable feeling inside from knowing that the program already has forty or one hundred or three hundred canned reports.

Table 3.1 contains a list of reports available in the low-cost (as low as $1,000) program HRSource from Auxillium West. The names and descriptions are the actual ones used in the program.

FINDING VENDORS

As an HR consultant and software reviewer, I often have people contact me for advice related to acquiring software. I advise them about the process. I caution about risks, such as, "That marketplace is very volatile right now, and there is a shakeout going on. Be careful which company you buy into." People often ignore these suggestions for advice on the process, useful as they may be. And they ignore the risks, too, at least at the initial stage.

What people want are names—names of companies and products. People often really don't know where to start. If they are looking for software for 360-degree performance evaluations, they want to know, simply, "Who is offering those?" Once they know, they can launch into the process. Without names, they are flailing around and not getting anywhere. When starting, whatever else you might say, it's all about names. Also helpful is some kind of quick summary, so you can understand a product's positioning and its specialization. In this book, you find out some of the best ways to get started with names of HR software providers. You will also begin to see how to go beneath the surface and find out the "real skinny" about products.

There are guides for finding HR software. For the most part, they are not very comprehensive and, in that respect, not entirely reliable. They are likely to list the more "extroverted" products (the ones with strong marketing and PR departments) and to pass over some of the engineering-driven companies that don't necessarily pay appropriate attention to marketing.

Personnel Software Census

Two excellent guides for HR software are *The 1999 Personnel Software Census, Vol. 1* (www.hrcensus.com/P1main.html) and *The 2000 Personnel Software Census, Vol. 2.*

Table 3.1. Reports Generated by HRSource

Report Name	Description
AAP Applicant Detail	Details the applicants selected for the AAP Applicant Summary report
AAP Applicant Summary	Counts applicants by EEO category, ethnicity, and gender for a specific time period against requisitions that have been filled for AAP purposes
AAP Hire Detail	Details the employees selected for the AAP Hire Summary report
AAP Hire Summary	Counts employees by EEO category, ethnicity, and gender who have been hired during a specific time period for AAP purposes
AAP Promotion Detail	Details the employee selected for the AAP Promotion Summary report
AAP Promotion Summary	Counts employees who have been promoted during a specific time period by EEO category, ethnicity, and gender for AAP purposes
AAP Termination Detail	Details the employees selected for the AAP Termination Summary report
AAP Termination Summary	Counts employees who have terminated during a specific time period by EEO category, ethnicity, and gender for AAP purposes
Accrual—Sick	Generates a report listing the usage of employee sick leave since the prompted date and calculates current accrual balance
Accrual—Vacation	Generates a report listing the usage of employee vacation leave since the prompted date and calculates current accrual balance
Activity—Department Totals	Active employee headcount by department and EEO category
Activity—Department Details PIT	Provides headcount as of a prompted date and a detailed listing by employee of hire and termination activity since that date

Table 3.1. (Continued)

Report Name	Description
Activity—Department Totals PIT	Provides headcount as of a prompted date and a summary listing of hire and termination activity since that date
Activity—Division Totals	Active employee headcount by division and EEO category
Activity—Hires	Year-to-date employee hires by division
Activity—Terms	Year-to-date employee terminations by division
Applicant—Interviewed (No Offer)	Generates letters to inform interviewed applicants they were not selected for the positions
Applicant—No Interest	Generates letters to inform applicants that a position with your company is not available given their specific skills
Applicant—No Openings	Generates letters to inform applicants that there are currently no openings available in their career field
Applicant Search Results	Conducts keyword search (enter up to two keywords) of applicant resumes pasted into HRSource
Birthday Listing	Lists all active employees by birthday, month, and day
Bonus History	Lists information on employee bonus awards
COBRA Six-Month Notice Letter	Generates a letter that notifies COBRA continuees that their coverage expires in six months. This report must be run between six and seven months prior to COBRA expiration
COBRA Cancellation Letter	Generates letters to inform COBRA continuees of the cancellation of their coverage
COBRA Election Form	Generates COBRA Election Forms for employees who become COBRA eligible. This report is run by clicking the Enroll Form button on the COBRA Participant Information screen.

(Continued)

Table 3.1. Reports Generated by HRSource (Continued)

Report Name	Description
COBRA Log	Lists COBRA Status history by employee
COBRA Premium Chart	Generates a chart of all active employee benefit plans for COBRA premiums (102 percent applied to premium)
COBRA Premium Due Letter	Generates letters to remind COBRA continuees that their premiums are due and includes a premium payment coupon
COBRA Premium Late Letter	Generates letters to advise COBRA continuees that their premiums are overdue and includes a premium payment coupon
COBRA Premium Summary	Lists the COBRA Premiums due and paid by employee
Directory with Dependents	Lists employee directory information, including a picture of the employee and information on the employee's dependents
Directory Without Dependents	Lists employee directory information, including a picture of the employee
EEO-1	Counts employees by EEO category, ethnicity, and gender for Affirmative Action and EEO-1 reporting
Employee Benefit Listing	Lists all active employees with their current benefit plan enrollment
Employee Education	Lists employees and all of their education records
Employee History by Code	Run the Employee History Report macro to generate this report; lists employee history, sorted by event type
Employee History by Date	Run the Employee History Report macro to generate this report; lists employee history, sorted by event date
Employee History Report (Macro)	Macro that combines pay, job, and department history into the two reports listed above

Table 3.1. (Continued)

Report Name	Description
Employee Leaves	Lists all employees or selected employee and their leaves for a specified period of time
Employee Phone Book	Generates a company phone book
Employee Stock Report or Employee Stock Report 2	Generates a stock option status report for two different stock option vesting schedules
Employee Turnover	Calculates employee turnover percentage since prompted date, subtotals by department
Employees by Alpha	Reports information on employees, sorted by last name
Employees by Alpha with SSN	Reports information on employees, sorted by last name similar to the report above, except this report includes Social Security number
Employees by Dept	Reports information on employees, sorted by department
Employees by Job Title	Reports information on employees, sorted by job title; includes number of employees, average salary, low salary, high salary, and salary range
Employees by Training Course	Reports information on employees, sorted by training course for a specific period of time
Health Verification	Generates a confirmation letter that the employee has changed his or her benefits enrollment (used with SelfSource)
Home Address	Lists all active employees with their home addresses
Insurance Census	Lists all benefit-eligible employees by Social Security number, including applicable insurance census information
Jobs by Title	Lists job-related data such as salary range
Labels—All Active Employees	Generates 1" x 4" labels for all active employees, sorted by mailstop

(Continued)

Table 3.1. Reports Generated by HRSource (Continued)

Report Name	Description
Labels—All Active Home Address	Generates 1" x 4" labels for all active employees, addressed to their home, sorted by name
Licensing and Certification Due Within Two Months	Lists licensing and certifications due within two months (typically used in Auto Alert function)
Licensing and Certification Report	Lists licensing and certifications due within a prompted range
LOA	Reports all employees who have been on a leave of absence during a specified time period
Med Plan Certification	Generates a Certificate of Group Health Plan Coverage for loss of medical coverage, run by clicking the Term Letters button on the Termination Process screen (You may need to verify prior plan coverage manually)
Monthly Benefit Billing	Generates a report for reconciling monthly benefit premium billing
Monthly Benefit Billing—Terminations	Generates a report of terminated employees for a specified month to reconcile monthly benefit premium billing
New Hire Notification	Sample cover letter for insurance enrollment submission, run by clicking the Hire Letters button on the New Hire Process screen
New Hire Payroll Notice	Includes a variety of information on new hires as typically needed by payroll; can be used as a file list, or as a transmittal document of new hire information for payroll (if you do not utilize the HRSource electronic payroll interface option)
New Hire DE34 (CA)	Required government report of new employees, run by clicking the Hire Letters button on the New Hire Process screen (This is a federal requirement, although this form has been modeled after the one used in California)

Table 3.1. (Continued)

Report Name	Description
Offer Letter	Sample offer letter for new hires that uses data entered on the Hire Wizard screen, run by clicking the Offer Letter button on the New Hire Wizard screen
OSHA101	Generates the government OSHA 101 form for a specified period of time
OSHA200	Generates the government OSHA 200 form for a specified period of time
Performance Review	Generates a letter to inform managers of their employees' upcoming performance reviews
Personnel Action Notice	Generates a personnel action notice to make changes or corrections to current employee information
RSalary Worksheet Export (Query)	Generates a query used to paste employee data into the "Salary Worksheet" spreadsheet for salary increase allocation, analysis, and budgeting
Requisition	Generates a report of all open requisitions and calculates the number of days the requisition has been open
Requisition Applicant	Lists applicant activity by requisition
Salary History	Lists employee salary history
Salary Review	Generates a worksheet for managers to complete and return to HR for their employees' upcoming salary reviews
Salary Reviews Due Within Two Months	Lists employees due for a salary review within two months (Typically used in Auto Alert function)
Salary Worksheet with Bonus	Generates salary worksheets with bonus information for all employees sorted by department and job title

(Continued)

Table 3.1. Reports Generated by HRSource (Continued)

Report Name	Description
Salary Worksheet with Bonus by Dept—TComp	Generates salary worksheets with bonus information for all employees sorted by department and job title; totals bonus and salary data
Salary Worksheets	Generates salary-input worksheets for all employees sorted by department and job title; allows managers to allocate salary increases quickly and equitably and submit the results electronically
Shift Lead Differential	Indicates base salary and total salary for those receiving differential pay
Stock, Salary, and Bonus	Lists employee stock, salary, and bonus information on a single report
Termination Benefits	Sample termination notification letter for insurance carriers, run by clicking the Term Letters button on the Termination Process screen
Termination Participant Data	Sample termination notification letter for the retirement plan administrator, run by clicking the Term Letters button on the Termination Process screen
Total Days Employed	Lists total length of service for employees, considering rehire dates and leaves of absence
Training Courses	Generates a list of all available training courses
Vacation Accrual Reminder	Generates reminder letters to employees who are within 10 percent or their vacation accrual maximum that they should schedule vacation time
Veterans-100 Report	Creates a report to fulfill the Vets-100 reporting requirement

(www.hrcensus.com/P2main.html). Prepared by Richard B. Frantzreb, these volumes are a comprehensive listing of software. If you don't know where to begin or who is doing what, they are indispensable. Frantzreb also offers other tools to assist you in locating HR software, such as a CD-ROM of eighteen HRIS systems priced under $2,000. You can check out his offerings at his website, www.hrcensus.com.

SHRM and IHRIM Websites

The two leading HR service organizations—the Society for Human Resource Management (SHRM) and the International Association for Human Resource Information Management (IHRIM)—both offer websites with useful product information. At the SHRM site (www.shrm.org) you can locate SHRM's Online Buyers' Guide, which highlights more than eleven hundred of the foremost companies offering products and services to the human resources profession. IHRIM (www.ihrim.org) offers its Online Products and Services Directory with information on more than 3,500 HR information systems, software, and systems consultants.

Other HR Websites

You can also locate information at HR websites. Although some such sites have disappeared or have been reorganized following the dot-com shakeout, some are still functioning nicely. One of the best known is the eMarketplace on HR.com, where you can find "hundreds of products and services."

There are a number of places to locate basic, directory-style information about HR products. I believe those I've listed are great resources. Of these, the Frantzreb volume in particular has great virtues. It is comprehensive, even though it is impossible to list everything in a marketplace with thousands of products and a continuous swirl of change. Nevertheless, it is a reasonably complete listing, with the obvious advantages you enjoy from such a listing. For one thing, you can discover the "sleeper" products that may not market aggressively and may not know how to achieve high placement on Internet search engines but may, nevertheless, be very strong technical products.

What, then, is wrong with these listings? Well, "wrong" is the wrong word. What is the tradeoff for using them? First of all, they take their information from the vendors. What the vendors say is what you get. From a vendor-prepared self-description, you aren't going to find out that a particular product has a weak benefits module. You aren't going to find out that "The pricing is way out of line for what you get. The product has strong loyalty from its installed base, and it leverages that. But you can get the same functionality for a whole lot less money if you go with a less famous company." You aren't going to find out, "The company has been acquired, and it has languished since being acquired. The product has lost its pioneering zeal, and the product architect has left the company. His successors don't understand the product or what made it good." You do find valuable information in the guides, of course. But you won't find analytical information.

Attempting to select HR software can at first be as bewildering as walking through a strange city in an unfamiliar country and trying to make sense of it. Where do you begin? What do you look for? What are known highlights and lowlights?

CONCLUSION

The purpose of this chapter has been simply to give you a bit of a feel for what HR products actually do and for the directories that help you find vendors. It's difficult to give much other information about HR software, such as how to prepare a needs analysis or how to view product demos, until you have a feel for what the products do. In this chapter, a basic orientation, you've had a chance to gain a solid sense of what an HR product might actually do for you. Now you are ready to begin to analyze your own needs, as explained in the next chapter.

Working with Consultants

Quite possibly, your whole point in using a book like this is that you want to do the complete software selection yourself, thus saving on consultants' fees. But considering the points at which you *might* use a consultant can also help show you what to do when you assume the complete consultant role yourself. In some situations you may decide that the consultant is cost-justified—that the expert you bring in saves you more than enough time and money to justify the cost.

In this chapter you take a close look at the value of a consultant at each stage of the process—from the needs analysis to the final negotiations and beyond. You may be able to do without the consultant. On the other hand, the consultant may make the difference between success and failure. Whether or not you decide to use an outside consultant, you owe it to yourself and to your company to consider all that a consultant might bring to the table. One way or another, you probably ought to provide for the expertise, objectivity, and leverage the consultant would give.

A FEW CAUTIONS ABOUT CONSULTANTS

As you evaluate and select software, you as the HR professional ought to be as fully involved in the process as possible. Said Richard B. Frantzreb in an interview with this author, "A consultant will ask you, 'How are you using your HR information now? What's your wish list for the future?' But an insider has to go through the process and identify users, uses of the system, what you are doing now and how that is likely to change, and try to match [that insider's] needs to system capabilities [being offered.]" You might well turn to the consultant to guide you through the process, but nobody from the outside knows your company the way you do. Whether you use a consultant or not, you should be intimately involved with defining needs and matching software to those needs.

Besides knowing your own company better than an outsider does, you stand to learn a good deal by going through the evaluation process yourself. You can use your experience to the benefit of your company in the future. If you go through all the stages of evaluation and purchase by yourself, you will have the most thorough understanding of your software and how to use it. You may make some mistakes that a consultant could help you avoid, but after all, mistakes are a great way to learn. Consultants may feel that you should not take on too much for yourself. Consultant alumnus Pat Phelan, research director with The Gartner Group in Stamford, Connecticut, advises, "Unfortunately, this is the most common pitfall of not having an expert assist—the company is not trained in how to select software for the business area involved, and therefore they either don't execute the selection project correctly or they evaluate at the wrong level of detail."

Keep in mind the following cautions if you do intend to work with consultants:

First, do your best to qualify your consultants in advance. Check their credentials, obtain references, and check references to see that the consultants can deliver as promised. Even if you are working with a "big name" consulting company, you may want to do some checking about the consultants being sent. Experience is key. If you are working with a less-experienced consultant, you may want to ask to have an experienced consultant as an adviser to the less-experienced consultant. Warns Phelan, "To get a true understanding of the proposed team's capabilities, check individual references for each team member."

Then, besides checking references, be clear about possible conflicts of interest. "It is advantageous to hire a consultant who is not aligned with any vendor," caution John A. Hinojos and Moira Miller (1998). "Objectivity of the consultant is important." Some of those who go by the name "consultant" are actually system integrators affiliated with a particular vendor. At least one prominent HR software company, for instance, distributes and supports its products through a network of third-party system integrators. Such a distribution approach offers many advantages, including software support available in your own region. But don't mistake the system integrator for a consultant, and don't think of such a reseller as in any sense an "objective" third party. (You can benefit nicely, though, by hiring a consultant who knows the vendors involved and is willing to call them on their weaknesses.)

In some cases, generally with smaller software firms, a technical expert will openly admit to being a salesperson for a particular vendor. A consultant who discloses such affiliations may still be a useful resource for you, but you should know about the consultant's ties with vendors. (Vendors often are willing to pay finder's fees to those who connect them with customers. However, consultants can have the option of passing those fees along to you, the buyer, as product discounts. That is, you can gain a financial advantage by using a non-affiliated consultant. In fact, your cost savings may enable you to pay the consultant's fees.) Also, says Phelan, "The big five and other large consultancies would blanche at the thought of taking kickbacks from a vendor, since they are typically aligned with several competing vendors."

Here are a few other considerations to keep in mind when searching for consultants:

- Rates for consultants vary, so you may want to do some comparative shopping to find the best rates. Phelan cautions, "High rates do not equate to high quality." You cannot be sure you are receiving high quality just because you are going with a big-name firm or a firm with high rates. Check referrals if possible. Take a close look at the consultant's experience. Practice some standard "due diligence" to assure that your person can do the job.

- Although consultants are industry experts, they are not necessarily expert on what you want from them and on how you want them to work. Your company and your industry have specialized needs, and the consultant may not know them in advance. Manage your consultants, and be clear in what you expect from them.

- Be aware of your budget. Smaller companies in the habit of doing most things for themselves may have to do their consulting for themselves. A small company just may not have the budget for an outside person and, of necessity, may go it alone. Consultants advise that their information applies as well to small companies as to large, and I would tend to agree with them. Nevertheless, consultants simply may not be cost-effective for a company of fifty or one hundred people. Large companies, however, may well find cost efficiencies by going to a "hired gun" who can execute a specified job at a specified rate and return results perhaps better than those from any non-specialist within the company.

In some cases, even the smallest companies can find the consultant to be cost-effective. The consultant may be a "software solution in a jar," guiding you through all stages of the process so that you find a solution that works. Once you're up-to-speed, you no longer have to retain the consultant, possibly saving you the cost of a full-time employee.

Here is one additional thought on the topic: If a consultant seems outside your budget, ask about getting shorter, specialized reports or services instead of full-fledged consulting. A consulting company may be able to share a report with you, for a reasonable fee, that it may have compiled in working with companies similar to your own. You lose some of the personal tailoring to your exact needs, but you have the benefit of the expert attention.

GENERAL REASONS FOR TURNING TO CONSULTANTS

With these few cautions in mind, you may well benefit greatly by calling in consultants. Phelan's insights on the topic, shared throughout this chapter, begin with the general guidelines for turning to consultants expressed below. She explains three of the occasions when you might want to turn to a consultant: when you need expertise, when you don't have the time to do the work yourself, and when you want the advantage of a valuable, third-party opinion.

When You Need Expertise

In all probability, you are an expert at some aspect of human resources. But perhaps you suddenly have decided (or been told) to select and implement HR software. You know nothing at all about software. Or selection. Or implementation.

In this case, the professional world does offer quite a few candidates for consultation (see Table 4.1 at the end of this chapter) who have the expertise you lack. They can help you find the answers to all the following questions:

- Do you know what extensible markup language (XML) is and what it could possibly have to do with your HR system?

- What are the advantages of client/server over PC LAN computing, and which do you have at your location?

- What do e-commerce and application service providers (ASPs) mean for HR at your location?

- What's the difference between Java and JavaScript, and why should you care? What's an applet?

- What's an object structure? How does it affect your HR application?

- What's IVR (interactive voice response), and do you care about it for your HR system?

- What's the difference between employee self-service, manager self-service, and a comprehensive HRIS?

- What's the difference between "Web-enabled" and "Web-native?"

- What is ERP (enterprise resource planning), and should you be taking it into account as you plan your HRIS system? How useful is ERP for small to mid-sized companies?

- What is a Web portal? What's the next step beyond a Web portal?

- Why is a keyword search less powerful than a general search (if it is)? And, as always, why should you care?

- What is SQL, and what does it have to do with HR systems? How does an HR system relate to a database, and how do databases work anyway?

- What is workflow, and what do you lose if you don't have it in your HR system?

These are just a few of the almost endless technical questions you might encounter as you evaluate HR software.

If you do not know enough to be conversant with the answers to such questions, you may not have the expertise to take full responsibility for your company's decision about implementing HR software. After all, you are an HR specialist, not a specialist in databases and other technologies.

So you may want to call in a consultant when you feel that your own HR department (understandably) lacks the technical expertise needed for the software selection process. According to Phelan, you would bring in a consultant when "either you don't have the resources internally, or your team doesn't have the domain expertise" to work in a certain area.

The consultant may have expertise not only about the particular technology you are evaluating but about other areas that may come up. Consultants can point you toward technical areas you ought to consider if you have not done so already.

As a further form of expertise, consultants have often "been there, done that." They often know the technology, not just on a theoretical level but on a practical level. Does a particular product have an earlier DOS version buried at its core, and will that inner core slow performance and make upgrades difficult? You'd never discern that during an ordinary evaluation, but a consultant may have learned it through tough experience.

A Web-enabled product may perform nicely in an artificial demo situation. A consultant may be able to ask the questions that show its limitations and show the importance of being Web-native. (Upgrades may be slower with the Web-enabled product. Compatibility issues may arise with possible companion products. You may not have the option of owning the product instead of "renting" it from a service provider.)

There is often no substitute for training and real-life experience, and the consultant may come with plenty of it.

When You Lack Time

Technical expertise is not the only asset that the outside consultant may bring. Consider, too, that your own people probably are facing severe time restraints. If you're like most companies, you've already been downsized, streamlined, and otherwise reorganized so that people are up to their eyeballs in their present responsibilities. Everyone probably has a line outside his or her door.

You have ten new hires to orient, and that just can't wait. You have to work with those new benefits providers and send the information on the providers to company employees. (That can't wait either, and you are the only one to do it.)

Management has insisted that you analyze skills available at the company and restructure training to help address the needs for certain skills. You don't have to do it today, but you'd better do it by next week. (And you are the only one who has access to the right information to do it right.)

You have been outsourcing your hiring, but you haven't been getting the results you wanted. Management is upset at the high cost of the outsourcing, and it wants to know what to do about it. You have to report to management . . . fast. You know the probable solution: Do the hiring in-house. And you ought to be in charge of it.

A disgruntled employee has a good foundation for a sexual harassment suit, and another might cause the company difficulties under EEO. You can nip the problems in the bud, saving the company thousands and perhaps hundreds of thousands of dollars. But to do so, you have to invest the time.

The time has come, you well know, for some serious compensation planning. The current system is not really fair, and it is rewarding longevity and punishing risk taking. You know you have to remedy it, but that will take . . . time.

An improved stock option plan would do wonders for employee morale, help greatly with retention, and give the company a powerful weapon in recruiting.

The list goes on and on. If any of these situations sound familiar, you almost certainly know what it means not to have enough time to focus on evaluating and selecting software. The very nature of software selection is that it can wait a day or two. But it shouldn't wait. The time savings and cost savings of having HR software are so significant that they could shorten your to-do list substantially and make you much more effective at the items that remain on your list. Nevertheless, implementing software is somewhat long-term, while answering the question of the person outside your door is immediate.

As day follows day, you might find yourself again and again putting off evaluating and selecting software. However, if you hire a consultant, software selection can be that person's top priority. Slipping through the cracks for months, it might suddenly become an urgent, immediate matter. You cannot manufacture any more time out of your own schedule, but you can buy the time of an outside expert.

When You Want Someone to Drive the Process

One of the most common reasons that software evaluation fails is closely related to the issue of time. Often a company has the desire. It has the expertise. It has HR people who could spare enough time to participate in committees, meet with vendors, and help plan implementation. The company has all the pieces, but it has no one to pull all the pieces together. "They lacked someone to drive the process," observed consultant Kenneth D. Myers of Vision Technologies in Minneapolis, when looking at one company that had been putting off the decision to purchase HR software.

Does the company have someone who can interact with all the parties involved—with management, HR, IT, payroll, employees, and vendors? Does it have someone who has the inclination to do so? Does the company have someone who will be accountable for seeing that the whole selection process takes place? Often, HR is accountable for so much already that it makes little sense to have the department be accountable.

A consultant sometimes is little more than a catalyst. The outside person may have no more expertise, time, or any other special qualification than people already inside your walls. But the consultant will focus on the matter of software selection and move the process along. Hiring such a person can make the difference between acquiring HR software and putting off a decision indefinitely.

When You Want a Valuable Third-Party Opinion

If your consultant is what his or her name implies—a disinterested third party—then another possibility arises for using a consultant. You may want to perform a "reality check" on your own conclusions.

Vendors, after all, are by definition salespeople. Their job is to present their products in the best possible light and convince you to purchase them. They may succeed in pulling the wool over your eyes in certain respects, such as these:

- Do they have a breakthrough technology, or are they doing what everyone else is doing?
- Is their support as great as they claim it is?
- Are they the *only* one doing what they are doing? Really?
- Does the training really require only two days?
- Is the interface so intuitive that you can start using it right away?
- Do they have what they say they have, or are they selling a small degree of "vaporware"?
- Is their pricing the best in the industry or is it in fact rather high?

- Is that special search capability they are talking about truly unmatched anywhere else or is it pretty commonplace?
- Are they the only ones who do COBRA so thoroughly?
- Is it really not important which version of Microsoft SQL they are using?

Vendors become so expert at putting the best possible "spin" on their products that they may not truly have any perspective. No one trains them in how other products are superior to theirs, only in how their products are superior to everyone else's. To gain objectivity, don't turn to the vendor.

What about your own internal person who has been working on software evaluation? Surely that person is objective. Perhaps, but a number of conditions can overshadow the objectivity of the internal person:

- Perhaps the internal person has a particular technology axe to grind. Maybe the person knows MS-DOS, likes it very much, and likes older technology that still features MS-DOS. Maybe your internal person has gone to great time and trouble to master Internet programming and is attached to a product that allows Internet customization, even though no one else in the department will have the first clue about how to use it. Maybe your internal person has had training in Crystal Reports and very much prefers products that utilize that popular report writer, even though other products might possibly be easier to use. Perhaps your internal person is in a rush to get onto the Internet, even with a product that doesn't have the functionality you need.
- In an extreme example (entirely fictitious), perhaps your internal person is feuding with IT so openly that the HR person will take almost anything other than what IT recommends . . . just to spite the technology department.
- In a quite common and natural instance, perhaps the internal person has been "snowed" by vendors and, not wanting to reopen the issue, has already made up his or her mind about what product to recommend.

Neither vendors nor internal people have guaranteed objectivity. What about management? Management often has a preoccupation with cost savings and may present unnecessary hurdles to products that cost a bit more. Or, wanting to keep peace between feuding departments, management may find itself unconsciously dragging its feet as you attempt to reach a product decision. Management sometimes forms unconscious loyalties to companies. Management certainly does have more objectivity than a vendor and probably has more objectivity than someone who has been involved in the process so far. Nevertheless, management may lack objectivity in some respects (besides, management may not have been participating and may not be particularly well-informed about the products being considered).

Being human, a consultant may also be subject to the same kinds of biases as any of your company's own people. But the consultant has a professional responsibility to be objective. Besides, the consultant represents a useful third-party opinion, not the final decision. "Most consultancies will not make the decision for you," says Phelan, "but they will tell you if they think you are making the wrong decision."

Often management may want to have the added assurance of a vote of confidence from a credible third party. (Keep in mind that management is often willing to pay for such a disinterested third party.) The presence of such a party may give credibility when the time comes to sell your project to management.

A consultant by herself hardly assures objectivity. Add a consultant to the team you already have in place—your HR person, your IT person, management, and whoever may be working on the project already—and you greatly enhance your chances of reaching an objective conclusion overall.

WHEN TO TURN TO A CONSULTANT

Consider bringing in a consultant at any of the stages—from the needs assessment right down to implementation planning, and at any stage in between. This section covers each of the stages of the project and some of your considerations in deciding whether or not to bring in a consultant for that stage. (As in the previous section, many of the ideas in this section come from Pat Phelan of The Gartner Group.)

Conducting a Needs Assessment

As discussed in Chapter 3, you really ought to decide what you want to accomplish before you start evaluating software. Therefore, you almost certainly ought to do a needs analysis.

Certainly, no one knows your company's needs better than the people at your company. Who, after all, is struggling with a spreadsheet list of the people in the company and trying to keep track of when performance reviews are due? Who has been negotiating with health providers and setting up ever-changing benefits programs? Your own people have been doing it.

The people in your company know their needs and have to be involved in any needs assessment. The first question may be, "You know your needs, but do you know anything about doing a needs *analysis*?"

"If you're going to go through a requirements analysis, consultants can bring predefined master lists of processes most companies perform and the requirements to support those processes," Phelan explains, "so you don't just start with a blank slip of paper." If you do start with a blank slip of paper, you may not think about some of the criteria you ought to list. Consultants, after all, are drawing on the collective experience of their many clients as they put together their list of requirements.

Companies are in the business of doing day-to-day work. You might almost say that they're in the business of losing sight of the forest and moving through the trees. Consultants are in the business of giving you a vision of the whole forest and the paths through it. Your staff may not have an idea of how an ideal company functions or of typical business processes that go on at just about any company (including, surprisingly, their own).

During a needs analysis, consultants can be helpful in additional ways that your internal people are not. Once you have drawn up a list of processes, consultants help with the next set of questions: "What do we like, and what don't we like about the processes in place now?" In other words, they can facilitate a discussion of "what works and what doesn't work." Sometimes, without a consultant present, discussing "what doesn't work" can appear to be simple griping. Or sensitive issues (such as, "We can't give you accurate numbers on number of employees, because IT won't give us access to the database") are avoided. When you do have a consultant present, you have to face up to the sensitive issues that may be holding back progress.

Consultants also can lead you in defining business objectives based on what is working and on what is not working. "Our workflow tends to hit a logjam when we request special reports from the payroll department," you may decide. You could then define an objective, such as being able to have any such reports on demand within two hours. Or you may say that it now takes you three weeks to get approval for a new hire, such a long period that some of the best candidates are gone before the approval comes through. You want to shorten the approval cycle to two days. Consultants may provide expertise in defining objectives and diplomacy in helping departments work with one another.

"Consultants may even lead you through some business process design at this time," Phelan adds. They can help you set benchmarks for tasks you are now doing and for what you want to do more of or do in a different fashion. You can even begin to move into the world of software by having the consultant preview for you how software might provide the capability to fulfill such benchmarks. Following is a summary of the questions consultants might help with as you prepare a needs analysis:

- What tasks do we do here now?
- What is working now, and what is not working?
- What business objectives would we like to accomplish?
- What benchmarks can we set to measure our success in reaching the objectives?
- How might software help us fulfill the benchmarks?

Devising Selection Criteria

When you begin to establish your criteria for selecting software, you again ought to be self-sufficient to some extent. You know what you want in your software. Do you absolutely, positively have to have an Internet-based system? Do you want to outsource any or all of the business process to an application service provider (ASP)? Do you have to have an ASP? Do you use only Microsoft Office? Are you a government? A manufacturing company? A service organization? A dot-com?

A consultant may have technical expertise to help you fine-tune your selection criteria. You may think you want Internet-based, but is "Web-enabled" good enough? Or do you insist on "Web-native"? Do you know the difference, and do you know what the difference means to you as a user?

You say you want an ASP, but do you know how to qualify the capabilities offered by an ASP? A mature desktop product may have search capabilities or reporting capabilities you just won't find with your ASP. Do you understand ASP pricing and know how to avoid excess pricing down the road, when you become dependent on the provider?

Perhaps you want to set guidelines for pricing, such as, "We cannot spend more than $50,000 for this system." Most vendors may claim they can meet that pricing requirement. Unless you have been through software selection before, you may not understand some of the subtleties of the pricing. Does the pricing include implementation? Training? Hardware? Are there other hidden costs such as annual maintenance fees that will come up later? A consultant may help you define a pricing requirement that will genuinely help you screen out vendors.

Consultants, too, are more likely to be current on technical matters than you are, simply because consultants are in the technology marketplace every day. You may want to open the doors to enterprise resource planning, or you may want to avoid it. In the mid- and late-1990s, ERP was all the rage. Suddenly, as the decade came to a close, so did all interest in ERP. Some were pronouncing ERP to be dead. Then the enterprise-wide technology began showing signs of life again, making the issue even more complicated. In the race to become Web-ready and to meet the needs of a changing marketplace, ERP vendors were presenting their plans to the public with what some regarded as undue haste. How is a user to distinguish "planned" technology from real? A consultant is likely to know where technology is lagging behind the sales hype and be able to help set criteria that will distinguish fact from fiction.

Vendor support, too, can be difficult to measure. Everyone has it on the books. Which vendors are currently effective in meeting the support needs of their customers? You may have difficulty knowing if you simply read company literature, but consultants know the word on the street and can help you set up criteria to distinguish among vendors. Sales is a world of hype. "A consultant can help you get to the bottom of the hype," says Phelan.

Because of their expertise, consultants can come forward with detailed questions that help you make meaningful distinctions. Working on your own, you might ask the question: "How do you track job and position changes?" The consultant might help you frame a question like, "How would you enter a job, salary, department, and company change for an employee when all four were changing effective the same day?"

Preparing the RFP or Demonstration Script

As explained in Chapter 6 in this book, the request for proposal (RFP) spells out the ground rules to vendors and specifies what you want to know from the potential providers. In many instances you may choose to use a scripted demonstration instead of an RFP, where you specify to a vendor what you would like to see in the product demonstration. Whichever process you use—RFP or scripted demo (or both)—you may want to turn to a consultant at that stage.

For one thing, you most likely will have to prepare an HR RFP only a few times in your career. Consultants have prepared such scripts routinely for numerous industries and vendors over years and months. Where you have to take the time to get "up-to-speed" and may well make mistakes in the process, consultants are already fully conversant with the typical requirements and uniqueness of the industry and the vendors.

In addition, consultants come to the table with sample RFPs in hand, saving you the time of starting from scratch. You work with the consultant to adapt the samples to your particular needs. Again the consultant's experience comes into play, helping you ask questions that will focus on the uniqueness of vendors or the differences among various vendors. For instance, you do not learn much if you ask whether or not a product does an applicant search. You would learn more if you ask how a product matches candidates to open positions or what fields can be used to conduct applicant searches.

Consultants are familiar with the similarities among products. Today products overlap about 80 percent in what they do. With a consultant's guidance, you can design your RFP so that you do not spend a disproportionate amount of time examining what everyone does (such as allow you to input and report on applicant personal information).

Consultants, too, can level the playing field as you compare vendors by forcing the vendors to address the same issues. Vendors have often developed specializations. One may be particularly adept at employee self-service. Another may excel at exploiting Microsoft's SQL database system. Another may have an extraordinarily well-developed benefits system. Another may have unusually powerful security. Theoretically, you could spend a complete session listening to vendors tout such specialties, yet end up with no basis for comparison. The experienced consultant can assure that vendors display common elements, even though they may be weak in them. Someone strong in benefits may not be strong at all in recruiting, for instance.

Finally, consultants can help to balance out a certain "winning through intimidation" sometimes unconsciously practiced by vendors. In touting their strengths, vendors can rather aggressively cover over their weaknesses. Unless you are familiar with those weaknesses, you may never know that you are missing key information. The consultant may well be familiar with such weaknesses and may be in a position to urge the vendor to address uncomfortable questions. By designing the RFP and holding the vendor to it, the consultant can help assure that the vendor addresses real questions instead of pulling the wool over your eyes in some respect.

Evaluating Vendors

Evaluating your vendors is "crunch time." A number of people begin to pay very close attention to you as you approach an actual decision. A salesperson or group of salespeople have commissions on the line (and, after all, they have families to feed). Your colleagues begin to pay attention because they want you to provide solutions to their problems and they don't want to be tied to a "wrong" decision. IT may begin to watch closely because it doesn't want you to make technical choices that add to its support burdens. Top management will look up from its strategy sessions or merger planning to see how much money you are about to spend and how you will be impacting the corporation. "The heat is on" as you approach a decision, and a consultant just may be a useful resource for you as the pressure builds. Here are some of the roles a consultant can play for you:

Scheduler

You can handle your Microsoft Outlook electronic calendar as well as any outsider. It's not the simple mechanics of scheduling that may drive you to a consultant. It's the logistics and some of the other maneuvering. "You have to get the vendors all scheduled and coordinated to come in at a certain time," Phelan explains. "Also, sometimes you have to break down a communication barrier to get the vendor scheduled." Because they are in the HR selection arena regularly, consultants often have the contacts and the leverage to accomplish what an "ordinary citizen" cannot. I have found that I may have difficulty getting a salesman I have never met to return a call. Perhaps I have dealt with the same company in another region, though. I can pull some of the information I need from a different salesperson, and I can ask the one I know to put in a word for me with the one I haven't met yet. It often works.

Ringmaster

The unexpected can happen during sales presentations. At a minimum, a vendor may diverge widely from an intended script. Or you, as the purchaser, may digress too widely yourself, perhaps dwelling on recruiting with a vendor who doesn't provide it or "beating a dead horse" on an issue like the need to have employee self-service in the future. If the vendors and you as buyer are the circus participants, the consultant can be the coordinator who keeps everyone more or less on task. "Consultants tend to be analytical thinkers," Phelan points out, and the consultant can analyze the ongoing events, compare them with the plan for the events, and steer them in a productive direction.

Bad Guy

Sometimes the consultant can move beyond being a ringmaster to being an outright "bad guy." Somebody has to do it, but generally only lawyers and other professionals (such as consultants) take to such activity with any kind of relish. For instance, the sudden race to the Web at the turn of the new century created a flood of convincing rhetoric from product providers. If you were to observe only the corporate vision of the vendors, you could readily be taken in by the rhetoric. However, behind the vision lay a difficult chore for those same vendors—converting massive technology written in C++ for client/server networks into massive technology written in Java and HTML for the Web. Sometimes the vision might tend to outstrip current reality, and the consultant could be the bad guy to step forward and point out that the vendor might be just slightly discussing futures as if they were "nows."

Discussion Leader

Similar to being a ringmaster is the consultant's role as a simple discussion leader. Both parties to the discussion—the vendor and the buyer—are deeply immersed in their own issues. The consultant can bring a measure of objectivity by supporting one party or the other, as conditions might justify, so as to generally maintain a level playing field.

Reaching a Decision

When the time comes to reach a decision, people at the company really ought to take responsibility for the outcome. Ultimately, the consultant is an outsider and typically will not make the final decision for you. But the consultant's educated opinion can count a great deal. The consultant's evaluation matrix can be a systematic, scientific method for reaching what may in the final analysis be a gut decision. The consultant's expertise can help assure that your decision in the company is the best one you can make. And the participation of an outside, qualified expert can lend credibility to your final decision.

Selling to Management

If you haven't used a consultant anywhere else along the way, you probably won't bring one in just for selling to management. But perhaps doing so would not be a bad idea. You do have to build a business case for selecting a particular vendor and for spending the money being requested. Also, perhaps you have reached an impasse after performing all the previous steps—the needs analysis, the RFP, the evaluation matrix, and the rest. Perhaps you have gone as far as you can go without management's buyoff. That is, perhaps you have decided that you want a particular product, but you need management to authorize the funds. A consultant can help lend weight to your position and prepare the kinds of materials that get the attention and approval of management.

Whether you bring in the consultant simply to sell to management or have brought in the outside expert at an earlier stage, he or she can be helpful as you sell to the decision makers. Here is some of what consultants can do to help sell to the folks at the top:

- *Identify the benefits of the project.* Management's job is to know what this project will do to help HR and what it will do to help the company overall. Having a vague idea of the value of the HR software really isn't enough when selling to management. A consultant knows how to prepare a systematic explanation of benefits, like those expressed in Chapter 11 of this book. Such a tool may be a useful weapon when dealing with the ones who make the final decision.

- *Articulate the challenges.* Management likes to know about risks. Bad news is immeasurably easier to take when it describes what *might* go wrong rather than what has already gone wrong. Consultants have the business expertise and the experience with other clients to be able to identify such risks, prepare management for dealing with them, and thereby remove possible objections on the part of management.

- *Formulate the business case.* Management has a formal way of thinking that may not be entirely the way that HR thinks. Management wants to go beyond the concerns of HR itself to concerns about the entire company. A consultant may have the expertise to present the business case in the style and language that management appreciates, often because the presentation ties the software purchase to the company's strategies and corporate objectives.

Also, if the consultant has been involved in earlier stages of making the selection, he or she probably has documentation to show what has gone on along the way. When you go to management for approval, you serve yourself well if you have a formal needs assessment document, an evaluation matrix, and other written documentation showing the formal steps you went through.

- *Lend credibility.* Credibility can be everything. Human resources certainly has credibility within its own organization, but there is also truth in the old saying, "You can't be a hero in your own town." The outside expert has a deserved credibility, but he or she also enjoys the perception of being credible. Obviously, an inept consultant could destroy that perception pretty quickly, but a competent professional consultant adds needed credibility as you attempt to gain final approval from management.

Closing the Deal

Negotiations can be tough. They call for expertise, leverage, and timing. If HR negotiates on its own with vendors, the two parties can become deadlocked or HR can miss opportunities to reduce the cost or increase the services being negotiated. A consultant can advise you on the kinds of discounts you might reasonably expect and may point out some other money-saving possibilities you hadn't considered. A consultant, familiar with the particular process, may be even more useful than an attorney (if that attorney is not expert in the particular issues). "I review software license agreements to identify areas where the company might 'get a better deal' or tighten the language that describes the vendor's commitment. I also provide negotiating points to people and sometimes sit right at the table and coach the client on what he should be asking for," Phelan points out. In the final analysis, you have to close the deal yourself, but there is nothing wrong with having the best possible guidance as you do so.

Planning Implementation

Even if you haven't used a consultant at earlier stages, you might turn to a consultant to help with implementation planning. Do you know the pitfalls you might encounter? Do you know hidden expenses that might come up? How do you tailor the software to fit your company? What kind of training is the best for you?

Implementation is much more complex than evaluation. All the reasons for using a consultant come up again as you plan your implementation. The consultant brings expertise, time, focus, and objectivity to a process with many twists and turns to it.

"Consultants are experts at implementing," says Phelan. "They can facilitate the entire process, help you really understand what is going to happen during each implementation activity, help you be prepared for it all." You have probably heard of projects that have been approved and been well into implementation only to stall and go no further. Perhaps even more alarming is the thought of an implementation that is not a stage but a permanent condition. If a consultant can help make an implementation speedy and effective, that outside expert may well be worth the cost.

FINDING A CONSULTANT

Referrals are one of the best ways to find consultants. If you know another company that has successfully used a consultant, look into using that same person. Consultants are often high-profile, successful people whose reputations precede them. If you don't know someone who has used the consultant directly, you may nevertheless find people who know of him or her by reputation. Phelan suggests these consultant evaluation criteria.

Strong in the following:

- HR/PR/BE package evaluation/implementation;
- Selection/implementation methodology;
- Industry experience in HR/PR/BE;
- Comfort with the personalities;
- Project manager;
- Samples (business processes, requirements, demonstration scripts);
- Geography (minimize travel, use local consultants where possible); and
- Global presence.

If you want to find a consultant in your part of the country, the Society for Human Resource Management (SHRM) provides on its website (www.shrm.org) a listing of member consultants.

Table 4.1 lists some of the most famous consulting groups, which may help you find a consultant who meets your needs. (Descriptions are from the companies'

Table 4.1. HR Consulting Groups

Consulting Group	Website	Description
The Aberdeen Group	aberdeen.com	computer and communications market research and consulting organization
Cedar Group plc	customer.cedar.com	specializing in concept-to-completion consulting services for the specification and implementation of client/server solutions for human resources management
Forrester Research	www.forrester.com	independent research company that offers products and services to help clients assess the effect of technology on their businesses (description from Yahoo.com)
The Gartner Group	www.gartner.com	independent provider of research and analysis on the computer hardware, software, communications, and related information technology industries
Grant Thornton	www.gt.com www.experio.com	an international accounting and management consulting firm
HRchitect	www.hrchitect.com	specializes in human capital management systems consulting
International Data Group (IDC)	idc.com	provides data, analysis, and advisory services on information technology (IT) markets, trends, products, vendors, and geographies

Table 4.1. (Continued)

Consulting Group	Web Site	Description
Meade Ink, Inc.	words@lisco.com	specializes in HR selection and implementation services
META Group	www.metagroup.com	information technology market assessment firm
SHRM	shrm.org	consultant's directory
VRC Consulting	www.vrcconsulting.com	strategic planning in the areas of human resource and financial management systems, information technology, finance, and marketing
The Yankee Group	yankeegroup.com	international organization specializing in the analysis of trends in strategic planning, technology forecasting, and market research

own Web pages or from Yahoo.com.) Consulting companies tend to be helpful and cooperative even if, ultimately, their services may prove to be "out of your league." If these companies cannot help you directly (and often they can), they may be able to assess your needs and point you in the direction of someone who can.

There are numerous other companies not listed here that are viable HR systems consultants. This list is meant as a jumping-off point for you, nothing more.

CONCLUSION

You may well have the expertise to be your own consultant. In the final analysis, you learn the most and prepare the best for using HR software by selecting and evaluating it yourself. However, you may not have the time, expertise, or leverage to accomplish what you want to accomplish. At any of the stages along the way, from the initial needs assessment to implementation planning, a consultant may prove to be helpful as you select and install your software. Whether you work on your own or with a consultant, you are going to have to decide what needs you want to address. The next chapter introduces the needs assessment.

PART
TWO

Collecting Your Facts

Becoming oriented, as you did in the previous section, is essential to carrying out effective software selection. Once you have a feel for the marketplace and trends, you are ready to get down to the real business of shopping. In this part you will explore the latest approaches for analyzing your own needs, soliciting information from vendors (without overwhelming either them or you), conducting demos where vendors address the questions you want addressed, and validating your own impressions by checking with reference accounts.

Do You Need a Needs Assessment?

Needs assessments are not particularly easy to start. The situation is one form of the old "the cobbler's children have no shoes." Companies are eagerly projecting outward and doing all kinds of business, but they have difficulty turning the cameras around and looking at themselves. People think that either they know what they need without defining it, or they can just plunge ahead without defining it. Or people sometimes prefer to implement whatever other people are doing, as if saying "That's good enough for us, too. We're typical."

"People call and ask what's the best HR software, and I say, 'For whom?,'" said Richard B. Frantzreb, editor of *The Personnel Software Census*, in an interview with this author. "They're trying to get around the difficult problem of defining what they're looking for."

It can be tempting, when making a purchase in any area, simply to begin shopping around, and I won't say that such an approach is entirely without merit. Sometimes, if you just start, you can fill in the needed pieces later on. Whether you do so later or at the beginning, though, at some point you have to decide what need you are going to address with your HR software.

"Use the right tool for the job," the old saying goes, and to use the right tool, you have to know what job you're trying to accomplish. You don't buy a bulldozer to help you drive nails into the house you're building. In the world of HR software, all kinds of software is available, and all kinds of companies are looking for it. A manufacturing company, for instance, might want a product that is strong in time and attendance. An accounting and consulting firm might be most concerned with succession planning or compensation analysis. It tends to make sense to set out your own needs at the outset; then, as you look at software, keep matching the capabilities of the software with your company's own needs.

To be realistic, you won't define all your needs at the outset, because the needs keep changing. Those requirements today, says consultant Vince Ceriello, head of VRC Consulting Group in Los Altos, California, are "a huge moving target." No sooner do you decide to get set up on your company's client/server computing than you move to Internet-based operations. You decide to use the Internet, but then the company decides it favors the heightened security of an intranet, and you have to make the small adjustments. You set up to serve people yourself, as the HR manager, and then the company moves to employee self-service.

Whether you are in a startup company in an emerging industry or in an established company in a slower-paced industry, your needs are going to change and evolve. Nevertheless, you are best off if you define those needs, at least in outline form, and plan for software that will meet the needs as they evolve.

SYSTEMATICALLY DEFINING NEEDS

Classically, HR needs for a company come in a number of specific categories. Above all, you probably want to define your own needs in the HR department. But you can't possibly purchase the right software unless you know the technical infrastructure at your company: that is, "What kind of computers are out there?" Taking a step further back, you probably have to understand the company itself and the industry you're in. (In spite of what anyone might say about offering software appropriate to any company, needs for a healthcare provider differ in some ways from those of an oil drilling company.) Here are the categories you should look at when defining your company's needs, along with a more detailed explanation of each.

Company Background

To begin with, you ought to know the size of your company and its projected growth. If you're small enough, you may not be a fitting target for human resources software. (Such companies might find some of the reports informative, they can probably meet most of their needs by using a spreadsheet.)

Jim Spoor, president of Spectrum Human Resource Software in Denver, says that his company's HRIS software typically serves companies with from 100 to 5,000 employees. "When you get below one hundred employees, people don't need much other than a payroll system," he says. "Somewhere between seventy-five and one hundred employees, companies start to have needs for meaningful HR information. At that level you need good, basic information. As you go more and more up the curve, your needs grow more and more sophisticated and elaborate. By the time you reach two hundred employees, you need a very rich product. You can no longer get by on basic entry-level products."

Although Spoor sets the minimum size for HR software at companies with one hundred employees, companies in the range from fifty to one hundred employees may find themselves overwhelmed with requests for information and may well turn to HR software. Some packages that don't require a client/server network, such as Abra HR from Best Software or People-Trak Human Resources Software, nicely work for even companies with fewer than one hundred employees. On the other hand, larger companies—with multiple departments, elaborate management structures, and much else to contend with—have to choose software designed for their considerable needs.

Company size is one variable. Also, the demands of one industry are quite different from those of another industry. A manufacturing facility has to be quite aware of the requirements of OSHA (the Occupational Safety and Health Administration). A strictly white collar company also faces occupational hazards on occasion, but EEO reporting may be a much bigger concern. Are you a hospital? A school? A service organization? Needs vary considerably by industry.

Management Considerations

In marketing, the famous slogan of the Marshall Fields stores in Chicago is, "Give the lady what she wants." The "lady," when you are selecting HR software, is management. If management *wants* human resources software, consider yourself fortunate. You have passed your biggest hurdle to software implementation. Often, top management even comes to HR and suggests that HR look for ways to automate.

Just as often, though, top management is unaware of the possibilities, indifferent to your plight (or so it may seem), or perhaps even resistant to investing in HR software. Whereas management often sees the payroll department as essential, sales as critical, and IT as indispensable, it may see HR as a group of "administrators" whose needs can wait until tomorrow.

If management is lukewarm toward HRIS software, then HR needs to use every means at its disposal to persuade them. Every step in a systematic software purchase may prove to be essential, from the needs assessment to the final recommendation—and even beyond. In some cases, too, management will demand a hard cost justification for the software. You may have to address questions like these:

- Will the software save on the number of full-time employees required in the HR department?

- Will it save time of existing people in the department so that they can allocate their time in more useful activities?

- Will it save on costs for training?

- Will it save on materials like paper?

"While you're conducting these [needs] sessions, be sure to ask how new features will affect costs and/or efficiency. This information will help you later when you prepare a cost analysis to justify the expense of the software," urges HR consultant F. Jay Fox (1998) of Working Concepts, Inc., based in Columbia, Maryland.

Technical Considerations

Your software has to run in a particular environment. Unless your department is completely self-sufficient with its own hardware, software, and network, you probably have to work with your IT department initially to become clear on the "backbone" for the software you want to select. As mentioned in Chapter 1, both software and hardware have become much more standardized in recent years than they were ten or fifteen years ago. You don't have to become a technical wizard yourself, but you do need to be careful, at the outset, to know the requirements of your own company. (Not that this would happen, but you wouldn't want to be evaluating a mainframe program, for instance, if your company doesn't have a mainframe and has no intention of ever having one.)

Here are the categories you'll probably want to examine:

Hardware. Does your company have personal computers exclusively or perhaps some blend of personal computers and other systems, such as mainframes or mini-computers? Chances are good these days that you will not have to worry much about this question, that your company uses standard PCs, but you may have a Macintosh environment or some other environment.

Operating System(s). What operating system do your computers run on? Microsoft's operating systems—Windows 95/98, Windows NT, Windows 2000, Windows XP—have become quite well-established. Most of the HR software you are likely to evaluate runs in the Microsoft environment. Other operating systems are widespread in the marketplace, though, such as UNIX-based systems. Make sure you know what your own operating system is so that you can clearly let vendors know your needs.

Networking. For HR software, two kinds of networking environments prevail—PC LAN systems and client/server systems. If your PCs are networked together in the most basic way, without using a server, then you have a PC LAN system. You will then be able to select certain offerings from HR software providers, but not some of the more advanced offerings. If your company is large enough and has its own IT department, you probably have a client/server environment. Windows NT is popular in client/server environments, but perhaps you have a UNIX environment.

Database. Your whole purpose in working with HR software will be to manage information—everything from the number of employees to the patterns being followed in performance reviews. That information will reside somewhere, and that place of residence is a database. Microsoft has recently become quite firmly established as a database of choice for many companies with its Microsoft SQL Server. SQL Server exists in various versions, however, and you need to know the version you have installed at your company so you can match that version with offerings from the vendors. Oracle also is a popular database, and a number of other databases exist as well. Whatever the database, your HR software will probably be able to work with it. But you need to make certain of that from the outset as you talk with vendors.

Software. What other software is installed in your company that you may want to work with? If your company is committed to Microsoft Office, as many are, you may want to choose software that integrates Microsoft Office. If you have other software that you may want to integrate with your HR software, be clear about it from the beginning.

Telecommunications. Many HR software applications don't directly involve your company's telecommunications system, but some do. If you are planning to use employee self-service, for instance, you probably want to make benefits enrollment available over the telephone using interactive voice response (IVR) and not just available from computer workstations. You should check at the outset about the telecommunications system at your company and any restrictions, or possibilities, it may pose for your HR solutions.

Possible Application Service Provider (ASP) Solution. With the Internet becoming universally available in business, you may not have to contend with any special technical considerations for your HR software. You can just choose to use an application service provider on the Net, such as EmployEase of Atlanta for comprehensive HR, or specialized products like eWorkforce from iCarian, Inc., in Sunnyvale, California, which offers staffing and hiring solutions on a subscription basis.

HR Considerations

You are the HR department, so your biggest responsibility is to meet the needs of your own function. You will probably find it worthwhile to step back and take a careful look at what you actually needs in terms of HR, so that you can demand as much of that functionality as possible from vendors. The following sections give you some guidance in steps you might take in evaluating your needs.

As I mentioned at the outset, businesses are often reluctant to pause and say, "What do we really do?" Answering the question can be difficult. Often the answer on an individual basis is, "I don't know. I don't know where the day goes. I start. People line up at my door. I answer questions. Every day is different." When you do begin to answer the question, you prepare yourself to make the best choice for an HR system and the best use of it once you install it. Following are some of the questions you probably ought to address in your self-examination.

"Where Is the Pain?"

You can become quite systematic in looking for your HR and business needs, and I show how to do that in later sections of this chapter. Also, you may have some fairly soft reasons for looking into HR software. Maybe you've just heard that HR software is a trend, and you think that you ought to be doing it. Maybe you have a vague idea that the software would help you, but you don't really care that much whether you automate or not. Maybe your manager has suggested that looking into the software would be a good idea, but perhaps there was no particular urgency.

Your quest for HR software truly becomes focused, though, when you're outright desperate, or close to it . . . when certain kinds of pressures have you at the end of your rope. If you stop and ask yourself, "Where is the pain right now?" you will have taken a giant step toward defining what you want to accomplish with your HR software.

Here are some examples, just to prime the pump of your own thinking and help you reflect on your own pain that you want to resolve:

- Every time someone comes up for a salary review, you have to collect folders to find out name and education, previous positions, salary history, performance reviews, and salary.

- The boss says he wants to know what the cost per hire was for the last month, and you have to start by trying to find out what you spent on newspaper ads, employee research time, and hiring time. You have little real data to draw on, and sometimes people provide information based on "best guesses."

- You want to "get real" about offering training, so you decide to look at what you are offering now. You spend two days looking through papers in employee folders, and you still aren't sure what people have been learning. You have no idea whether the training has been effective.

- Suddenly, a rumor hits that the company might be liable for a lawsuit under the Family and Medical Leave Act. You never thought that could happen to you. You thought you knew what the Family and Medical Leave Act was; actually, you haven't taken truly strong measures to be sure you are compliant.

- You put out a newspaper ad and received a resume back from the ideal C++ programmer. By the time you approve a requisition, set up the interview, and prepare an offer, the candidate has accepted a position with another company.

- Benefits enrollment at your company takes almost two months. Almost as soon as it is completed, employees come around and ask, "What is my dental coverage?" They don't really understand what they have and are spending so much time enrolling, not because the process is educating them, but because the process is just slow and inefficient.

What Daily Requests Do You Respond To?

Another way to begin to define what you need in your HR software is to look at what you do all day—a process that can be easier said than done.

Consultant Vince Ceriello uses a standard set of questions to help HR people take that step back and observe what they actually do during their often frantic days of attending meetings, answering phone calls, meeting with people, and filling out reports. Here are questions he asks first to help people see the kinds of "emergency" information they have to come up with, usually on short notice:

- When the "red phone" rings, what does the person on the other end want from you by way of information?

- What information do you need to have available in order to answer their questions?

- Where do you find the information?

- Where is it stored?

- Is it secure?

- Can you trust its accuracy?

- How frequently are you called on to provide this information?

- What kind of unpredictable requests have you had in the last year?

What Reference Materials Do You Use?

You don't know all the answers off the top of your head. As people come to you with questions, you have to come up with the answers from some sources—sources that, ideally, will be automated in your computer system. Here is the series of questions Ceriello asks to help identify sources of information:

- What forms, reports, listings, files, and so forth, do you maintain as reference materials?

- Explain each document used (frequency, format, content, sequence, complexity, and so on).

- How much time is spent on these documents in origination, review, analysis, approval, and dissemination?

- Where is historical data kept?

- When is it purged?

- What reports do you use?

Reports are the heart of HR, particularly in HR's role of supporting line management and top management. As HR becomes increasingly strategic, HR also has to become increasingly proficient in turning raw information into meaningful reports. Here are the questions Ceriello asks to help people identify the kinds of reports they create (and will want their HR software to create):

- What reports are produced that circulate either inside or outside the HR department? (Review for content, format, frequency, various audiences. Obtain a copy of each report.)

- What data is required to produce the report(s)?

- Where do you find the data/information?

- How long does it take you to put together the report(s)?

- How reliable/valid is this data/information?

- How do you determine who receives specific reports?

- What is policy regarding output distribution and confidentiality of data?

What Information Passes Through Your Unit?

Some information is data that you control as HR; other information passes through but originates in another department. Sometimes you may want to include all or part of that information in your HR reports. Here are Ceriello's questions that help identify such information that "just passes through":

- What information—reports, listings, approvals, etc.—passes through your unit? (Review purpose, history, format, sequence, frequency, to/from.)

- What computerized output do you currently receive from the present system?

- Who else receives it?

- What changes would you like to see in current output?

What Manual Records Do You Maintain?

Reference materials are one kind of information. Another kind you may have on hand are manual records—personal data, salary information, performance reviews, or any other data you maintain by hand. To have an effective HR system, you have to be certain to automate as much as possible of the information you now maintain manually. Also, when you have such manual information, you want either to avoid duplication or to make certain that duplicate records are as close to identical as possible. Here are Ceriello's questions that help identify such manual records:

- What kind of manual records do you maintain? (Review purpose, content, etc. How are files set up?)

- Who else has similar data on file? Why?

- How is it cross-referenced? Where?

What Other Considerations Will You Be Addressing?

A number of other questions can be key to successfully deciding on the right HR software for your company and to implementing that software. You should look at projected benefits, improvements over the present system, and other matters (not least of which, of course, is pricing). Here is a series of other questions Ceriello includes in his needs-assessment questionnaire:

- How would an HRIS most benefit your function?

- What will it do that present system(s) cannot?

- What are your major information needs?

- What could you accomplish if you had computer support?

- Do you need a cost-benefit analysis to sell to top management?

- Have internal data processing resources indicated a willingness and ability to help?

- What kind of prices/delivery have vendors quoted?

Pricing

As anyone knows, you can't be purchasing champagne on a beer budget. If you do have a champagne budget, why settle for beer? As with almost any other purchase you make, pricing has to be a consideration. Pricing will become even more central when you enter into formal negotiations with a vendor, but even at the outset you should have some idea of your budget. You can aim for very inexpensive software, even applying the concept of "throwaway software"—software so inexpensive that you could afford to use it for a time, then cast it aside. At the other end of the spectrum, you could commit to hundreds of thousands of dollars or even millions for a full-scale enterprise resource planning (ERP) system.

Chances are that most small to mid-sized companies fall somewhere between the two extremes of "throwaway software" and ERP systems. Here are some of the things to consider in setting out an initial budget:

- *Do we plan to take charge of our HR software or put someone else in charge?* Outsourcing can be a viable option for many companies these days. An outside company takes responsibility for having the right systems, software, and even business management systems. You simply ask for results and pay on a subscription basis.

- *Do we plan to buy or "rent"?* Purchasing software was the way of the world for some time, but the Internet is making ASPs much more popular. Yet, a backlash against the "rental model" during tight economic times has brought increased respect for the "own your own" model.

If you do plan to purchase your own system, consider these questions:

- *How much do we plan to spend for the software itself?* This is the obvious question you would not be likely to overlook. Remember, though, that the software may include annual licensing fees, support fees, database licenses, or other costs.

- *What are we prepared to spend for hardware?* If you're lucky, you may already have the computer systems in place for the HR software you plan to purchase. However, you may need to the following hardware: personal computers, servers, networking hardware (hubs, routers, and so on), or Internet connectivity (cabling, networking cards, modems).

- *Are we budgeting for implementation as well?* Some of the more disturbing estimates I have seen say that implementation can cost from two to three times the cost of the software itself. Some say the costs can be even higher than that! You may have to take on some costs to convert your existing data to the format used by your software or you may even have to arrange to key in some information now kept manually.

Training can be another major cost, and you may not want to settle simply for having people be able to use the software. Keep in mind, too, that your software doesn't have true value for you unless you squeeze the maximum value out of it. You may want to plan to have people learn to take advantage of such capabilities as the software's report writer. You may want to have at least one person who can administer the software (configure it for security, user privileges, and various setup considerations). Plan on having budget available for training, including such activities as visits to user groups where you can learn from others who are using the same software.

General Risks

Think about your own business environment and possible obstacles you may encounter there. These are risks that only you can know. Here are a few possibilities you might encounter:

- IT is overworked and reluctant to take on additional support responsibilities for HR software.
- IT currently controls all HR software and is reluctant to give up such control, believing that HR lacks the technical expertise to take charge of its own system.
- The budget is too restrictive, which may force HR to purchase software that will not meet its needs in two or three years, or even sooner.
- Planned hardware upgrades at the company may change the database environment, the networked environment, or both.
- Planned business expansion may make it necessary to collect information from a number of distributed sites.
- HR is currently so overworked that it has no one who could take responsibility for implementing the software or for training others in its use.
- HR may need to add an additional person or, more likely, to reorder the priorities of the people currently working there.

- Top management is skeptical about the value of the HR software and will need to see a convincing cost/benefit analysis before it will sign off.

- HR needs the software in place before some coming event, such as a major acquisition.

Priorities

Once you have defined your HR needs, pricing, and risks, you ought to go through and set up your priorities among all those needs. Priorities vary widely from company to company. If you do not yet have top management support, you may want to set as your top priority that you will win at least a neutral attitude from top management as you go through this process. IT, too, can be a major consideration. If you have IT's blessings and active participation, your whole project has a better chance of success. Look at your own needs within HR and set priorities there. What do you need most desperately? What can you live without if necessary? Look at your budget. You cannot accomplish much without a budget. If the budget is small, you can plan accordingly.

Go through all the considerations in your needs assessment and rank them in order of importance. Such a ranking will help you as you apportion your time, make decisions about software, and schedule the rest of the process. The ranking will also help you establish the right criteria for vendors to follow in showing you their wares.

SAMPLE REPORT

Samples of reports from other companies can provide excellent models for your own needs assessment. Following are, first, a brief list of sample needs, then a complete sample report (Exhibit 5.1).

User Needs

Often the best way to see how to do your own needs questionnaire or assessment report is to look at what others have done and use their work as a model. Here, for example, is a list of user needs for software for medical and dental plan administration (Hinojos & Miller, 1998).

- Automate monthly reporting process;

- Easily create and automate production of monthly premium reports for all plans;

- Ability to electronically transfer eligibility and claim payment information to carriers;
- Maintain and easily report on the following information:
  - Census (demographics),
  - Monthly premiums: employer versus employee,
  - Payroll deduction changes; and
- Track Section 125: pre-tax medical and dental contribution.

Needs Assessment

Exhibit 5.1 shows a more detailed example of a needs assessment report done for an imaginary company.

 You will find some additional vendor-provided needs analysis forms on the CD-ROM.

 ### Exhibit 5.1. Sample Needs Assessment Report

Company Background

Imaginary Dot-Com is a leading-edge Internet marketing company of seventy-five employees. The company plans explosive expansion over the next two to three years. In addition to headquarters in Madrid, New Mexico, it will open offices in Tucson and Los Angeles, and may go international as well.

The HR department has one person, who works with a hiring manager as well. Human resources is beginning to be overwhelmed by the demands of rapid growth on all fronts—recruiting, employee tracking, benefits, specialized management reports, external reports, and more. Imaginary Dot-Com wants to implement an HR software solution that will support the HR department in all its needs.

Management, Project Team

Top management initiated the process of evaluating and selecting HR software to help the HR department meet its rapidly growing needs. All involved

---

Exhibit 5.1. (Continued)

departments buy into the process—HR, hiring, IT, operations. The departments cooperate fully and support one another, and resources of IT are available to HR on an as-needed basis throughout evaluation, implementation, and use of the HR software.

Technology Needs

For HR software, Imaginary Dot-Com's IT department sets these preferences:

1. All Microsoft environment

   - Microsoft Office

   - SQL Server

   - NT client/server network

2. Web-based application

3. Open system that might tie in to company's own ERP system

4. Scalable product that will grow as the company grows

5. Security of data (essential)

6. Compatibility with outsourced ADP payroll system (required)

7. A Web-based application service provider (ASP) might be acceptable, with the service provider primarily responsible for technology

HR Needs

Imaginary Dot-Com has all the standard HR tracking and reporting needs that any company its size has. The company is growing so quickly that it wants to cover not only the currently identified needs but all the needs that may arise as the company grows.

Current Situation

The HR department currently has no HRIS system but uses spreadsheets to track data. For recruiting, the department uses Microsoft Outlook. The hiring manager categorizes e-mails into a series of Outlook folders and has virtually no capacity for automated searching and filtering

(Continued)

Exhibit 5.1. Sample Needs Assessment Report (Continued)

Capabilities Desired

General HRIS

- Employee information, including personal information, standard information such as hire dates, job title, and so on;
- Standard reports such as number of employees; and
- Tracking of retention and turnover rates and meaningful reports on those.

Recruiting

- Automated posting to multiple job boards;
- Resume management system;
- Keyword indexing and search;
- Prescreening and qualification (by geographical area, skills, and so forth);
- Requisition management;
- Reports such as recruitment cost per hire, applicants per position, acceptance rate, sources of successful hires, time to hire;
- Referral program, with metrics; and
- Reminder system for contacting possible future hires.

Benefits

- Enrollment;
- Tracking of medical, dental, and cafeteria;
- Management reports, such as cost of benefits per year;
- Information on W4s;
- Tracking of 401(k), stock option plans; and
- Automatic tracking of bonuses, given out after specified periods.

Exhibit 5.1. (Continued)

Time and Attendance

- On-demand reports for:

  Vacation days

  Sick days

  Personal days

  Billable versus non-billable time.

Calendaring/Scheduler

- Ability to print out quarterly reports showing forms due, filings to be done.

Managing Performance Reviews

- Tracking of due dates, who has submitted reviews, what reviews are outstanding from which managers.

Compliance

- EEOC reporting and
- Other reporting.

Compensation

- Management, planning, and reporting.

Testing

- Testing of technical candidates and
- System of benchmarks, measuring of candidates against benchmarks.

Training

- Individualized training plans;
- For each employee, which courses taken, when, cost;

(Continued)

Exhibit 5.1. Sample Needs Assessment Report (Continued)

- For company, overall training provided, cost; and
- Perhaps assessment of training (skills) needed for individuals, overall company

Needs for Report Writer

- A system containing a strong collection of pre-designed reports, as well as
- Flexible, easy-to-use tools for preparing ad hoc reports on any subject.

Ease of Use

Imaginary Dot-Com is seeking HR software with a report writer that is as easy to use as possible. System should be intuitive and offer a standard interface available from all locations (as in a Web browser). Ideally, a non-technical HR person, with no training or only an hour or two of training, would be able to use the report writer to create meaningful ad hoc reports.

Pricing Considerations

Like any fast-growing, innovative company, Imaginary Dot-Com is budget-conscious. The company will seek aggressive, competitive (that is, low) pricing from its providers of HR software.

Highest Priorities

- Internet based;
- Ease of use overall;
- Ease of use for deployment (installation) and training;
- Recruiting module; and
- All other modules also key, close second to recruiting.

Risks

HRIS Versus Specialized Packages

General HRIS packages may be best-suited to the overall needs of the company and may provide the flexibility to meet future needs, but they may not have the

Exhibit 5.1. (Continued)

functionality needed to meet special needs in recruiting, benefits, or other areas. Imaginary Dot-Com may have to consider specialized software to meet such needs. Such additional packages might create issues of compatibility (including issues relating to the desire for a single, standard interface).

Vendor Reputation and Longevity

HR software is a growth business. New products are appearing daily, some of them excellent. Imaginary Dot-Com will want to take precautions either to purchase from a company with an established user base or from a company that provides other assurances. Internet-based HRIS systems, almost by definition, are new and somewhat untested in the marketplace.

Entering and Maintaining Data

HR software systems depend on data, much of it now residing on spreadsheets or even on paper. HR must plan to import data into the system, or key in data from hard copy, and to continue to maintain the data over time. Vendors may offer the ability to import data from spreadsheets, but Imaginary Dot-Com should make certain that the promised import capability meets expectations.

Training

Imaginary Dot-Com will want to assure that users are proficient in using the software and its report writer. Vendors may claim ease of use, but Imaginary Dot-Com should test the product with real users to see whether or not training will be necessary.

Testing

HR may want to work with IT to set up a system of testing the software with multiple users before purchase. Users may want to validate ease of use, helpfulness of help files, ease of navigation, ease of creating reports, and the value of the documentation. Although Imaginary Dot-Com should not plan to perform true software testing, nevertheless the company can determine whether or not the software has a tendency to "crash," lose data unexpectedly, or put up strange or difficult error messages.

(Continued)

Pricing

Among considerations in pricing are these:

- Use of an ASP would, in some instances, avoid expensive start-up costs, but monthly costs might end up being substantial.

- Costs of installation and training often come in at two to three times the cost of the software itself. Imaginary Dot-Com may want to seek methods to control that cost. (One vendor, for instance, promises to come in with a firm bid that covers implementation as well as purchase.)

Conclusion

Imaginary Dot-Com is a dynamically growing company with a strong management team, strong technical basis, knowledgeable HR management, and a strong vision for its future. The company is ideally situated to benefit from HR software, but the software must be the right software addressed to the right needs—the needs outlined in this document.

CONCLUSION

As when you look at a map at a highway rest stop, you have to know where you are before you can figure out how to get to the next place. This may seem obvious, but we all tend to overlook it at times. If something is a hot trend in HR software, people decide that "we must have that need as well" and begin to evaluate the software without first deciding on the need.

Advice from consultant Jenni Lehman, research director with The Gartner Group, is that HR departments should, above all, "Stay focused on what you're tying to achieve from a business perspective."

Explains Lehman, "Over and over I talk to companies who are saying, 'How can I do a cost justification to add ESS [employee self-service]?'" or similarly ask about trendy software. Her standard response is, "What business objective are you trying to achieve?" Often, says Lehman, companies respond, "I don't know. We just think it would be cool to have ESS; our employees would think it is cool." Cautions

Lehman, "HR organizations often aren't focused enough on what it is that their company is trying to achieve and what the value of that is to their organization."

Looking ahead to the possibilities is natural and fun, but doing so can prove costly down the road if you install software you don't need or, worse, fail to install the software that you do need. The best way to avoid such missteps is to go systematically through the process of a needs assessment to identify your general business, technology, and HR needs and balance them against such considerations as your budget and your degree of management support.

In short, you may not feel inclined to break down your department's activities into measurable bites. You may not feel that you need the needs analysis. The experience of most companies, however, indicates that the best thing to do is to bite the bullet and do it, because, yes, you need the needs analysis. Once you have your needs analysis, you are ready to request information from vendors. If you ask in the right way, you will obtain useful information without being overwhelmed. The next chapter reviews one way to request information from vendors: the request for proposal (RFP).

The RFP: RIP?

R equests for proposal (RFPs) have a long history as valued documents in the search for software. The theory behind the RFP is simple enough. First, from your side, you systematically set forth what you are looking for from vendors. You send out the document to a group of vendors, who then take the time to respond painstakingly to your requests. You then have the basis for sifting through materials and reaching a short list of vendors from whom to see formal demonstrations.

A good way to understand the classic RFP is to look over a few of them. You can see examples of classic RFPs on the CD-ROM. In this chapter, we'll first review the sections in the standard RFP. You'll also find out what you might put into the shortened form of the RFP that is coming into vogue, and you'll find guidelines for creating your own RFP as well as pitfalls to avoid.

WHAT TO PUT INTO AN RFP

The theory behind the classic RFP is good, but the trend lately has been toward streamlined versions or even toward no RFP at all. Nevertheless, if you remember that the RFP has a long tradition as a useful document, you may want to think about including some or all of the standard ingredients in a document that you send around to vendors. The following two sections summarize the standard ingredients in an RFP.

One Set of Possible RFP Ingredients

RFP expert John A. Hinojos, president of Triangle Business Solutions in San Diego, recommends these ingredients (Hinojos & Miller, 1998):

Data You Should Provide

- Size, annual sales, and all locations of the company;
- Overview of the project;
- Technical requirements;
- Project scope;
- Training, staffing, and maintenance requirements;
- Timelines and critical success factors; and
- Documentation requirements.

Data to Request that the Vendor Provide

- Length in business;
- Annual sales and number of employees;
- Ratio of income to R&D;
- Product information;
- References;
- Cost proposal (this you may not receive); and
- Technology supported today and in the future.

Hinojos is one of the world's foremost experts on RFPs. These suggested contents for an RFP are about as solid as you could find anywhere. If you want to give your vendors the confidence that you know the right things to ask, you might work from such a list. However, you don't have to feel obligated to use any that are not meaningful to your company. (For instance, your company may not have multiple locations.)

An Alternative Set

You can find a second list of recommended RFP ingredients in a white paper prepared by the Society for Human Resource Management titled "18 Steps to Selecting a Human Resource Information System." Here are the recommended RFP ingredients from that source:

- An overview that describes your company;
- A description of your software need and the employee population it will support;
- Desired system functionality;
- Required technical environment/specifications;
- A request for pricing;
- A request for customer references;
- Details on customer service/support available from the vendor; and
- A request for sample contract terms.

Notice that these two lists, although similar, are different. The Hinojos list, for instance, requests much more in terms of specific company background from the vendor. Either set can work nicely as a starter for your own RFP, but *your own RFP should be your own.*

TEN COMMON ERRORS IN RFPS

If you're going to send out an RFP, you can make it most effective by keeping a few simple guidelines in mind as you work. Here are some of the cautions I've picked up in talking with various vendors, consultants, and candidate companies. I've listed these more or less in reverse order of importance.

1. Asking for Too Much Detail

RFPs often go into a frightening level of detail, such as, "Do you allow five character fields for middle initials of job candidates?" or "Do you distinguish between upper and lower case in passwords?" If some such detail is critical to your business, then by all means include it. Many vendors, though, may simply toss your

RFP aside at the outset as not applying to them. You may miss out on the best suppliers in that case.

For the most part, for small to mid-sized companies, the RFP is an initial screening, not a final screening. You may want to know such things as, "Do you support Microsoft Word?" or "Do you have a candidate search capability?"

I recommend using the RFP to make broad distinctions among candidate companies, not to go into excruciating detail.

2. Not Asking for Enough Detail

A salesman from PeopleSoft once cautioned me that a too-general RFP will result in no screening at all. If questions are too general, he said, companies will just put "y," "y," "y," and plan to explain more to you during the product demo. That salesman recommended that companies request a good deal of narrative from vendors. "It's an incredible amount of work for us," he said, "but it's probably better in the long run. It allows companies to make genuine distinctions."

Of course, PeopleSoft does benefit from such screening methods. PeopleSoft is a product bursting with detail. It has hundreds of built-in reports, for instance, and hundreds of data fields. It would probably be the lead qualifier if you were looking for detail in the product.

If the details are not the right details for you, though, then your screening may not get the right results. And if the product you purchase has too many reports and data fields that you don't use, your product is cluttered and not as easy to use.

Therefore, though you may want to take that salesman's cautions to heart, you should consider the source as well. Some small, elegant products don't have a lot of built-in detail, but you can easily set them up to have the detail that you need.

In short, you may want to ask for some detail, but try to make it the right detail, and leave it at that.

3. Bashing Them with Boilerplate

Vendors who reply to numerous RFPs have libraries of boilerplate on all the items listed above as standard content. Similarly, companies who send out RFPs can have boilerplate on the company-supplied information, such as the company history.

Some boilerplate shows preparedness and professionalism. But control it, and keep it to a minimum. Read it yourself when you put it into your RFP. If your own eyes glaze over as you read it, expect the same from your audience.

4. Not Being Organized

Decide on the categories on your RFP, and stick to them. For instance, you may have these categories:

- Company History
- Technical Requirements
- Employee Tracking
- Benefits Tracking
- Pricing

When working with any of the categories, focus on that category. One vendor reported to me that he found it distracting when an RFP would "mix in pricing all over the place." Read over your completed RFP and ask others to read it over as well. Keep it well-organized and simple.

5. Not Having an Open Mind

One of the key reasons for the selection process is to balance out any pre-dispositions you may have. Sure, you may already like the personality of a particular company rep. Another may have been rude to you some time in the past. However, when all is said and done, the one who was rude once may actually be best for you most of the time. Approach the RFP with the open mind of a scientist. Be fair. You'll obtain the best results if you do so.

One of the most certain ways to begin with a closed mind, perhaps unintentionally, is to work with the sample RFPs that vendors provide you. Often vendors will do so, and you may benefit by looking over their suggestions. But I wouldn't work with just one such sample. Vendors invariably build their own product strengths into the RFP. Collect a number of such RFPs from competing vendors if you want to remain open-minded as you compile your own RFP.

6. Relying Too Much on the Numbers

In the abstract, almost everyone loves the idea of an evaluation matrix. (You can see a sample on the accompanying CD-ROM.) The matrix would appear to make your assessments quite objective and to prevent you from putting undue weight on one consideration or not enough weight on another.

However, one vendor in particular protested vehemently to me that such matrixes were unfair to his product. His product—a neat program for performing 360-degree evaluations—was creative. You had to understand the concept underlying it before you could evaluate it. "We have wonderful built-in tools," he explained, "and people don't even realize that they are in there." Also, he said, people rule them out based on price, even though their price/performance is actually superior. A matrix, he insisted, can be really misleading. And, he added, "People tend to ask the wrong questions with a spreadsheet. They tend to be mechanical about it." A spreadsheet, then, can give a false sense of preparedness and objectivity. Don't feel that, simply because you have one, you are truly being thorough and fair to a vendor.

What's the solution? For the vendor mentioned here, the suggestion was simple: "We want to sit down and talk with them. We need conversation so we can explain what we have. When we can do that, we almost always win."

7. Not Knowing Your Priorities

You're not looking for the right product. You're looking for the right product *for you*. Technical requirements, such as SQL 7 compatibility, may be critical, or they may not be so important at all. (You can elect an ASP solution and not have to be concerned at all about the technical environment.) You should go in doggedly looking for certain features that matter to you, such as, perhaps, competency-based training. Know what's important to you as you go through the process.

8. Asking for Information You Don't Care About

As HR becomes more savvy, this situation may become less common. A couple years ago a vendor said to me, "Someone in HR is asked to do this. They don't know anything about software. They go to IT, who gives them a list of questions. They cut and paste the questions into an RFP, such as the question 'What power backup features does it have?' They don't know what the questions mean, and they don't really care at all about them."

Take charge of your own RFP. Know what you mean in the questions you ask. If IT supplies questions, make sure you understand them. If you don't, seriously consider leaving them out of the RFP (because you won't understand the answers either).

9. Not Really Knowing What You're Looking For

You need a point of reference. If you are requesting information from vendors, you have to know what you're going to do with it. What problems do you want to solve in your HR organization? Do a thorough needs analysis so that you can decide what's missing. Then, in interrogating vendors, ask them for the information that you truly want.

Now, I can imagine a situation where you aren't sure what you want, and you'd like to have vendors begin to tell you what you want. To some degree, I think you might allow that. Vendors are in the business, after all, of supplying user needs. I recommend, however, that you balance such a process in two ways. First, gather such advice from multiple vendors—and multiple vendors of different styles (such as, for instance, one who recommends the ASP option, another who is purchase only). Second, once you have gathered such "hints" from a number of sources, use them to jump-start yourself. Then sit down and do your own needs analysis, drawing on all those useful suggestions.

10. Making an RFP at All

Because the RFP has become a time-consuming, bureaucratic process in many instances, you may serve yourself well simply by avoiding it altogether. The RFP does help protect against the danger of simply turning to one vendor and accepting whatever that company says. However, if you can trust yourself to locate several qualified vendors and to work with them, you save yourself months of valuable time if you bypass the RFP altogether.

TEN USEFUL GUIDELINES FOR AN RFP

If you do decide to make an RFP, here are a few suggestions to keep in mind:

1. Work from your needs assessment.

2. Ask IT for advice, but don't put IT in charge.

3. Ask top management for its requirements. You won't get anywhere if you don't have management's backing.

4. Ask how the vendors will meet your *business* needs. You want to solve problems, not put a pretty system in place that no one uses.

5. Get organized.

6. Ask about price.

7. Ask for reference accounts.

8. Be fair.

9. Be objective.

10. Be willing to look beyond the RFP.

THE ARGUMENT FOR A SHORT RFP

As you contemplate your own RFP, you may want to consider a shorter document than the classic RFP of old. Hank Riehl, CEO of SkillView Technologies, Inc., of Plaistow, New Hampshire, suggests that a full-blown RFP may be overkill. "If I told you how much money and effort some of these companies spent evaluating products, writing elaborate RFPs, and then *not even buying anything,* you'd be sick," he says.

"Our company no longer responds to elaborate RFPs because so few ever get awarded to anyone (and they are a challenge to respond to). By the time proposals are in, a 're-org' or some other shift in priorities takes the entire initiative off the table. We've seen twelve-month, even eighteen-month buying cycles. In my opinion, these RFPs are perfect examples of how NOT to do it. Seriously, these companies spent twice as much in staff time evaluating products as the products themselves cost.

"If you want to give good, useful advice to buyers of this sort of software, here's my version. Cut the evaluation time from months to weeks, and evaluation costs from tens of thousands to a few thousand. This approach serves both the vendor and the buyer. This is premised on what I think is a fundamental fact: There are probably several, perhaps many, vendors whose product(s) will serve this need just fine. In the final analysis, a Ford is not that much different in its utility from a Chevy. Both are competent and viable. Many buyers think they are 'unique,' but they are (almost always) not."

Mr. Riehl suggests the following steps to short-cut the RFP process:

1. Create a short wish list of the strategic business objectives this software should help address. The list should probably not have more than three to five entries.

2. Create another short list of the general, high-level attributes/modules/ features the software should possess. The list should have maybe eight to

twenty entries. Keep the list small, including the things that *really* matter. Don't worry about including every bell and whistle.

3. Using the lists from 1 and 2, research the market for a list of potentially viable vendors. Although more vendors may be available, keep this list to the best five to eight, using whatever elimination criteria is deemed most important but keeping analysis at a high level. Vendors should be selected/rejected in this phase from their product literature and/or websites.

4. Research these vendors and their offerings more thoroughly to cut out half to arrive at a short list. Even in this phase, product demos are premature (because seeing eight different demos will just confuse matters rather than clarify them). Digging into eight different companies and their products will result in some obvious "keepers" and "rejects" without having demos.

5. Now with the short list of two to four vendors, have them make presentations/demos. Be sure to share with them your criteria from steps 1 and 2 so they are not shooting in the dark. They are not adversaries; they are potential partners. Make sure they know what you are trying to achieve so they can show you how they can help you get there.

6. Make your vendor selection on a trial or pilot basis. Negotiate a no-cost or low-cost deal where you can try out the software for thirty to sixty days to really find out how easy it is to "live with" and how well it serves your needs. This is where the real analysis belongs.

"I liken this whole process to buying a car," says Riehl. "No matter how many reviews one reads, or test-drives one takes, one never *really* knows whether the car was a good choice until a few weeks after the purchase. For my last few purchases, I've rented that model for a week just to see how it was to live with. Twice, I've switched selections because of what I discovered during a rental. So it should be with software. The essence of all this is that too many software buyers over-analyze. Intricate feature lists and RFP specs cloud the much more strategic issues:

1. In the main, does this software serve our strategic needs?

2. In the main, does this software deliver all/most of the attributes/features we desire?

3. In the main, is the vendor behind the software one we can see ourselves doing business with?

Says Riehl, "Find a vendor for whom all three are a 'yes' and go with them." Riehl is the voice of experience in the process, and perhaps a voice of sanity as well.

WHY YOU MAY NOT NEED AN RFP

The RFP, then, is a formal process for collecting information in a systematic fashion and tracking your results as you do so. You go through steps more or less like these:

- Send out an RFP document to a list of vendors.
- Vendors respond to your questions.
- You compile the responses when they come in and compare the various vendors.
- You draw up a list of top candidate companies, which you can then call in to demo their products.

Some such process is the ideal for the RFP, but, as you can perhaps infer from this brief description, the whole concept lends itself to wasting precious time. Often you can narrow your list of candidate companies to the right ones without actually sending out a request. For example, if you insist on a vendor who is compatible with an Oracle database, many on your list of candidates may not be eligible. Or, in the world's most common screening method (cost), if you have only $25,000 to budget for purchase of the software, you really don't have to take the time to consider all those who cost $50,000 and above.

I will concede that the RFP is great for accountability after you have completed software selection. If you were in charge of the process, with an RFP in hand you can readily respond to questions such as, "Did we ask about proper support when we sent out the RFP?" or "Is this time and attendance piece the right one for us. Did we check on that during the RFP?" However, in many cases in the modern, fast-paced economy, nobody will be looking backwards anyway to see what you should have done. They'll be looking forward, using the software you've selected, and thinking about what they should do with it.

For a large company, the RFP may be nothing short of essential. For the small to mid-sized company, though (the targets of this book), the RFP may be more an obstacle to success than a steppingstone. Author Richard B. Frantzreb summarized the situation nicely in a conversation with me. "For a big firm, a lot is at stake in software selection. Prices of the software they're purchasing are high. They get great value by going through the RFP exercise, with the help of a consulting firm. But that model applies only at the top end, or at the mid- to top end of HRIS.

"For specialized and lower-priced systems—for example, for an HRIS system for five hundred to one thousand employees—they are not going to put out an RFP. The software might have a base price of $2,000 to $5,000. They're going to end up putting out ten times that much in consulting fees."

F. Jay Fox, a consultant with the firm Working Concepts, Inc., in Columbia, Maryland, made a similar point in the August 1998 issue of *HR Magazine*: "Traditionally, the next phase [after compiling a short list of prospective vendors] would require that you issue a request for proposal (RFP), in which you draw up a list of requirements and submit them to selected vendors. Then, interested vendors send you a bid for delivery and completion of the requested product(s) and or services. This approach is time-consuming. I recommend skipping the RFP and contacting the top three or four vendors that have the best chance of fulfilling your needs."

I don't particularly like the idea of RFP for smaller companies. Perhaps I tend to be impetuous, impatient, and eager to "get on with it." I don't much like the idea of sending out something in the mail, then waiting days and days for people to respond. Experts like Fox and Frantzreb agree. If you want to purchase HR software, get on with it. You don't have to bury yourself in the paperwork of creating, sending, receiving, compiling, and evaluating RFPs.

CONCLUSION

On your own, you can probably narrow down your list of likely software providers to four or five. Use a directory like the Frantzreb directories listed in the References at the end of the book. You can even do preliminary research on the Internet. Once you have your list of vendors, establish some criteria, then give the vendors a chance to present their wares to you.

If you bypass the RFP in the right way, you can save weeks of frustration—on your part and on the part of the vendors. You can get past the boilerplate and get down to the nitty gritty of matching a vendor with your own needs. Once you receive information from vendors in one way or another, you are ready for product demos. The next chapter tells how to prepare your own script for the demos from vendors.

Scripting the Demo

"Demo script." It is not an everyday term in HR software selection, as is, for instance, "RFP" or "needs analysis." A scripted demo is an in-person demonstration of the product that follows a clear agenda (in fact, a written script) that you have prepared for the vendors. Vendors may be caught off guard when you first suggest the demo script to them, and they may try to discourage you from it. "Oh, you don't need a demo script for this, because . . . blah, blah, blah." They may say that the material is too straightforward or that the important thing is to see the standard demo of the product. "We'll have time for questions afterward," they may say, even though people often get tired, demos run long, and the question period often receives short shrift.

The time you actually spend in person with vendors is precious. On the occasion of the live demonstration (demo), vendors can present their living product as you will see it when you use it. You, for your part, can evaluate the product dynamically in terms of the real needs of your own company. As F. Jay Fox (1998) notes in "Do It Yourself HRMS Evaluations," "The scripted demo is the heart and soul of the evaluation process." In spite of what vendors may say about the script being out of fashion or whatever, the demo script is a powerful evaluation tool for you.

In this chapter, I acquaint you with some of the background issues related to scripted demos. I tell you why you ought to script the demo, what to cover, and how to avoid common pitfalls (such as using somebody else's demo script that doesn't fit you). I conclude with a sample demo script that might serve as a model (but not a straightjacket) for your own.

WHY TO SCRIPT THE DEMO

Scripted demos are not necessarily a standard approach among HR departments. Payroll departments or IT departments, more technical by nature, tend to prepare scripts for the product demos they receive. Human resources departments, more human and "right-brained," do not always take the time to break out product demos into a series of steps for the vendors to follow. There is a clear advantage, however, to scripted demos.

The biggest advantage I see to the product demo is that all the key players are present in one place to view a live version of the product. At the demo you can have HR managers, IT representatives, payroll, top management, and, in short, everyone who will be benefiting from the software. The vendor may bring in a team as well. At a minimum, the vendor will have a prepared presentation that represents the overall thinking of his or her company. In putting the vendor through his or her paces, you find out systematically how well the product meets your own needs.

Any demo has the advantage of bringing all the players together. A *scripted* demo, though, has added advantages. "What's the difference between a sales presentation (a canned demo) and a scripted demo?" asks Fox (1998). "In a canned demo, you see only what the salespersons want you to see. By requiring a scripted demo, you tell them what you want to see. This puts you in the driver's seat."

A second benefit of the scripted demos is that you assure that the vendors you evaluate all treat the same material. After all, you have to reach some kind of a fair decision. One vendor may have great reference accounts and great pricing, and the presenter could spend three hours talking about the success of the product at other companies. Then the vendor could nail down a sale by offering aggressive pricing. The approach might be great for the vendor, but it might not cover what you wanted to know.

A second vendor might do a beautiful job presenting his product's elegant technical architecture (its coding, its use of databases, its links to other software) and his product's simple-to-use interface. This vendor might be every bit as persuasive as the other one, just mentioned, who focused on reference accounts. What would happen when you wanted to compare Vendor A with Vendor B? You would be comparing apples and artichokes. You would not be being fair—above all to yourself.

Also, by allowing vendors to form their own agendas, you would not assure completeness. Perhaps the vendor with the strong reference accounts is weak on ease-of-use (or vice versa). Left to "fly on his own wings," the vendor is going to talk about his product's strengths and, as much as possible, downplay the product's weaknesses. (That's OK for the vendor. It's his job. But it is your job, as the purchaser, to see the full picture.)

If you script the demo yourself, you are much more likely to see what you need to see for your company. Leave the vendor on his own to script the demo, and you will see whatever makes that company look the best (even if it is more suited to a manufacturing company when you're a service company, or to a start-up when you're a long-time, true blue player).

WHAT TO COVER

If you are scripting for your own company, then, of course, you will cover your own specialized considerations. There are no hard-and-fast rules as to what to cover. If you've done a needs analysis, you have already nailed down the needs at your company. *Those* are what you want this vendor to address, not the needs at the last company he did a demo for or at the hypothetical company he has presented in the slide show that he has on his laptop.

Review both your needs analysis and your RFP, if you have prepared one. If you've done these steps, then the script for the demo need not be a major undertaking. Go through the criteria you have set up and adapt them to the format you and the vendor have planned for the demo. Keep the following guidelines in mind:

- Be sure the vendor has enough time to cover what you want to cover.
- Help set priorities, so the vendor will know which things to cover in greatest depth.
- Help adapt the presentation to the audience. Perhaps you say, "Finance is attending this demo today. Please be sure to cover in-depth the connection between HR and finance in your software."

Here are some basic topic categories you may want the vendor to include:

- Vendor and product background;
- Human resources solutions;
- Reporting;
- Ease of use;
- Technical basis; and
- Pricing.

As I've mentioned, the priority of each topic depends on the particular needs of your company. Here are a few things to consider within each topic.

Vendor and Product Background

Human resources software, at this time, has many newcomers and few established names. Even PeopleSoft, the longtime king of human resources, came into existence only in the 1980s. It does not have the longevity of IBM or AT&T. You cannot hold your HR software vendor up to too high a standard for longevity. However, you do want to have confidence that your vendor is a reliable company with a solid reputation.

Also, companies have varying visions. One prides itself on knowing HR inside and out. Another, while knowing HR, prides itself on its technology. Finding out about the vendor right at the outset is just like a good introduction when you meet a person. As the rest of your meeting takes place, you have an idea of whom you are dealing with.

Human Resources Solutions

The essence of all the rest that you are doing is, most likely, solving human resource problems. Your department has real business activities, and you want to automate them. If you did a needs assessment like the one outlined in Chapter 5, you have spelled out your human resource needs. You know what you are doing manually that you want to do automatically. You know what you would like to be able to do if you only could (such as see at the touch of a key a list of all those managers with performance reviews that are overdue).

Focus the presenter on your real needs and how her software would meet those needs. The meeting will be meaningful for you, perhaps inspiring, and you will be taking a major step toward successful implementation later.

Reporting

The true power of your HR software is its reporting. Initially you may be interested in just basic reports, such as a listing of all employees in certain departments. Quite quickly, though, you will be wanting specialized reports such as the average "time to hire" for new employees or the comparative costs for benefits providers under your cafeteria plans.

You will want to look closely at both standard and ad hoc reporting (reports you prepare yourself on specific questions) features. Look at both the overall number of reports and at the categories of reports available. If you need extensive reports on labor relations, for instance, make sure those are available.

Many products use built-in report writers such as Crystal Reports for their ad hoc reporting. Not all use the standard report writers, however. Sometimes a product creates its own original report writer designed to be easier to use. You will want to focus on the ad hoc report writer closely enough to see any particular enhancements or advantages a particular vendor may provide.

Ease of Use

Products have become quite standardized over the past few years. Microsoft Windows 95 and its successors became a standard, and Internet browsers (Netscape Navigator and Internet Explorer) have become standard as well. A product no longer has an edge in ease of use because it allows you to click on menu choices or use a mouse.

However, products vary widely in how well they exploit the standard environments. A product may use a Web browser as an interface, yet require several steps for you to move from one place to another. You may have difficulty going back to where you were in a previous step. Online help may not be adequate. With one product you may be able to right click and see a useful list of choices; with another product you might not have the same shortcuts at hand. Have clear ideas of what ease of use means to you, and find out how well the candidate's product lives up to your standard.

Technical Basis

The Internet has recently become the medium of choice for many users, yet only a short time ago a client/server environment was as technically advanced as you could get. Suppliers are eagerly demonstrating that their products are Web-ready, but not all are. In some quarters, a backlash against the Internet has led to increased appreciation of client/server.

You will want to check both the technological vision and the technological reality of your candidate product. Whether the issue is Web readiness or something else, technology continues to evolve at a furious pace.

You probably ought to call in your IT people to help you ask the right technological questions in your demo script. You don't want your demo session to turn into a purely technological discussion (which could easily happen). You want the emphasis on HR solutions. However, unless your candidate products address key technological needs, all the rest of your inquiry is for naught.

Also, you will probably want to tie technology to the solution at hand. The presentation may degenerate into a discussion of "backbones," "coding," "object models," and other technical matters. As the HR person, don't be overwhelmed by the discussion. The software, after all, is for you and to solve your problems. Don't be shy about asking politely, "How does this technology help solve our problems in HR?" And don't just settle for the response that the software is reliable, that it is flexible, or that it is fast. Ask how it helps you perform actual business activities.

Pricing

Shopping for HR software is like shopping for anything else. Pricing, ultimately, has a good deal to do with the final decision. You probably don't want your discussion to begin and end on the question of pricing, because you want to find a product that will meet your needs. Perhaps your company is not particularly price-sensitive. You are more concerned with meeting your needs than with saving $30,000 or $40,000 on the purchase price of a product. Nevertheless, you want value for your money. Management is going to want to know that you are spending money wisely. Don't be shy about asking about pricing during your product demo.

AVOIDING PITFALLS

Once you decide to script your own demo and settle on what to cover, you still face certain risks. Here are a few of the most common risks, with thoughts on how to avoid trouble.

- First, don't just take a demo from a vendor and use it as your own, possibly for presentations from several vendors. Using a vendor's own script is only one step better than simply turning the floor over to the vendor in the first place. You want the vendor addressing your questions, not doing his own "dog and pony show."

- Second, don't take a standard script from the Internet, from your IS department, or even from this book and use it as your own. One vendor told me that HR departments often came to him with scripts that the IS department had provided them, and the scripts would be filled with technical questions that did not mean much to the HR department. Human resources may have thought it was going by the book, but, in fact, it was removing itself from the process (or making the whole process ineffective).

- Third, go over each step in your demo script and make sure it is meaningful to you. If you see something you don't understand, ask for an explanation. If you adapt a script from a vendor or from your IS department, adapt it freely. Adapt it so that it truly does reflect your concerns and address your real needs.

- Fourth, share the script with your team members. If you can, obtain participation and buyoff from everyone. If people have not seen the script before the session, they tend to just give themselves over to the vendor. You may never have a chance to cover some of the points in your script.

- Fifth, give the script to the vendor beforehand, and have him or her agree to follow it. Have the script handy at the time of the presentation. Vendors, believe me, don't really want to follow your script. They probably have a canned presentation, developed over months and months of planning. They position their product in certain ways. They emphasize strengths and gloss over weaknesses. Besides, tailoring a presentation to one audience takes time and thought. They don't want to do it, but you want them to.

- Sixth, don't be shy about having a script and wanting to use it. True, the vendor has demo'd the product perhaps hundreds of times, and this is your first time to see it. But you will be paying. This is your day, and you should receive answers to your questions.

- Last, of course, allow the vendor time to go into a "dog and pony show." (He'll do it whether you allot time for it or not.) Do allot time for it, but have it be just one of the points covered, as in answer to a question such as, "What are the particular strengths of your product in relation to the competition? What makes you special?" Have that be one question out of many. Don't allow it to be the only subject of discussion.

CHECKING OUT A VENDOR'S SCRIPT

One vendor has kindly shared the script shown in Exhibit 7.1 with us. The vendor, Performance Software of Hasbrouck Heights, New Jersey, provides payroll and human resource software using standard Web tools and technologies. As you look over the flow of this demo, you can see two different things. First, the demo does nicely cover the material that the vendor wants to cover. Second, the demo does not necessarily cover everything that you might want to cover. To be able to see the capabilities that you have in mind, you have to ask for them.

Exhibit 7.1. Sample Vendor Script

Preparation

- Set up e-mail for report group to e-mail reports to prospect.
- Create two batches: 1 spreadsheet and 1 time card. Create checks for one batch.

Brief Technology Background

- JAVA and HTML, ability to run a whole payroll over the Internet, not just some of the system.
  - No transmitting data. All one database.

Review Main Menu Items

- Global Setup
  - Deductions

    Taxes

    All other employee deductions-unlimited

    Deduction types tie into formulas
  - Formulas
  - System administration

    User setup

Exhibit 7.1. (Continued)

Data filtering

User roles

- Basic security

Firewall, network, DynaSuite, database

Report writer uses same security for end user report writing

- Company information
- Employee information

Hire wizard

Employee summary history

Employee check history detail

- Create/edit trial payroll

Show spreadsheet and time cards

Walk through menu options

Show checks and check detail

- ACH

Show ACH detail

- Finalize payroll

Track status of batches as they process

- Reports

Show sorting and grouping options for reports

Talk about report writer

- End

Remove client from group e-mail address

CHECKING OUT A GENERIC SAMPLE SCRIPT

Although your own demo script should truly be your own, you can find good ideas of what to include by reviewing other demo scripts. Vendors will occasionally provide you with samples. Consulting companies (discussed in Chapter 4) may provide you with samples as well, although consulting companies often require a fee for such materials.

Exhibit 7.2 shows one sample I have prepared, aimed at a small, growing ad and PR agency. Note that the script truly is a script. It sets the times for discussion, sets priorities by allocating more time to certain events and less to others, and plans the sequence of events. (The sample, which you may adapt for your own purposes, also appears on the CD-ROM.)

 Exhibit 7.2. HRIS Product Demonstration Script

BACKGROUND FOR PRESENTERS

The Company: A_STARTUP

A_STARTUP is a creative organization of departmental teams that work in harmony to deliver solutions. It is

- Fast-growing

- Based on accountability

- Already established with ten key clients

Currently it has one location, in Topeka, but plans to add locations on both coasts and possibly in the Far East.

The heart of all that it does is its people, whom it seeks to attract, manage, reward, retain, and inspire.

Key to working successfully with its people are its human resources and hiring departments.

The purpose of today's demo is for you to show how your product is the best possible choice to help A_STARTUP's HR department fulfill its contribution to a fast-paced, ever-changing, creatively charged company whose heart is its own people.

Exhibit 7.2. (Continued)

The Purpose of the Script

The purpose of this script is to assure that competing vendors address the same issues, allowing A_STARTUP to make a meaningful comparison afterward.

Also, this script seeks to focus vendors on the issues of importance to A_STARTUP. Priorities and times are those preferred by A_STARTUP. Total time allocated for your presentation is three working hours.

Both vendors have met rigorous pre-qualification. We're not encouraging "opponent bashing," but we are interested to determine what distinguishes your well-qualified product over the other well-qualified product.

PART I: INTRODUCING YOUR PRODUCT VISION (15 MIN)

Introduce your product and your company. Explain:

- How you exploit the Web environment

- What you provide that gives an edge to an advertising and PR company

- How your product makes HR more efficient, more effective, and a better strategic contributor to the company

- What above all distinguishes your product in the marketplace

PART II: FILLING A_STARTUP'S HR AND HIRING NEEDS (45 MIN)

The purpose of automating A_STARTUP's HR is to speed up and simplify the real tasks that HR does, while at the same time increasing HR's accuracy, accountability, and effectiveness. Show how your software would accomplish the real A_STARTUP tasks in the following categories.

Hiring

Managing Requisitions

- Show how you set up a requisition.

- Show how you send a requisition for approval and what happens if the requisition is not approved.

(Continued)

Exhibit 7.2. HRIS Product Demonstration Script (Continued)

Collecting and Assessing Candidate Information

- Show how you would perform automated posting to multiple job boards.

- Show how you collect resumes, route them to the appropriate managers, and track them so as to avoid duplicate interviews.

- Show how you would pre-qualify an applicant. Does the system have the ability to ask an applicant questions about his/her skills before the resume is sent? Does it have the capability to reject a candidate based on his/her answers, before the resume gets through to the recruiter?

- Show how you place applicant information into a database.

- Show how the hiring person locates applicants. Do you search by keywords, codes, or by plain text?

- Demonstrate searching for a candidate qualified by geographical area and skills.

- Show how you would maintain a reminder system for contacting possible future hires.

The Hiring Decision

- Show how you would schedule interviews with candidates.

- Show how you formally hire applicants.

- Do you support the ability to send out letters to applicants automatically?

- Show how to maintain a referral program. Would the program include metrics? What would they measure?

Employee Tracking

Putting in Information

- Show how to put applicants into the database.

- Can your program feed in data from the hiring portion?

- Can your program import data from a spreadsheet? (Show either here or in implementation section, Part V.)

Exhibit 7.2. (Continued)

Displaying Information

- Show how you would display employee information, such as personal information, standard information such as hire dates, and job title.
- Show how you put in a salary increase and change a department.
- Demonstrate how to view an employee history, and show how to correct the history.

Terminating an Employee

- Show how you terminate an employee, and tell what happens to employee data at that time.

Benefits

Enrolling an Employee in Benefits

- Show how to enroll an employee into benefits, including medical, dental, cafeteria, insurance, and stock options.
- Show what happens when you attempt to enroll an employee in a plan for which he or she is not eligible.
- Show how to add a new benefit to the system.
- Show how you prepare employee benefits statements.
- Do you offer employee self-service?

Tracking Benefits

- Show how you track medical, dental, cafeteria, and other benefits.
- Show how to automatically track bonuses given out after specified periods.
- Show how to track 401(k), stock option plans.

Changing an Employee's Benefits

- Show how to change a benefit, such as a change in dependent coverage for medical insurance.

(Continued)

Exhibit 7.2. HRIS Product Demonstration Script (Continued)

Preparing Management Reports

- Briefly introduce benefit reports here, but cover them in detail in the Strategic Reporting section of Part III.

Training

Tracking Skills

- Demonstrate how the system tracks employee skills.
- Demonstrate how the system tracks prior work experience.

Assessing Training Needs

- Show how the system assesses training needs, both for the individual and for the company.

Preparing Individualized Training Plans

- Show how you would use your system to prepare individualized training plans and distribute them for review and approval.

Tracking Employee Training

- Show standard reporting available for each employee, indicating courses taken, when taken, and cost.

Succession Planning

- Show how your system supports management succession planning.

Preparing Management Reports on Training

- Introduce the subject here but cover in detail in the Strategic Reporting section of Part III.

Performance Reviews and Tracking

Show how you track due dates, who has submitted reviews, and what reviews are outstanding from which managers.

Exhibit 7.2. (Continued)

Time and Attendance

Show how you display an employee's vacation days used and available.
Show your system's compatibility with external payroll packages such as ADP.
Show how you display the following information:

- Sick days used and available.

- Personal days used and available.

- Billable versus non-billable time.

Compensation Analysis and Management

Show how with your system you input a salary increase and break the increase into merit, promotion, and adjustment components.
Does your system support multiple bonus plans?
Do you keep historical records for individual employees and for each bonus plan?

Testing

Show how you would test the skills of technical candidates.
Demonstrate your system of benchmarks and methods for measuring candidates against benchmarks.

Other Possible Activities

Please briefly explain any other key HR-related capabilities (such as organization charting) you may have built into your product.

Break

PART III: REPORTING: COMPREHENSIVENESS, FLEXIBILITY (30 MIN)

The A_STARTUP HR and hiring departments face both standard and specialized reporting tasks, related to all the HR scenarios in Part II above and more. A_STARTUP is seeking an HRIS program with built-in reporting that draws on extensive industry experience and, at the same time, provides the capability to generate ad hoc reports quickly and easily.

(Continued)

Exhibit 7.2. HRIS Product Demonstration Script (Continued)

Built-In Reports

How many built-in reports do you offer? Please explain your thinking in providing the built-in reports that you do.

Show how A_STARTUP might adapt a standard report to meet its special needs. Show how you report on the following:

Recruiting

- Recruitment cost per hire

- Applicants per position

- Acceptance rate

- Sources of successful hires

- Time to hire

Employee Tracking

- Number of employees

- Retention and turnover rates

Benefits

- Indicate your standard benefits reports.

Training

- How would you prepare a report showing for each employee courses taken, dates, and cost?

- Indicate your other standard training reports.

Compliance Reporting

Please demonstrate your readiness to meet government requirements in the following areas or any others you may address: EEO, FMLA, OSHA, COBRA.

Exhibit 7.2. (Continued)

Ad Hoc Reporting

What distinguishes your built-in report writer?

How would you create an ad hoc report to show all employees with Java programming skills, their years of experience, salary, current department, and EEOC classification?

Key question: How would you create a dynamic HR calendaring system that each quarter would automatically tell the HR manager all forms due and filings to be done (including performance reviews, filings with benefits providers, and more). How would the HR person re-design the system on the fly, as needed?

Strategic Reporting

In a company like A_STARTUP and an industry like the Internet industry, HR seeks to be much more than a successful clerical activity. It seeks to be a strategic partner with top management.

Give examples of the kinds of strategic reports you might offer, including:

Benefits

- Show how you would report on cost of benefits per year.
- Show how you would report on provider prices and overall cost effectiveness of provider.

Training

- Show how you would report for the company on overall training provided and the cost.
- Show an assessment report showing skills needed for individuals and the overall company.

(Continued)

Exhibit 7.2. HRIS Product Demonstration Script (Continued)

Break for Lunch

PART IV: EXPLAINING YOUR PRODUCT ENVIRONMENT (30 MIN)

Special Focus on Ease of Use (15 min)

A_STARTUP HR is busy, focused, and productive. To be useful, the HR system should require the least possible training and allow users to accomplish even advanced tasks with relative ease. Please demonstrate your product's ease of use in the following areas or any others you may have developed:

- Ease of use in exploiting the browser interface.
- Ease of use through understanding of HR and providing shortcuts to accomplish routine activities.
- Ease of use in standard reporting (allowing users to find reports readily).
- Ease of use in ad hoc reporting.

How much training is generally required to use your report writer? What makes your report writer easy to use?

Administering the HR System (15 min)

A_STARTUP wants to be able to adapt its HR system to meet its changing needs as it grows. For instance, A_STARTUP might find itself going international and might want to add or change certain display fields. A_STARTUP could add departments, change benefits procedures or salary review procedures, and much else.

- Briefly introduce your system administration capability.
- Show what makes the capability easy to use.
- Indicate the amount of training needed to use it.

PART V: PRESENTING TECHNICAL AND IMPLEMENTATION CONSIDERATIONS (30 MIN)

Technical Infrastructure (15 min)

All candidates to be the A_STARTUP HRIS provider meet the basic requirements of being Web-based, using Microsoft NT and SQL Server, and providing ADP

Exhibit 7.2. (Continued)

compatibility. Please state what you believe distinguishes your product in exploiting the required technical environment.

Web-Based

- How does your product exploit the Web environment and avoid its limitations?

Microsoft NT/SQL Server

- Show how your system, based on Microsoft NT and SQL server, is an open system that might tie in to A_STARTUP's ERP system.
- Discuss your product's scalability.

ADP Compatibility

- Describe your product's ADP compatibility.
- Show how your product handles W4 forms.

System Security

- Describe the measures your product takes to ensure security of information.

Implementation (15 min)

Rapid implementation is essential. A_STARTUP wants to be performing the HR activities outlined in the morning session as quickly as possible.

Key Question: What would be the projected time to implementation?
Please introduce key implementation considerations, including:

Ease of Implementation

- To what degree can A_STARTUP HR people carry out implementation themselves?
- To what degree is IS needed?
- To what degree must the vendor participate?

(Continued)

Exhibit 7.2. HRIS Product Demonstration Script (Continued)

Data Import

- How would A_STARTUP import current data on spreadsheets?

- What is involved in inputting manual information. Do you have guidelines and procedures for doing so effectively?

System Administration Setup

- How much training is required to set up system administration initially?

- How much time is required for HR to continue to perform system administration?

Implementing Regular Upgrades

- Can A_STARTUP implement regular upgrades, or do you advise that the vendor be involved?

Break

PART VI: PRICING AND REFERENCE ACCOUNTS (15 MIN)

Pricing

Purchase Options

- Please introduce your pricing and any special approaches you may take to pricing (such as a "fixed bid" approach or possible exchange of services).

- Show pricing in relation to all the following:

  The software itself

  Implementation

  Support

  Licensing and upgrades

Possible ASP Option

- Describe your ASP option and its pros and cons for A_STARTUP.

> **Exhibit 7.2. (Continued)**
>
> ---
>
> ### References
>
> Can you provide the names of three to five reference accounts of those who have purchased and implemented your system?
>
> ### PART VII: FINALE (15 MIN)
>
> Summarize why your product is the right one to fulfill A_STARTUP's purposes as a dynamic, competitive, Web-based company.

CONCLUSION

Demo scripts may not be as commonplace in software evaluation as the over-worked RFP. Vendors may act as if they are unusual, downright strange, and unnecessary. You, though, profit in several ways by using one. You prepare yourself. You prepare your evaluation team. You focus the vendor on what is important to you. And you assure that the needs analysis and RFP you have prepared do not go to waste. You find answers to the specific questions you have in mind, leading to meaningful decisions as you select a product.

In addition to scripting the demo, another way to obtain useful information about vendors and their products is through references, which is the subject of the next chapter.

"Word on the Street": References

You can spend months or years evaluating a product and trying to figure out what it does or does not do. You can ask yourself, "Does it really do what it claims to do?" Yet you can have difficulty finding out for sure whether the product lives up to its billing. The vendor claims it is ridiculously easy to use, but is it? They claim that the company's support service is truly superlative, that you always get a live person, and that the person always knows the answers. But how good is the service really? The company claims that it already has a stored version of just the specialized report you are going to want. But does it work out that way?

You can go round and round trying to answer such questions or, on the other hand, you can sit down and talk with someone who has already spent months or years figuring out what a product does or does not do. You can talk with real users.

Real users of a product are an incredible asset in the software selection process. Vendors, by trade, are supposed to make their products sound like the solution to all problems. Vendors are salespeople. Users, though, are hard-headed realists. In science, a researcher takes a hypothesis and tests it in the lab. In the business of HR technology, real users are the lab that tests the claims of the vendors.

Here is a joke that has been making the rounds recently. It applies directly to the situation you are in as a prospective HR software purchaser:

> A middle-aged man dies and soon finds himself with both St. Peter and the devil. St. Peter asks his name. And he says, "Bower, Johnny Bower." And St. Peter says, "Johnny Bower? Oh, I'm so sorry, you're not supposed to die for another five years. We'll have to send you back down."
>
> Mr. Bower is overjoyed, but he notices the two doors leading to Heaven and Hell and hears what sounds like a party behind the door to Hell. He asks if he can go over and just look around. The devil says, "Of course, but just for a few minutes." So he goes over and finds an incredible party going on, with wonderful food and drinks, and everyone obviously having a great time. He says to himself, "If this is Hell, I want to be part of it!"
>
> So when he gets back to earth, he sins his brains out for the next five years, doing every immoral thing imaginable to be sure he winds up in Hell. And sure enough, five years to the day later, he's facing the devil again in front of the door to Hell. As the door opens, he hears no music, and there is no food or a party. There are just these flames leaping out from the door. In disbelief, he asks, "Where's the party? Where are all the people having fun?" The devil grins and says, "Oh, you fell for that? Well, five years ago you were a prospect. Now you're a customer."

As a software purchaser, you don't want to be deluded by the promise of a great party with your new technology. You want to get a view of the reality you will face after you have had the product installed. There is no better way to get that view than to talk with real users. In this chapter are some guidelines on where to find the reference accounts, what to ask them, and how to get the most out of dealing with them.

FINDING A LIST OF REFERENCES

There are a number of ways to acquire a list of reference accounts, and you may have to resort to all of them. The first method is simply to ask a vendor to provide you with such a list. The vendor has a definite motive to satisfy your request, namely that the sale may depend on providing the information. Here are a few other reasons to turn to the vendor for your reference list:

- Vendors, of course, have access to the complete list of users;
- They know which users are willing to participate and which are not; and
- They know which users match up with your particular needs.

Vendors have leverage with their users and often can persuade them to take on this activity, which, after all, is a favor to you and to the vendor and does not offer any clear return for the reference account itself. The limitation of a vendor's hand-picked reference account, though, is that it is a vendor hand-picked reference account. Is a vendor going to choose someone disgruntled as a reference account in a sales situation? Probably not. If he did, he probably wouldn't be in business for long.

Some products have active users' groups. If you can contact the users' group and find a few names of users to talk with, you may be able to find reference accounts that way.

You also may know sister companies that are using the product that interests you. If there is any way that you can locate users "through the grapevine," you gain the advantage of talking with a more random sampling of users. That is, you can find users who are not necessarily the vendor's hand-picked favorites.

Sometimes the website for software or the vendor contains testimonials from users. You don't have to settle for the packaged set of information on the website, though. Call the user directly. You may end up speaking with a different person from the one on the website, or things may have changed from the time the material was placed on the site.

THE KIND OF REFERENCES TO LOOK FOR

Obviously, you gain a great deal if you can speak with other users in your same industry. If you are in manufacturing, you learn the most by talking with someone else in manufacturing. If you are in pharmaceuticals, you can find out a great deal from someone else who is using an HR product in a pharmaceutical company.

Even if you don't match up with a company by industry, you would like to match up by size. Software products often target particular market segments. ADP specializes in smaller companies; PeopleSoft specializes in larger companies. Those software companies may serve their target markets better than others. (Some companies, like Spectrum Human Resource Systems Corporation and NuView Systems—to name two—specialize in the mid-market but will serve almost any size company.) You would like to talk with users in your own market segment to find out how well the vendor serves your segment.

In sum, you want to look for a user from your industry, with the same technical environment as your company, and of similar size to your company. If you can, locate a user in your geographical area. You may find an onsite visit to be worthwhile.

However important finding a reference account in your industry may seem, welcome the opportunity to speak with just about any real user. Much of what you want to know does not depend on industry or company size or any of the other direct parallels to your own company. You can ask any user, for instance, how good the service has been from the provider. And the answer will be valuable for you. For almost any question that you ask, the experience of any user is useful. You should try to speak with at least one reference account from your own industry, but don't hesitate to speak with users from across the board. You may even learn something surprising and valuable from someone at a company in an industry completely unrelated to your own.

THE KINDS OF QUESTIONS TO ASK

If you have a really cooperative reference account, you may ask them to respond to any of the questions you have compiled in your needs analysis and your RFP. Perhaps you would show them an evaluation matrix (see Chapter 9) you have prepared and ask for their input on it as well.

The reference account is doing you a favor, though, and you may not want to put up too many obstacles to his or her participation. You can't really expect the third-party reference to devote the time and energy to you that the vendor will. General impressions from the user are valuable. Often the key information is simply a chance remark or even something that is not said. "We had a problem at first, but it was cleared up," the user may say. Ask them about it, and you'll find out something about technology (the actual problem that came up) and service (how the vendor responded).

I recommend nothing more in some cases than just a good chat with the user. You'll learn volumes. "So what did you want to accomplish with this software?" you might ask to get the ball rolling. "We had information in about five different places," the user may respond, "and it took us hours to prepare a report that should have taken minutes." Continue with the conversation in an easy way. But do have particular questions in mind. You can direct the reference to them as appropriate, and you can turn to the list when there is a lull in the conversation. Following are some of the questions I like to ask reference accounts:

- What problem were you trying to solve with this software? Did it solve the problem?

- What would you say are the product's greatest strengths?

- Is it easy to use?

- How is the support from the company?

- Did you encounter any problems with the product or the service?

- Did the implementation go smoothly, or did you encounter unexpected snafus?

- If you had it to do over again, would you choose this product again? Why or why not?

- What advice would you offer to someone like us as we begin the process?

You may want to match up your technical person with the reference account's technical person. Such a conversation would be quite revealing, as technical people are not in the habit of "sales patter." Your technical expert (who may be you) can come away with a solid sense of how well the product truly functions.

Even something as simple as the reference's "bottom line evaluation," however general, is invaluable. Some references will say, "I love this product. It's unbelievable." Others may say, simply, "I can't complain much, really, except for that one thing that happened."

Users, even hand-picked users from the vendors, tend to be quite independent in their thinking and quite honest. Vendors might wish that they could write scripts for their users, but they do not have such control. Reference accounts tend to give you the straight story, which is precisely why you should take the time to talk with them.

A FEW CAUTIONS ABOUT TALKING WITH USERS

Although sessions with users are invaluable, there are some cautions to keep in mind:

Some Aren't Easy to Connect with at First. These reference accounts are doing you a favor, as mentioned. There is no money in this for them. Sometimes they may even be competitors of yours, and they don't want to help you. You may encounter a few voicemail messages as you chase down users, and their attempts to connect with you may be half-hearted at best. Their reluctance is just natural. You are the pursuer in this situation. People are almost always friendly and forthcoming when you finally do connect, and remember that their information is worth the trouble it takes to nail them down.

Some Are Reluctant Because They Don't Want to Imply Endorsement. Perhaps you are talking with a large company, such as Johnson & Johnson, or with a government agency. On the other hand, the HR software product you are looking at may have only ten users and may come from a thirty-five-person company. The large company knows that its public endorsement would work wonders for the vendor and could even result in some form of liability. The user may not want to talk, even if the vendor has already provided you with the name. Often, you can get cooperation if you assure confidentiality, possibly in writing. Sometimes, too, you can ask the vendor to persuade an otherwise reluctant user to talk with you. But sometimes, especially with big, famous companies, you just have to give up and talk with someone else instead.

Some May Not Be Very Talkative at First. Be prepared to warm someone up. Some users are chatty, and some are a little on the morose side. Often the morose ones have the most information if you get them warmed up. Have your list of questions handy, and be prepared to carry the ball in the conversation.

References Selected by the Vendor May Be Biased. As mentioned earlier, the reference accounts sent by the vendor often are "teacher's pets." They are the ones the vendor expects to say the right things. Perhaps the vendor and user even have some form of understanding, as in "You scratch my back, I'll scratch yours." Maybe the vendor provides certain benefits to the user, such as paid speaking appearances or something else. Such things are possible, but vendors are not that much in the habit of paying their users. Usually the arrangement works the other way. I find that, for the most part, users are unbiased, even hand-picked ones.

References Don't Want to Offend the Vendor. Reference accounts want to stay in the good graces of the vendor. They don't want to say something that might offend the vendor and possibly damage the relationship. For instance, they wouldn't want to have the vendor fail to provide as good service as in the past. With such accounts, you may have to learn from what they do not say as much as from what they do. One way or another, you can generally tell whether they have been satisfied with the provider or not.

The Actual Expertise You Encounter Varies Considerably. There are users, and then there are users. Some have had the system for only a month and are still in the glow of the honeymoon. Some have no technical expertise and know no more than what they see on the screen: "I do one report. I point and click, and I get it."

Other users may be so expert that they'll quickly go right over your head. They may have the ability to design products similar to the one you are investigating. They'll know the inner structure, the outer performance, and the business implications of the whole thing. With such users, don't hesitate to ask them to explain things that you do not understand. They don't know that you don't know something unless you tell them.

Whatever the level of expertise of the user, the user is likely to be valuable. Naïve users can tell you a good deal about ease of use and support. Advanced users can be almost like unpaid consultants who help launch you on your way.

You Have to Talk with More than One. If you speak with just one user, you may end up with a distorted picture. "This product is supposed to be self-service," someone may say, "but at our company we use it for applicant tracking." This imaginary scenario may not seem to make sense, but any given company may have any kind of idiosyncrasy in how it uses a product. Similarly, any one user may say, "Boy, this is just an amazing product" or "I'm surprised they had you call me. We're taking the product out." However, if you talk with as few as two or three users, certain patterns begin to emerge. You'll see a fair picture.

CONCLUSION

As vendors and others lay out the formal steps for evaluating HR software, they often tend to downplay the importance of talking with users. Perhaps vendors would prefer that you talk only with them, where the message is controlled. Perhaps they don't like the inconvenience of having to identify and encourage reference accounts. Or perhaps they simply overlook the reference account as a key stage in the process.

Although vendors may overlook the reference accounts, you should not. You can learn more in fifteen minutes talking with an experienced user than you might in fifteen hours of demos with the vendor. You can draw on the real-world experience of the user. Nothing is better than that to balance out the abstract theory of a vendor's sales pitch. As you gather your materials from vendor demos and reference accounts, you reach a point at which you should be serious about making a decision. One of your best tools for comparing the offerings from multiple vendors is the selection matrix, discussed in the next chapter.

Moving Toward Implementation

Collecting facts is essential, of course, but you cannot continue indefinitely with mere information gathering. To accomplish the objective of selecting software, you have to reach a decision about your software and actually implement it. In this section you find out about a useful decision-making tool—the selection matrix. You receive tips on negotiating on HR software. You look into the all-important question of winning management approval. And you take a preliminary look at the mission-critical matter of planning implementation.

Preparing and Using a Selection Matrix

Grids are great, aren't they? On a grid you can see in one glance information that might take up pages and pages of text. You can run your finger along the top of a grid to find whatever column head interests you, such as "Internet ready." Then you can run your finger down the column to see who fits the category and who does not. Grids are great for summarizing information and for displaying results quickly. Grids, too, allow you to assign numerical values and reach quantitative decisions about what might otherwise seem a chaotic mass of material you have received from vendors.

In this chapter you will have a chance to see the selection matrix in a number of different forms—as a simple checklist, a questionnaire, and a table. The samples of these matrixes are also on the CD-ROM.

THE MATRIX AND HOW TO CREATE IT

A selection matrix is a table. Often people create them on an Excel worksheet. Typically, creating the matrix is a three-step process:

1. List vendors as column headings.

2. List criteria as row headings.

3. Fill in the matching cells.

Table 9.1 shows a sample of a very simple matrix:

Company Criteria	Great HRIS, Inc.	Also Good HRIS, Inc.	Competitive HRIS	Another HRIS
Table 9.1. Sample Selection Matrix				
Priced Below $5,000	X	X	X	
Microsoft Environment	X	X	X	
Offers Employee Self-Service	X		X	X
Pure Web Solution			X	

A quick look at this table tells you that only Competitive HRIS meets all of your criteria.

HOW IT'S USED, AND BY WHOM

You use the matrix in several different ways. First, in compiling your information, the selection committee simply uses the matrix to organize. You can keep track of the companies you are reviewing and the criteria you want to track. You can add and delete companies or criteria as your research evolves.

Second, the committee might use the developing matrix during information gathering. Often gaps show up on the matrix, and the committee can call vendors to gather additional information such as, "Do you offer employee self-service?"

Third, you can use the matrix during the demos to compile information and to focus the vendors on the issues that matter to you.

Next, you can use the matrix to help with decision making. For instance, you can assign weighted values to each of the boxes, based on the quality of a vendor's offering. Table 9.2 shows an example.

Table 9.2. Selection Matrix with Weighted Values

Criteria \ Company	Great HRIS, Inc.	Also Good HRIS, Inc.	Competitive HRIS	Another HRIS
Priced Below $5,000	2	2	1	0
Microsoft Environment	3	1	1	0
Offers Employee Self-Service	2	0	2	2
Pure Web Solution	0	0	2	0
Score	7	3	6	2

Using a weighted system, you can see that Great HRIS, Inc., "scores" the highest, even though it doesn't meet one of the criteria. This means that it does the things that it does do better than the competition. You and your organization then need to decide whether that superiority is worth the tradeoff in missing criteria.

PITFALLS OF THE SELECTION MATRIX

The selection matrix looks glamorous and, in fact, downright authoritative. There is no question that it is a great way to organize your material. The matrix has great utility in helping you compile your material, put together a rating, and find information at a glance. What could be the possible drawbacks to such a thing?

You do encounter certain risks. If your matrix is too detailed, and you ask the vendors to fill them out, they may do whatever it takes to "get a foot in the door." More than one vendor has told me, in fact, that they simply check off all the boxes when asked to list their capabilities. They can do everything one way or another. Most programs, even the least expensive ones, offer user-defined fields, which make it possible for the vendors to appear to adapt to almost any need. (But often a user-defined field is not the same as a fully defined function to carry out an activity.)

Here, then, are some of the cautions to observe with these tools, powerful though they are:

- Sometimes HR may be filling out a matrix that it has not prepared and does not understand. How could the outcome be meaningful to HR?

- Sometimes HR tries to squeeze products into the matrix, thereby missing the big picture and the subtleties.

- Detailed as it is, the matrix may not include the qualities that are most important about the product, and that would be most important to you if you addressed them. Perhaps you particularly need the ability to prepare your own ad hoc reports. Perhaps a matrix provided to you by IT or another department does not have that capability on its list. There are many possibilities for your needs that may not match with categories on a matrix provided from outside.

- As mentioned, the vendor may be able to answer "yes" to all categorics on the spreadsheet, making them more or less useless in the process. (To eliminate this risk, you may want to complete the matrix yourself rather than having the vendor do it.)

SAMPLE SELECTION MATRIXES

You can collect sample matrixes from vendors, consultants, your own IT department, and possibly other sources (HR websites, other HR folks, and so on). Vendors are often particularly willing to share such samples. Consultants may be the least willing to do so for no cost, because the matrixes are part of their practice. On the following pages are three sample matrixes from vendors—a checklist, a questionnaire, and a table. When doing your own evaluation, you can adapt such models to your own purposes.

The Selection Checklist

The basis of any comparison matrix is the initial checklist. You begin with a checklist, which may then become the items in a left-hand column on a matrix. Later, you can put the names of a number of companies across the top, and complete the checklist for each of the companies. Exhibit 9.1 is a simple checklist, suggested by PerfectSoftware, makers of hrWindows. Clearly, as with any vendor, the checklist is geared to the company's own offerings. To make it meaningful for you, delete and add items so that the checklist reflects your own needs in a software product.

Exhibit 9.1. Sample Selection Checklist

Does the system offer the following?

- ❑ Accrued Vacation Liabilities
- ❑ Additional Compensation
- ❑ Attach Word Documents
- ❑ Attendance Reports
- ❑ Attendance Tracking
- ❑ Automatic Benefit Eligibility
- ❑ Automatic Benefit Recalculation
- ❑ Automatic New Hire Function
- ❑ Automatic Termination Function
- ❑ Automatically Create Open Positions
- ❑ Benefits Reports
- ❑ Benefits Statement
- ❑ Benefits Administration
- ❑ Bonus Tracking
- ❑ Budget to Actual
- ❑ Calculate Adjusted Dates of Hire
- ❑ Career Development
- ❑ Change Field Labels
- ❑ Client/Server Version
- ❑ COBRA
- ❑ Company Holidays
- ❑ Company Property
- ❑ Company Property Reports
- ❑ Compa-Ration Analysis
- ❑ Compensation Reports
- ❑ Context-Sensitive Help

(Continued)

Exhibit 9.1. Sample Selection Checklist (Continued)

- ❑ Custom Attendance Formulas
- ❑ Custom Benefit Formulas
- ❑ Custom Code Tables
- ❑ Custom Design Fields
- ❑ Custom Preferences
- ❑ Custom Queries
- ❑ Custom Reports
- ❑ Custom Salary Grades
- ❑ Default New Hire Information
- ❑ Departmental Budgets
- ❑ Dependant Tracking
- ❑ Disability Tracking
- ❑ Disciplinary Actions
- ❑ Documentation
- ❑ Education Tracking
- ❑ EEO Reports
- ❑ EEO, AAP, and Military
- ❑ Electronic Notes
- ❑ Electronic DOL Handbook
- ❑ Electronic Manual
- ❑ E-mail Account Tracking
- ❑ Emergency Contact
- ❑ Employee Correspondence
- ❑ Employee Photos
- ❑ Employee Skills Development
- ❑ Expire Employee Benefits
- ❑ Export to ASCII

Exhibit 9.1. (Continued)

- ❑ Family and Medical Leave
- ❑ Field Level Security
- ❑ Fill Open Positions
- ❑ Financial Planning and Projections
- ❑ Full-Time Equivalency
- ❑ Global Update
- ❑ Graphs
- ❑ Grievance Tracking
- ❑ Handicap Information
- ❑ Headcount Analysis
- ❑ I-9 Information
- ❑ Illness Tracking
- ❑ Import from ODBC
- ❑ Imputed Income Calculations
- ❑ Incentive Pay Tracking
- ❑ Internet Updates
- ❑ Job Analysis
- ❑ Job Electronic Notes
- ❑ Job History
- ❑ LAN and WAN Versions
- ❑ Licensing
- ❑ Manager Level Security
- ❑ Mass Increase Salaries
- ❑ Mass Salary, Job, and Benefit Updates
- ❑ MS Access Database
- ❑ MS Visual Basic 5.0

(Continued)

Exhibit 9.1. Sample Selection Checklist (Continued)

- ❑ Multiple Phone Numbers
- ❑ Name/Address/SSN
- ❑ Open Positions
- ❑ Organization
- ❑ Organization Planning
- ❑ OSHA 200
- ❑ OSHA Tracking
- ❑ Output to Excel
- ❑ Output to Excel, Lotus, ASCII
- ❑ Output to Word
- ❑ Pay Period Dates
- ❑ Payroll Input Screen
- ❑ Payroll Interface to ADP
- ❑ Payroll Interface to Ceridian
- ❑ Payroll Interface to In-House
- ❑ Performance Reviews
- ❑ Plan Definition
- ❑ Position Control
- ❑ Remove Unused Fields
- ❑ Report Grouping and Sorting
- ❑ Report Record Selection
- ❑ Review and Effective Dates
- ❑ Salary Administration
- ❑ Salary History
- ❑ Salary Mid, Max, and Min
- ❑ Security Users and Groups
- ❑ Select Active or Terminated Employees

Exhibit 9.1. (Continued)

- ❏ Self-Service Module
- ❏ Seniority Dates
- ❏ Shift Information
- ❏ Skill Development
- ❏ Skills Tracking
- ❏ Split Cost Center Job Information
- ❏ Succession Planning
- ❏ System Audit Function
- ❏ System Tutorial
- ❏ Track Dependant Coverage
- ❏ Training
- ❏ Turnover Analysis
- ❏ Union Participation
- ❏ Unlimited Employee Records
- ❏ User-Defined Fields
- ❏ User-Defined Screens
- ❏ User-Defined Tables
- ❏ User-Level Security
- ❏ Vacation Accruals
- ❏ Visual Attendance Input
- ❏ W4 Data
- ❏ Wage and Salary Administration
- ❏ What-If Calculations
- ❏ Windows 95 Compatible
- ❏ Windows 98 Compatible
- ❏ Windows NT Compatible
- ❏ Workers' Compensation

The Selection Questionnaire

You may want to have the members of your evaluation team complete evaluation questionnaires. You can later compile the questionnaires to reach a quantitative analysis of the vendors. Exhibit 9.2 is a sample of such a questionnaire, suggested by vendor HR MicroSystems of San Francisco.

Exhibit 9.2. Sample Selection Questionnaire

HRIS Needs Assessment

Technical

- ☐ Database capabilities must support company growth to a minimum size of 1,000 employees. Will the database support company needs?
- ☐ Interface with ADP—automatically receive updates from ADP downloads
- ☐ Match company specs
- ☐ Internet-based
- ☐ WAN environment
- ☐ Merging records
- ☐ Purging records
- ☐ Data migration path
- ☐ Upgrade path
- ☐ Security

Company D Standard
- ☐ SQL 6.5 or 7.0
- ☐ NT 4.0 Server
- ☐ SP 5
- ☐ Compaq Proliant 3000r
- ☐ Dual PII 333 MHz-450MHz
- ☐ 512 MB Ram

Exhibit 9.2. (Continued)

❑ A mirrored 9GB HD for operating system

❑ RAID 5 Arrary of 18 GB usable HD for data

Rating (1–5; 5 the best):
Comments:

Recruiting

❑ Resume scanning quality—types of scanners that are compatible; e-mailed resumes acceptable for scanning; in batches; procedure to clean up errors on scanned resumes

❑ Resume attachments

❑ OCR quality—time it takes to recognize resumes and word recognition stats

❑ Ability to upload to job boards

❑ Document attachments

❑ Number of colleges in skillset engine

❑ Profiles for technical companies in skillset engine

❑ Easy to find candidates—how does a user go in to find a candidate?

❑ Ability to track candidates offer/acceptance by other companies

❑ E-mail response capabilities to candidates once resume received

(Continued)

Exhibit 9.2. Sample Selection Questionnaire (Continued)

- ❑ Recruiting source tracking—where a candidate was sourced and cost of that source

- ❑ Candidate tracking—notes section to keep track of dates contacted, interviewed, assign recruiter, interviewers, interview feedback, hiring manager, and so forth

- ❑ Schedule and e-mail interviews for candidates right from the database—link to recruiting calendar

- ❑ Ability to post positions internally/externally

- ❑ Ability to retract an acceptance

- ❑ Skill set searching capabilities—word for word or by groups

- ❑ Requisition tracking—tie candidates to a certain requisition, multiple requisition; search by requisition; track time to fill a req; reopen a closed requisition; attach resumes to req

- ❑ Cost per hire reporting

- ❑ Employee referral tracking—by employee and cost of referral

- ❑ Contact tracking

- ❑ Easy way to code/label contacts

- ❑ Download info from Access DBs and other sources

- ❑ Reference check tracking

- ❑ Phone interview tracking—create phone interview questions and use while speaking with candidates

- ❑ Web access so that multiple offices can use the same database or access remotely; web-based inbox or database inbox that could directly be submitted to the database

- ❑ Accessible to multiple users

- ❑ Speed

- ❑ Easy work flow

- ❑ Able to do different mailings/campaigns

Exhibit 9.2. (Continued)

- ❑ Recruiting reports available—weekly volume report
- ❑ Visa transfer checkbox
- ❑ Have all types of rejection letters
- ❑ Grade level field
- ❑ Offer letter templates
- ❑ Online employment application
- ❑ Able to assign tasks (Outlook)

Rating (1–5; 5 the best):
Comments:

HUMAN RESOURCES—GENERALIST/CORPORATE

A. New Hire

- ❑ Integrate with recruiting side (once a candidate hired, will the information be transferred to the HR portion, or downloaded from ADP)

B. Benefits

- ❑ FSA tracking—employee deductions and reimbursements
- ❑ Benefit plans, entry date, changes tracking; when changes made, are previous plans still tracked or are they deleted

(Continued)

Exhibit 9.2. Sample Selection Questionnaire (Continued)

- ❏ Dependent & spouse coverage tracking—by benefit, is type of plan trackable

- ❏ Beneficiary tracking—something employees might access via self-service tool if they would like to make changes

- ❏ Tuition tracking & reimbursement tracking—ability to track actual classes taken, grades, and reimbursements made

- ❏ COBRA tracking—terminated employees who opt for COBRA, tracking of payments received

- ❏ Total benefits tracking/individual statements—print individual statements for employees with detailed benefits explanation, including company expense

C. Compensation

- ❏ Salary history tracking by employee with dates and reasons and changes

- ❏ Review tracking, when occurred, by whom, and overall rating

- ❏ Profit sharing tracking—bonuses paid to each employee and percentage of salary

- ❏ Grade tracking—track grade ranges and employee's fit within range

- ❏ Manager & service line tracking—field that might be needed to create necessary reports

D. Terminations

- ❏ Tracking terminated employees—in the database and for how long

E. Self-Service

- ❏ Quantity of items available to employees—the interface look and what it includes

- ❏ Security issues, log-in requirements—what employees need to do to access information

F. Reporting

- ❏ Quality of reports available—easy-to-read and attractive
- ❏ Customize capabilities—new reports; can information from all tables and fields be linked to create certain selection requirements, sorting requirements, and group requirements
- ❏ Customize capabilities—current reports; can change current reports to match certain reporting needs
- ❏ Reporting capabilities are Company D standard

G. Bells & Whistles

- ❏ Org chart capabilities, customizability
- ❏ Job descriptions
- ❏ Task reminder—for certain HRIS-specific tasks; work with Microsoft Outlook
- ❏ Company inventory—laptops, cell phones, AMEX cards
- ❏ Manager access to subordinate salary history and so forth

Rating (1–5; 5 the best):
Comments:

The Selection Table

You can begin with an existing table and complete the table for each vendor. Exhibit 9.3 shows a sample suggested by another vendor, Open4 of Addison, Texas, makers of a Windows-based HRIS system with optional payroll as well.

Exhibit 9.3. Sample Selection Table

General	OPEN4	Vendor A	Vendor B	Vendor C	Vendor D
32-bit object-oriented	Y				
Truly OPEN system (runs on over 200 computers)	Y				
ANSI-standard relational database technology	Y				
100 percent 4th generation language (PROGRESS)	Y				
Centralized data dictionary	Y				
Multiple companies, divisions, branches, and departments supported	Y				
Number of employees limited only by disk space	Y				
Over 150 information tables included —most are user-modifiable	Y				
User can define unlimited additional tables, without programming	Y				
50+ information categories set up and ready to use	Y				
User can define unlimited additional information categories without programming	Y				
Category screens modifiable by end user without programming	Y				

Exhibit 9.3. (Continued)

General	OPEN4	Vendor A	Vendor B	Vendor C	Vendor D
User can define additional new data fields without programming	Y				
Full-featured REPORT WRITER included	Y				
Full-featured online QUERY included	Y				
Full integration with OPEN4 payroll system (optional)	Y				
Pay changes, promotions, transfers, and benefit enrollments may be scheduled in advance	Y				

Security	OPEN4	Vendor A	Vendor B	Vendor C	Vendor D
Work group security controls data access (display, update, query, and report writer)	Y				
Group security can control access by category of information	Y				
Group security can control access to notes, independent of information category security	Y				
Group security can control access to any individual field(s)	Y				
Standard menu item selection security is also available	Y				
Access can be limited to specific companies, divisions, branches, and departments	Y				

(Continued)

Exhibit 9.3. Sample Selection Table (Continued)

History	OPEN4	Vendor A	Vendor B	Vendor C	Vendor D
Unlimited history of all category information is possible	Y				
History can be tailored to retain information for different periods of time for each category	Y				
Can retain all pay changes, terminations/rehires, reviews, disciplinary actions, transfers, etc., for employee's entire time of service	Y				

Query	OPEN4	Vendor A	Vendor B	Vendor C	Vendor D
The online query displays or prints applicants or employees based on the contents of selected data fields. Multiple conditions may be connected to form a complex query	Y				
Queries may be performed on the basic person record or on any person category	Y				
Results of a query automatically lists names and employee numbers and may be printed	Y				

Report Writer	OPEN4	Vendor A	Vendor B	Vendor C	Vendor D
WYSIWYG (what you see is what you get) display	Y				
Report writer can access all authorized data	Y				
Work group security controls what fields may be selected for printing	Y				

Exhibit 9.3. (Continued)

Report Writer	OPEN4	Vendor A	Vendor B	Vendor C	Vendor D
User-defined conditions can control what is printed	Y				
Conditions can compare to other fields, constant values, or entered runtime variables	Y				
Multi-level user-defined sorting	Y				
Multi-level user-defined totaling	Y				
Multi-level user-defined page and line control	Y				
Accumulations, counts, minimum value, maximum value, and averages are supported	Y				
Supports variable runtime entry parameters	Y				
Supports hide of repeating values	Y				
Automatic column labels (user can change labels)	Y				
Print fields may be placed in specific locations (the system doesn't force its own spacing)	Y				
Page headers and footers can be copied from an established library	Y				
A file viewer is part of the product and allows the controlled viewing of reports sent to a file	Y				
ALL reports included in the OPEN4 HR system were produced by the report writer	Y				

(Continued)

Exhibit 9.3. Sample Selection Table (Continued)

Report Writer	OPEN4	Vendor A	Vendor B	Vendor C	Vendor D
Summary or detailed reports may be produced	Y				
Print All or Exception reports may be produced (outer/inner joins)	Y				
Mass update facility built into report writer (access controlled by security)	Y				
An optional upgrade is available that allows the OPEN4 report writer to access any other PROGRESS database	Y				
Output can be printed, viewed, sent to a file, or passed to Excel	Y				

Basic Person Information	OPEN4	Vendor A	Vendor B	Vendor C	Vendor D
The person information screen can display persons on file in several sequences: by name, by applicant or employee number, or by social security number (user-selectable)	Y				
The person information screen also provides display options: applicants only, employees only, or termina-tions only, as well as any combination of the three (user-selectable)	Y				

Note: OPEN4 stores only those category records in which the applicant or employee has had activity. For example, an active employee won't have a COBRA or terminated record (unless a rehire) and an employee with no military service will have no military record. When there are multiple occurrences of a category (absences, for instance), we automatically show a count of records and if you access the records, they're automatically presented in a latest-to-oldest sequence. Please read on—recognizing that we've omitted a great deal in the interest of space and have only presented highlights that we feel best represent the OPEN4 functionality.

Exhibit 9.3. (Continued)

Categories	OPEN4	Vendor A	Vendor B	Vendor C	Vendor D
Absences					
User-defined absence codes	Y				
Automatically shows day of the week for each absence	Y				
Automatically shows cost of the absence using the employee's rate information	Y				
Addresses					
Can retain unlimited addresses including: residence, mail, forwarding and others	Y				
Applications					
Stores position applied for (with multiple records possible) as well as shift	Y				
Carries user-defined recruitment source as well as several types of recruitment costs	Y				
Interface (optional) to Microsoft Word for rejection letters, etc.	Y				
Benefits					
Benefit information stored at company level and copied to employee (plan number, premiums) with employee override for insurance amounts, deduction periods, etc.	Y				
Related deduction data populates OPEN4 payroll for both employee and employer deductions	Y				

(Continued)

Exhibit 9.3. Sample Selection Table (Continued)

Categories	OPEN4	Vendor A	Vendor B	Vendor C	Vendor D
Dependent/beneficiary information retained in record including Medicare databank data. Beneficiaries automatically copied from family records	Y				
If benefit is terminated, a termination effective date and termination reason are available	Y				
Future benefits can be established with audit listings when ready to apply	Y				
All changes tracked via Benefit-Change Category for historical purposes	Y				
COBRA Stores the qualifying event code, type, and date as well as the continuation period and expiration date, and disabled code	Y				
Interface (optional) to Microsoft Word for COBRA letters	Y				
Court Orders Carries issuing authority, case/cause information, payer/payee name and addresses, and amounts for child support, garnishments, and liens	Y				
Discipline User-defined infraction codes, counseling information, scheduled review date, and recommendations	Y				

Exhibit 9.3. (Continued)

Categories	OPEN4	Vendor A	Vendor B	Vendor C	Vendor D
Access to OPEN4 payroll check history can display or print all earnings, tax, and deduction detail from history (when OPEN4 Payroll is in place)	Y				
Education Institution, degrees, GPA, user-defined educational codes as well as majors, minors, start and finish dates	Y				
Emergency Phone number and address of person to notify, blood type, allergies, personal physician, special instructions	Y				
Family Carries name, address, phone, birth date, Social Security number, age, and COBRA information for each dependent or beneficiary	Y				
Address updates from the person file can be copied into family member records	Y				
Family Medical Leave Act (FMLA) Includes information on both originating request and records of leave taken	Y				

(Continued)

Exhibit 9.3. Sample Selection Table (Continued)

Categories	OPEN4	Vendor A	Vendor B	Vendor C	Vendor D
Originating request includes qualifying reason, dates employee notification/certification requested/received, any temporary job assignments, paid leave used, second and third opinion, and entitlement in days	Y				
Records of leave taken includes number of days taken, when employee will return, and remaining entitlement	Y				
Health Height, weight, hair and eye color, smoker status, physical exam dates, and ADA disability or impairment information and special accommodations (this category can be specially secured)	Y				
Wellness participation tracking (for flu shots, exercise programs, etc.)	Y				
I-9 Information Includes resident type and supporting documentation	Y				
Injury/Illness Covers accidents, treatment, lost time, cost, OSHA reporting, and workers' compensation	Y				
Injury/illness information includes date and time of incident, injury or illness flag, location of incident, body part affected, description of incident, chemicals/equipment involved, and events leading to incident	Y				

Exhibit 9.3. (Continued)

Categories	OPEN4	Vendor A	Vendor B	Vendor C	Vendor D
Treatment information includes probable cause, injury type, affected body part, initial treatment, health care provider's name and address, offsite facility name and address, hospital in-patient flag, and date of death, if applicable	Y				
Lost time and cost information includes first day of work missed, number of days missed, number of restricted days, date returned to work, value of time missed, medical costs, and total cost	Y				
OSHA record includes OSHA case number, on-premises flag, illness or injury and illness type for OSHA 200 reporting, illness class for OSHA 300 reporting	Y				
Workers' compensation information includes date workers' comp was filed, file i.d., file status (open/closed), employee's job title, and department assigned	Y				
Interviews Unlimited records detailing interviewer name/title, dates, and comments	Y				

(Continued)

Exhibit 9.3. Sample Selection Table (Continued)

Categories	OPEN4	Vendor A	Vendor B	Vendor C	Vendor D
Jobs					
Master company-level job table carries exempt status, work hours, shift, pay type and pay frequency, EEO job category, AA job group, work comp code, salary ranges, and more for each job/position	Y				
Information is automatically copied into employee-level job record, where the individual employee's pay is stored in hourly, daily, pay period, monthly, and annual pay fields along with percent of mid-point	Y				
Job history is automatically retained for a user-specified period of time, tracking job changes along with reason for change	Y				
Multi-dimensional Pay Grade and Step tables also support geographical differences	Y				
Counts of authorized, budgeted, currently filled, and available positions retained at company level	Y				
Provides a link to position control and corporate hierarchy (with optional link to ORG PLUS)	Y				
License					
Stores issue and expiration dates, user-defined license types, license suspension flag, issuing authority, and employer/employee costs	Y				

Exhibit 9.3. (Continued)

Categories	OPEN4	Vendor A	Vendor B	Vendor C	Vendor D
Maintenance Audit Records all changes made to employee's data records (including records added, deleted, or changed); displays date, time, user, category, field, old data, new data	Y				
Military Branch of service and rank achieved, discharge type, and VETS-100 information, as well as service-related awards, disabilities, duties, and remaining commitment	Y				
Pay Changes Can be tied back automatically to benefits, so benefit coverage and employee/employer deduction amounts can be correspondingly changed	Y				
Future pay changes can be established with automatic activation at appropriate time along with audit trail of change	Y				
Prior Employment Details unlimited previous employers, positions held, earnings, reason left, and contact information	Y				
Reviews Unlimited user-defined rating tables with weights by review category, ratings totals	Y				

(Continued)

Exhibit 9.3. Sample Selection Table (Continued)

Categories	OPEN4	Vendor A	Vendor B	Vendor C	Vendor D
Unlimited history of reviews, w/unlimited reviewer remarks	Y				
Separate scheduled and actual review dates allow reporting of upcoming reviews as well as reviews that were late	Y				
Security Information includes vehicle descriptions, assigned parking, issued credit cards, equipment, and confidentiality agreements	Y				
Service Separate record for each hire/termination period, along with computed length of service for each period	Y				
Skills Unlimited number of user-defined skills with related user-defined proficiency levels and experience	Y				
Stock Purchase Stores information relating to the employee's purchase of discounted stock under a company's stock plan	Y				
Company table stores information about plan year, beginning share price, ending price, deduction limits, deduction identifier, earnings code for refunds; employee record stores percent of salary committed, base annual salary, purchase dollars available, number of whole shares, and payroll deduction amount	Y				

Exhibit 9.3. (Continued)

Categories	OPEN4	Vendor A	Vendor B	Vendor C	Vendor D
Calculation of deduction or refund can be done for individual employees with a "calculation button" or en masse via a batch program; system creates payroll transactions for those requiring refunds	Y				
Termination Carries rehire eligibility, reason for termination, exit interview data, and last check information	Y				
Testing Can be used for pre-employment, drug screening, etc.; also supports cost analysis of testing	Y				
Training Type, course format, awards, CEUs awarded, costs, and approval information	Y				
Can interface with internal classes (company level)	Y				
Enrollment at company level classes, as well as wait-list flag	Y				
Transfer An individual record for each transfer, showing both from and to locations as well as the effective transfer date and transfer reason	Y				

(Continued)

Categories	OPEN4	Vendor A	Vendor B	Vendor C	Vendor D
Exhibit 9.3. Sample Selection Table (Continued)					
Can transfer within divisions, branches, and departments	Y				
Transfers are interfaced with OPEN4 payroll	Y				
Unions Includes union number, classification, seniority dates, and ability for automatic pay increase by contract	Y				
Vacations Scheduled begin and return dates, the dollar cost of the vacation (using employee's pay rate) and remaining accrued days; also stores leaves of absence	Y				
Workers' Compensation Claims Provides detail record of claim and payments	Y				

CONCLUSION

The selection matrix is a useful tool in software selection. It displays your information in a format that allows you to readily compare products with each other and readily detect any holes in a product's offerings. You can use the matrix to come up with a numerical value for a program, which again allows you to readily compare results from one vendor with those from another. It's important not to be too carried away with the sense of finality about a matrix, though. The matrix is useful, but not necessarily definitive. On the basis of the matrix and the rest of the steps you have gone through, you can decide on the preferred vendor or a short list of vendors. You are then ready to negotiate a deal, as described in the next chapter.

Negotiating the Agreement

Y ou think you're done with software selection when you decide on the product you want. Perhaps you've even settled on a price with the vendor. When the time comes to put the informal agreement onto paper, though, you may feel as if you are starting all over again. Suddenly, with formal commitment staring them in the face, everyone from the president of the company on down begins to see the selection process with a whole new seriousness. The negotiating process, you find, is the selection process itself . . . but intensified.

Matters that seemed to raise little concern before suddenly become monumental as the formal close begins to arrive. Your company may end up saying to the vendor, "We know you told us that you could integrate time clock information. Now we really want to know *how* you will do it." Or you may say to the vendor, "You have insisted that the report writer is so easy that an idiot can use it. Would you mind giving us a sample one-hour training session to prove that?" Everything takes on a whole new importance now that the game is truly on the line.

For his part, the vendor has to begin to take a whole new look at promises he was tossing off rather easily early in the process. The vendor may have checked off everything in an evaluation matrix you gave him, but now he has to fess up. "Yes, I said we could integrate your offbeat/weird payroll information. Well, the thing is, we can sort of integrate it, but you'll have to hire consulting time with us, and it may not be everything you thought it would be." Or the vendor may say, "Yes, we said that we could provide onsite training, but actually, to get it for the price you want, you have to do it on *our* site." You may be thinking, "But that isn't really onsite," and you're right; words begin to distill down to their real meanings as crunch time approaches.

Companies may be inclined to sign a contract without clearing up last-minute issues, but, says analyst Rick Fletcher, vice president and rounder of HRchitect, Inc., of Cambridge, Massachusetts, "The 'need for speed' is an admirable project team trait, but don't rush the license negotiation process. Project teams often underestimate the importance of doing their full due diligence during this final phase of the software evaluation. Remember that the software evaluation is not over until the license agreement is signed" (Fletcher, 2001). Whether you fall into last-minute due diligence by accident (not the right way to do it) or perform your licensing due diligence by design, you should give the process full opportunity to run its course.

WHY TO HAVE A CONTRACT

You probably don't have many reservations about having a contract. It's standard, and it protects both you and the vendor. Here are some of the reasons you definitely want to have a contract when you buy your software:

- It tells what the software company is going to do for you;
- It specifies what the product is going to cost;
- It spells out the support you will receive, which may be more important than the product itself;
- It spells out any exceptions or special requests you may have made (If there is no written record, promises may not hold. Often they do, but why not have it in writing?);
- It gives you a basis for suing later (just kidding, but it does give you a document you can use if you have a formal grievance).

WHOM TO INCLUDE IN NEGOTIATIONS

You probably do not have to worry too much about finding the right people for negotiations. Often, they find you. If you have to get formal signoffs on your purchase, you will meet all the right people for your negotiations along the way. Here are some of the obvious ones, suggested by Fletcher and Katavola (2001) and, of course, common sense in some cases:

- Head of the HR department;
- Payroll department, if affected;
- IT department;
- Finance department;
- Legal;
- Top management; and
- External consultants.

Others may well give you the opportunity to take your best shot at getting the right deal in place. You may think that you are truly the negotiator, and you may be. But others will nevertheless get into the act, perhaps well after you think you have a deal in place. Each of those listed above will offer advice from a different perspective. Any one of them might make or break your deal. Here is what each brings to the negotiating table:

Head of the HR Department. You may be that head. Or you may have disparate functions within HR—someone doing union agreements, someone focusing on benefits, someone in charge of training, someone doing hiring, someone tracking attendance, and so on. What you purchase has to meld in with the rest of what the department is doing, even if you are purchasing software for just your function. The HR manager can make sure that what you do fits with what the rest of the department is doing—or at least does not work at cross purposes with the department.

Payroll Department. You may know quite clearly that "HR is not payroll" and vice versa. You may or may not much like the payroll department and (again) vice versa. You may be selecting combined HR/payroll, or you may be selecting HR that simply integrates with payroll. The two functions overlap too closely, though, for you to simply select HR without taking payroll into account. At a minimum, you may have to be able to integrate your HR application with the payroll application for such things as basic personnel data.

IT Department. HR software is a technical purchase. The people who are selling it to you have technical knowledge. They know the technical strengths and weaknesses of the product. You want to have resources available that, from your side, can assess the strengths and identify the weaknesses of the product (which, after all, the vendor may be in no rush to identify on his or her own).

Finance Department. Often, HR and finance have close ties. Human resources is involved in compensation management, one of the key items to impact finance. HR manages benefits, another major cost to the corporation. Finance understands money, and your purchase involves money. You may not want to have finance as an ongoing member of your negotiating team, but you may at least want to consult them.

Legal. A funny thing happens in negotiations when an attorney is present. Those across the table begin to become much more careful, and sometimes they remember options they had overlooked in the past. Fletcher (2001) offers this advice: "Your legal counsel should be considered as the company's ultimate authority on legal issues, whereas when it comes to business issues, HR should be the final test of which business terms are acceptable."

Top Management. Top management, of course, will not participate in the day-to-day negotiations, unless you are a smaller company (if then). But its signoff will be essential. If you have the opportunity to apprise top management of the progress of negotiations, seize the opportunity. You will get indications if you are heading off the track, for example, exceeding your budget. And you may get indications of the best path to follow if you are to obtain approval.

Consultants. For all the reasons mentioned in Chapter 4, consultants can be useful. They can provide technical and legal know-how. They can provide experience. After all, you may be buying software for the first time. The consultant may have been involved in software purchases dozens of times. People like to do things on their own, and that is fine. Often, though, a consultant can more than earn her fees in the discounts she can negotiate for you.

KEY NEGOTIATING POINTS

Negotiating is all about price, right? What else is there? We often tend to think of price as the only thing that matters, as if everything else in the contract is pure boilerplate. As a matter of fact, I am often of that opinion myself. Get the price right, and everything else follows as the night the day. However, there are other things to keep in mind, and they may become bargaining items you can use as you go through the process. Here are some of the things you may want to consider:

- *What you get.* Really it's all about the product. What will you get (for what cost)? Products often come with multiple modules, and all are not necessarily automatically included. Make sure you are receiving the ones you expect.

- *What you get, part 2.* You are not just buying a product but services that can include support, training, and implementation. The product is worth nothing if you cannot get it to work right. Do you think that "Well, that never happens"? It does. People buy software and never use it. Or they buy it, struggle with it, and abandon it. It's often the support, not the product itself, that is the obstacle to success.

- *When you get it.* Everyone is always busy. Everybody always has to set priorities. The software company that is selling to you is also selling to someone else. Be sure to obtain a commitment, in writing, about when you will be receiving the product and the services. One principle is as true as ever in the world of business: the squeaking wheel gets the grease. You want to be in a position to squeak effectively if your product and services do not come through on time.

- *What you will not get.* If there are to be specific omissions or restrictions, be sure the contract spells them out. If you will receive support only for one year, be sure you know that. If your package will not include the applicant tracking module, be sure the contract specifies that. If your Internet-based recruiting package does not offer posting to Internet job boards, have the contract spell that out.

- *What it will all cost.* You probably do not need this particular caveat. People tend to read the pricing listed on contracts even if they read nothing else. Nevertheless, here is the caveat anyway. Be sure the pricing on the contract is right, and get opinions from everyone on the team to be sure it is right.

GETTING DOWN TO IT: NEGOTIATING PRICE

Negotiating may not be all about price, but, on the other hand, it may be. Vendors are selling you software—a bunch of code. Their costs are hourly costs that have gone into building the product. They do not have costs for components and such. In other words, they have some room to negotiate on price. They may or may not admit that, but you can generally shave a bit off the initial asking price if you approach it properly.

"You have the greatest leverage with the vendors before your team identifies a final preferred vendor," Fletcher (2001) points out. He would not be so crass as to say that you should play the vendors off against one another. You would not want to alienate them, after all. However, a vendor who is still on the fence is a receptive vendor. One who is already in control has no reason to compromise.

Fletcher (2001) recommends that you rank your finalists. If you have not yet made a commitment, you can use the oldest of all bargaining approaches. "Your competitor has agreed to offer us this," you can say. Maybe the competitor is including the applicant tracking for no additional cost. Or maybe the vendor is throwing in a second year of phone support for no additional cost. Or maybe, simply, the competitor has a lower base cost.

I have never much liked to negotiate with no real leverage. I don't like to say to someone, "Well, would you take half?" I like to say, rather, "I already have an offer for half of what you are asking. Can you match it?" Nor do I like to bluff. I like to really have such an offer in hand and be able to point to it. You may be more adept at bluffing, and you may be able to negotiate the price down even if you do not have competing offers. But the old, tried-and-true methods of free enterprise and competition can serve you well in a software purchase.

Price may not be everything, but some think it's the only thing. At the very least, it's the best game in town when shopping for software.

WHAT ELSE TO INCLUDE

You are likely to negotiate over deliverables, price, and the other items listed above. Here are a few other matters you will want to cover in your contract:

- *Rights.* What can you do with the software, and what can't you do? How many people can use it? Can you copy it? Is it all right to have it on your server or do you have to have it on a single machine?

- *Warranty.* If it breaks, will they fix it, and for how long from the time you sign?

- *Terms of separation.* If you are going to part company, what can you keep? What goes back? What do you have to destroy? Prenuptial agreements are a good idea these days.

- *Little idiosyncrasies.* Little things matter. Small is beautiful. Maybe it matters to you that a particular trainer come to your company. Maybe you want the vendor to promise that in writing. Who knows what the idiosyncratic item will be? It will matter to you, though, and you may want to spell it out.

A FEW GOTCHAS

What can go wrong in this most delicate of the steps in evaluating and selecting software? Any number of things. Here are some of them, most suggested at least in part by Fletcher (2001).

Sabotage from Within. "Be alert to team members who are trying to sabotage the negotiation process because their favorite HRIS vendor was not chosen," Fletcher cautions. You would not think one of your co-workers would do such a thing. But it happens. People, even professionals, can sulk. They can refuse to cooperate. They can look for ways to detour or even derail the process if they do not get what they want. Try to keep such people happy in the first place. Think in terms of consensus rather than simple democracy. Listen to people's opinions along the way to avoid having malcontents who may block progress at the end.

Negotiation Fatigue. "The finalist vendor should not have to navigate through successive levels of negotiation meetings," says Fletcher. It can happen, and it can "squeeze" a vendor. If you squeeze too much, even big, grown-up vendors can become dispirited. They may begin to become less responsive. They may even decide that the deal is no longer beneficial for them, and they may drop out of the process.

Starting Before You Sign. "Don't make the too-often mistake of starting the implementation design phase or attending the vendor training without a signed contract," says Fletcher (2001). A honeymoon often begins well before you sign a contract. The vendor has charmed you, and you have impressed him. You feel like best friends, even brother and sister, and you can't imagine anything going wrong. So you want to start, even before things are signed. Doing so is a good formula for problems. You lose negotiating leverage. You may start and have to cancel. You may start in the wrong direction and have to make costly adjustments. You may take on unexpected costs that you later find are explained in the contract. Top management may nix the deal, leaving you embarrassed . . . or worse.

Not Yielding an Inch. "Make sure that your 'needs' are met with the vendor contract and be willing to bend on the 'wants,'" Fletcher (2001) advises. Negotiating has to involve give-and-take. Generally, both sides understand that. People like to treat others with respect and feel that they are being treated with respect. People like to come away from negotiations with something to show for it. Neither side is happy if it gives away too much.

Being Mean. "Keep a positive tone with the vendor; don't create an adversarial relationship," Fletcher (2001) cautions. "You are entering into a relationship with this vendor that will last for years to come." People help others and "go the extra mile" generally because they want to, not because they have to. If you and the vendor establish a trusting relationship, the sky is the limit on how much you might do for each other. Create an atmosphere of distrust, though, and you are likely to receive only what you are clearly entitled to, nothing more. And the distrust can take the fun and creativity out of the relationship.

Losing Control to Another Department. Setting up your team does not have to mean losing control. Payroll may be quite powerful, and it may want you to use the HR system put out by the payroll provider. IT may be forceful, condescending, insistent. It may want to wrest control of the process, but it does not know HR the way you do. And it is HR software you are selecting. Do have members of your negotiating team from multiple departments, and use them to advantage. Do what you have to do, though, to keep them from taking control entirely.

CONCLUSION

Negotiating is in many ways the heart of evaluating and selecting software. Demos may seem to be a key piece, but demos can have quite a bit of "fluff" in them. They are part of the getting-acquainted process. Negotiating, however, is the final step leading to a permanent relationship. It is delicate from the very beginning. Start early. Involve the right people. Use your leverage. Follow the golden rule, and treat your vendor as you would want to be treated. But be sure to play out the process fully. Negotiations should not be slighted. Nor should you slight the next major step in the process—selling the concept to management, as discussed in the next chapter.

CHAPTER

11

Selling to Management

You have received sales pitches from multiple vendors. You have hammered out with software providers and with your own staff both your needs in HR software and the solutions that vendors can provide. You have been systematic throughout the selection process. Now, as you approach management for its signoff, you have to be more systematic than ever. If you have been doing things thoroughly so far, then you should not have much trouble being businesslike at the end. But take the time and the care to prepare your presentation to management fully. Without final approval from management, all the rest you have done is for naught.

Human resources professionals John A. Hinojos and Moira Miller (1998) make the same point in an article in *Solutions* magazine. "A well-thought-out process will help you select the best solution for your organization," they say. Adding, "It will also prepare the selection team to articulate the decision to management— the strengths, weaknesses, and tradeoffs between solutions. The documentation will be in place to build a business case, including a return on investment (ROI) analysis."

When you present to management, draw on the expertise you have compiled in all the previous stages of the process. Make your business case.

DON'T JUST REPORT; SELL

Probably no one has to tell you this, but put on your "Sunday best" in all respects when you present to management. Do not think of this as simply another humdrum report. Think of it as your moment in the spotlight. Think of it as a selling situation, because you cannot just pass along a few memos and leave matters at that. You have to sell management on purchasing the software.

"Management has a short attention span," notes consultant Vince Ceriello, and you know that yourself about management. You do not generally have a long time to develop your case with management. You have to make your points quickly (with solid backup evidence for them to turn to if they wish).

Think as a marketing person as you prepare your presentation. What does management like? What does it want to hear? Marketing people have concluded that "marketing pull" (selling what people want) is much more effective than "marketing push" (trying to convince them to do something they do not already want to do).

You are best off, of course, if you have management support from the beginning. But even if you have that support, you have to present your case well or you could lose the sale. If management does not particularly want an HR system, you would have to think long and hard about whether you even wanted to evaluate systems. You may have difficulty ever putting one into place. Or you may want to aim for small, affordable systems . . . perhaps modular systems that you can expand as management acceptance grows.

The best sell is one that you do not have to make at all. If you do have to convince a skeptical management of the value of HR software, you should know that you have to make a strong presentation specifically tailored to them. Whether or not management seems to be on your side, you should make the best case that you can. If at all possible, develop a strong PowerPoint presentation. In the presentation, present the material described in this chapter—namely, the benefits of the product you are recommending, a summary of the process you have gone through, and a possible mention of return on investment. (The PowerPoint medium is good if your company is equipped for it, because it allows you to make your points, pause to discuss specific points, and demonstrate your preparedness for the meeting.)

EMPHASIZE BENEFITS, BENEFITS, BENEFITS

"Here is what our new HR system will do for us," you should say to management. As you present your HR system, begin by showing the benefits of the system. Everything else is secondary. Management may want to know that you have done good research, that you have compared multiple packages, that you have negotiated a good price. But management has to hear *why* it should care about all the rest that you have done. It should care because of the benefits to the company of the product you are recommending. Following are some of the possible benefits for the system you intend to bring in, presented in terms of the standard flow of HR activity.

Faster, Better Hiring

In economic good times, automated hiring enables you to compete in speed and quality of your hiring. In a downturn, your program may help you avoid the deluge of applicants and make intelligent choices. The right software may help you organize internally by helping displaced employees find suitable employment within the company, thereby avoiding a disgruntled employee on the one hand and, on the other, placing a strong employee into a suitable spot in the company.

Improved Efficiency in HR

Properly implemented, new HR systems almost always mean improved efficiency. Your company may have stacks of manila folders gathering dust, spreadsheets that only their creator could love, slips of paper, and simple human memory as the means to store important data. Putting together a report on, say, all employees whose performance reports are due, can end up taking a week. The HR system may make the same information available essentially on demand. Here are some of the other ways that the HR system may improve efficiency:

Finding Information

If an employee wants to know how much vacation time she has available, you can just click and give the response. She may be able to look it up herself. If the company wants to see the latest org chart, and it seems to change daily, you can just click to display it. If someone wants to know what training classes he has taken and which he needs to take to advance to the next position, the information is there for instant display.

Without an automated system, information lurks in strange places, if it resides anywhere at all. Sometimes it is just plain lost. The biggest single advantage of HR automation is the seemingly inglorious, clerical advantage. Information, finally, is at your fingertips.

Preparing Good Reports

Information displays as reports. Having good information almost automatically means that you can prepare good reports in answer to questions such as:

- Who are the top candidates for marketing manager in our company?
- How many employees do we have in a four-state Southern region?
- How many do we have from particular ethnic backgrounds, per EEO requirements?
- What have been the drug testing results in Cleveland for the past five years?

The questions you may ask are unlimited. The software allows you to reach out automatically and report the answers. You may have a good system of built-in reports. You may have reports already customized to your company, and you will do well to spell out to management exactly what the reports are. And you may have a built-in report writer that allows you easily to create whatever report you want. Point out that the report writer exists, and perhaps mention a sample report that management will appreciate, such as, "We can instantly create a report showing which employees have not used their medical benefits for the last five years."

Serving Employees

Ready information is not just for you and for management. It is for the employees. If they can find out what they want without difficulty, perhaps through employee self-service, they tend to be happy employees.

- "Am I covered for the surgery I am planning to have?"
- "Can I use some of my option money at this time?"
- "What happens to my premium when my child graduates from college and is not covered?"
- "When am I due for a salary increase?"

Answering these questions promptly and without hassle can help create a loyal base of employees.

Administering Training

Every company talks about doing training, but not every company lives up to its intentions. Often, the information needed for good planning is not available. Software may not automatically solve the problem either, but it can help. Trained employees are not only satisfied employees, they are better contributors to the company. If you show management that your program strengthens training, you will score some points with those powers that be.

Averting Litigation

One lawsuit can bring a company to its knees, even if the company wins the lawsuit. And there is so much legislation to keep track of—EEO, OSHA, COBRA, and more. Laws vary from state to state and from industry to industry. If software can protect a company against potential lawsuits, that alone may be reason to purchase the software.

Contributing Strategically

Long the company's glorified clerks, HR may be able to use software to become genuine members of the company's strategic team. Software now includes analytics, allowing HR not only to assess how well the company is doing but to make recommendations for improvement. How fair are our salaries? How strong are the skills of our employees? What can we do to strengthen the company over the next year? Such questions may well be the most important ones a company can ask, and automation equips HR to answer them. Here are two examples:

Planning Compensation. If your software helps you be fair in compensation and to satisfy employees that you are being fair, it is a great retention tool. Compensation is a company's greatest expense. If software helps you manage compensation effectively and perhaps save money, management will want to know that.

Planning Succession. Who is out there? Who deserves to move where? Who has been waiting how long? Everybody wants to advance in a company. Being passed over for an expected appointment is often grounds for leaving. Create order out of the former confusion about hiring, and you greatly benefit the company.

PRESENT THE RESULTS OF YOUR RESEARCH

You have accumulated documents during the systematic evaluation you have done. Once you have gained management's attention by talking about benefits, you can go through the nuts and bolts of what you have done to reach your conclusions. Here is some of what you may want to cover:

Needs Analysis. Show that you did not just work in a vacuum but developed an understanding of the needs at your specific company. Management wants to know not so much what you are going to do as what you are going to do "for us." In the needs analysis, you have identified those problem areas at your very company that the software can help resolve. The needs analysis begins to bring home to management the results of your work.

RFP. Make management aware not just that you researched the marketplace but that you researched it in a way that would serve the needs of your company. That is, you took the needs analysis and developed it into a document that you then circulated to vendors. The business process itself had value as you looked at the way things work at your company and received direct feedback from vendors as to potential solutions.

Demo Results. Show that you did your homework. You did not choose a favorite and simply go through the motions with the others. You compiled telling information from a number of well-qualified vendors.

Selection Matrix. With the matrix, you can show a meaningful comparison in a single table—just the kind of display management most likes to see. Management is likely to key in on the one or two most important strengths or weaknesses on the matrix.

Negotiation Process. Management may have been involved in the negotiations, or it may have simply passed along guidelines. In either case, it needs to know that you have negotiated fair pricing for the company. A company that overpays is not a well-run company.

Everything you have done to evaluate the software, then, is preparation for presenting to management at the end. And you should have all the results of your efforts compiled in a form that allows you to find information quickly and display it effectively.

LIGHTLY MAKE THE CASE FOR ROI

Perhaps "ROI" isn't even one of your everyday terms. Human resources, even "human capital management," looks at people and at people problems. Many of the benefits of HR software systems are "softer" benefits, such as improved employee satisfaction. They don't always have to yield the hard, "return on investment (ROI)" numbers.

But maybe your boss is a "strictly numbers" person. In most cases, you do not build the case for your HR system strictly on the numbers. Doing so in this instance may help your case with management. Ultimately, every business has to look at its bottom line. And the bottom line is all numbers. Following are some of the matters you may look at as you evaluate dollars saved through your HR system:

Managing Salary. A company always tries to keep these costs under control. Software may turn a "seat of the pants" affair into a scientific approach and save real dollars for the effort.

Managing Turnover. Turnover often leaves a company's managers scratching their heads: "Why don't they like us?" Software may bring real answers and real employee satisfaction, thereby lowering turnover and saving costs. For instance, software may allow companies to survey employee satisfaction or to survey employees who are leaving. Compensation analysis may indicate whether the company is being fair and whether the compensation is the type employees are looking for. Industry benchmarking may compare company statistics on salary and other matters with industry standards.

Lowering the Cost of Hiring. Preventing turnover may be the best way to lower hiring costs. You can also develop effective advertising, keep recruiter costs in check, develop a strong employee referral service, and otherwise lower the cost of hiring.

Saving HR Time. With employee self-service and manager self-service, you may be able to lower headcount in HR or at least protect against raising the headcount, even as the company grows. Top management is generally happy to see these dollars saved.

You could even develop dollar amounts for projected savings in each of the areas. Ultimate Software uses an ROI estimator from Giga Information Group to show potential cost savings from its software. Figure 11.1 shows sample results for a company, with savings in decreased turnover and improved use of HR time.

Figure 11.1. Sample Ultimate Software ROI Estimation

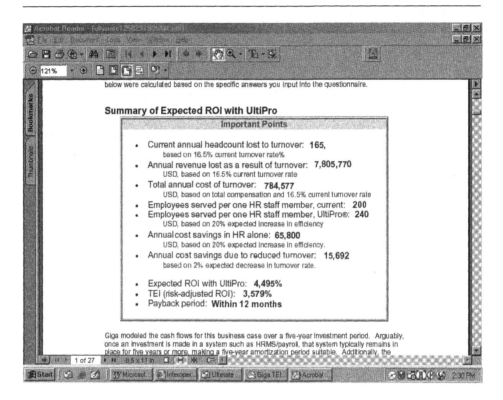

Figure 11.2 shows a table of the benefits of HR software in terms of direct cost reduction, efficiency gains, and positive business impacts. On the CD you will find a sample ROI report for the Ultimate Software product.

Best Software has prepared an estimate of the ROI on its software. As Figure 11.3 shows, the software estimates savings in benefit/costs administration; information/data gathering; recruiting costs; and turnover reduction.

If you can assign meaningful numbers to the cost reductions your HR software provides, you can help to build a telling argument for management. You do not have to feel that the success of your presentation depends on your ROI calculations. As mentioned, management is often more concerned with softer benefits of HR (such as improved record keeping, better reporting, and better service to employees) than with pure hard dollar savings.

Figure 11.2. Detail of Basis for Ultipro ROI

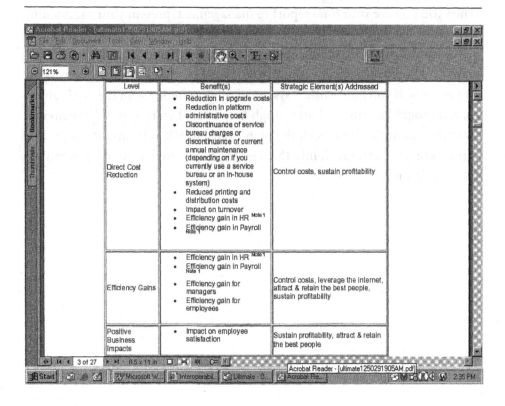

Level	Benefit(s)	Strategic Element(s) Addressed
Direct Cost Reduction	• Reduction in upgrade costs • Reduction in platform administrative costs • Discontinuance of service bureau charges or discontinuance of current annual maintenance (depending on if you currently use a service bureau or an in-house system) • Reduced printing and distribution costs • Impact on turnover • Efficiency gain in HR [Note 1] • Efficiency gain in Payroll [Note 1]	Control costs, sustain profitability
Efficiency Gains	• Efficiency gain in HR [Note 1] • Efficiency gain in Payroll [Note 1] • Efficiency gain for managers • Efficiency gain for employees	Control costs, leverage the internet, attract & retain the best people, sustain profitability
Positive Business Impacts	• Impact on employee satisfaction	Sustain profitability, attract & retain the best people

Figure 11.3. Best Software Estimate of ROI for Abra Software

Employee Size	Savings on Benefit Costs/ Administration	Savings on Information/ Data Gathering	Savings on Recruiting Costs	Savings as a Result of Turnover Reductions	Year 1 Total Savings	Abra Suite Investment*	Year 1 Return on Investment	Year 2-4 Savings
75	$3,082	$2,850	$10,566	$14,382	$30,880	$12,895	$17,985	$89,660
150	$7,344	$4,275	$13,133	$17,048	$41,800	$19,755	$22,045	$120,455
500	$14,750	$5,700	$18,000	$13,715	$52,165	$27,255	$24,910	$149,647
1,000	$42,620	$7,125	$28,000	$15,715	$93,460	$32,855	$60,605	$272,596

*Investment is total product cost and includes services which vary depending on the complexity of the installation or the services that are required.
(Investment = Product Cost x 2 + Support Cost + 1 training class)

The results contained herein are estimates only and Best Software, Inc. cannot guarantee that your organization will obtain the same results.

CONCLUSION

When you prepare your final report to management, present your most telling arguments first. But have the other information available as well, including ROI information. Consider the presentation to be a challenging sell, with a great deal at stake for both you and your company. You want to present the most convincing case possible. If you have worked systematically, beginning with the needs analysis, you should have more than enough firepower at your disposal to convince management to go ahead with the plan to install HR software. If you obtain permission, you can launch into the next big step—implementation planning, discussed in the next chapter.

Planning Implementation

You have been thinking about *selecting* and *evaluating* software, right? Not about implementing it. People have a tendency to think that, if they choose the right software, the whole technology system will simply fall into place automatically once they have it. After all, if you buy a Microsoft Windows program, you just click *Setup*, click a couple other buttons along the way, and watch the software install. Maybe you read a Help file or two to see how the program works, or you have a friend show you a couple things, and you are off to the races.

Implementation with your HR system, though, is generally bigger than for a word processing program or a money tracker or some small PC program. (If you are installing a small program, you may be able to just install.) You have to match the software with what you need and with what you do. The software probably will not have all the features activated in advance. If you do the implementation properly, this HR software will run your daily HR activities. It will track the information that you track, report on the information you report on, follow the business flow that your company follows, and meld in comfortably with the technology you have in place.

Or to look at the same matters from a negative point of view, if you do not take the steps to bring the software and your company up-to-speed with your new software, you may end up with a white elephant on your hands. Systems may be great, but systems that no one uses are a problem no matter how great they are. Does it happen that people purchase HR software and then do not use it? Of course it happens, and you have undoubtedly heard of such instances yourself.

Carefully following a few steps can help you succeed with your product and avoid the embarrassing failures that happen from time to time. Put a good team in place. Work with a realistic schedule. Anticipate and address your hardware and software needs. Train those who will be using the system. And, in general, be methodical and patient in planning a thorough, careful implementation of your product.

SETTING UP A PROJECT TEAM

Implementation—like the needs analysis, the RFP, and everything else—is not an individual undertaking. You need group participation and group buyoff. Following is a list of some of the people you will want on your team:

- HR—your HR manager and perhaps others to assure that all your HR areas have representation;

- Benefits—which may be different from HR or a department within it;

- IT—particularly for implementation, you need the support of those who understand the technology requirements and what it takes to meet them;

- Payroll—you are going to share data with payroll one way or another, so you want the department intimately involved to assure that the implementation goes smoothly;

- Outside consultant—if one stage of the process attracts consultants more than any other, that stage is implementation. Companies invest small amounts in the consultant to avoid losing large amounts in lost time or in a system that simply does not work properly. Consultants do implementation after implementation and know the risks you face. You, on the other hand, are likely doing your first and perhaps your only HR installation; and

- The vendor—the vendor has installed the system over and over and has designed the system and written the code. The vendor's guidelines are your Bible, but, at that same time, you want checks and balances on the vendor (such as your own management, IT department, and consultants).

SETTING THE SCHEDULE

In implementation, as in everything in business, work expands to fill the time there is to do it. Set realistic dates, but make them aggressive as well. Keep them posted openly for the participants on the team, and refer to them. If you miss some planned milestone, ask for an explanation. Adjust the schedule, and do your best to assure that you do not miss future milestones. Some of the milestones you might want to set would include the following: installation of first module, beta test for small number of users, installation of additional modules, further beta test, kick-off of training for individuals or the department, beta test for the entire department, final signoff after successful beta test, official rollout, six-month analysis of the system, one-year analysis.

PREPARING YOUR COMPUTER SYSTEMS

You have made sure during earlier stages of software evaluation to purchase software that is compatible with your hardware. And you are planning to use hardware that you either already have on hand or that is compatible with what you already have. Such earlier planning was theory. Now you face a good dose of reality as you actually put the system into place.

Hardware

Perhaps you have a PC/LAN system. You may have a client/server system. Perhaps you are installing on a single PC. Maybe you are installing on an Internet system that requires only a browser. Whatever the requirements, go over them clearly with IT. What seems simple may end up not being so. For instance, not all Internet products allow you to access them from just any browser. Sometimes you have to install special software on your PC. If you have multiple PCs in your department, you face additional challenges even for this simplest of tasks. The hardware on hand may not be sufficient. You may need additional software and possibly even hardware.

Software

Setting the software up to meet your needs can be the biggest challenge in implementation. There are three critical areas you will want to consider: data fields, reports, and importing data.

Data Fields

Your company works a certain way. Perhaps you track EEO in greater depth than most companies. Do you have the data fields to keep the detail that you want? Perhaps COBRA is important to you but is not addressed well by the software at hand. Perhaps you need more detailed recruiting information than comes with the program. You want to be able to track the geographical origins of the applicants, say, or the previous five employers for each candidate instead of the previous three. Perhaps you want special fields to assure that you have completed a thorough background check.

The possibilities are numerous, and you should go over your wish list point by point. You will have a system administrator from within the company (perhaps you, yourself) who will be able to make adjustments on an ongoing basis. You want to be sure that as much as possible is the way you want it in the first place, though.

Reports

No matter how many reports a system comes with, they are almost never the reports that you want. Even if you do set up canned reports that are the ones you want today, your boss will discover a need tomorrow that is not one of those reports. Nevertheless, you at least want to put reports in place that are as close to your needs as you can define them today. It is much easier to adapt an existing report to your needs than to create an entirely new report. Perhaps, for instance, a report shows EEO history for the whole company for the past three years. If you want to show a report for a single department instead, you have the basis for the second report.

You have probably defined your reporting needs during the needs analysis, and you have probably discovered other neat reports you would like to have during the demos and other stages. Reporting is the heart of the system. If you do not have the reports you need, you will not use your system—or at least not use it properly. Take the time during implementation—when your consultant, vendor, and IT department are readily available—to get your reports into the state you want them.

Importing Data

All the literature for your product probably talks about how automatic it is to import data from worksheets and other sources. Hah! Welcome to real life on the planet. Some of your data may be on paper only. Your spreadsheets may be a mish mash of half-baked sheets that only their authors could love. It might take longer to get the sheets ready for importing than it would just to key in the data in the first place. Importing data can be a nightmare. Address the matter carefully during implementation rather than facing the hard reality, later, that importing the data will be a real challenge. Reporting may be the heart of the system, but reporting has no value without valid data.

TRAINING HR AND USERS

Anything is easy to use *once you know how to do it*. Getting there can be the hard part. If you simply watched someone else demo your software, you may have the impression that "all you do is point and click to find out who is in line to succeed whom as sales vice president." When you sit down by yourself, though, you may scratch your head and say, "What do I point at?" "Where do I click?"

Your salesperson may have said, "You can readily add your own user-defined fields," but you may not have any idea where you do that or what you say when you define them. What is the right way to name a user-defined field, and is there a wrong way? You may have seen that you can nicely create little algorithms that will limit candidate searches, letting you find only those who applied from a certain geographical area during a certain time period. It looked easy when someone else did it. When you find that you have to work with Boolean expressions and actual codes, though, you may feel a bit wide-eyed and stymied.

Using the system is never as automatic as the instructions say it is, even if you do find it quite easy after a few days or weeks. But the pointing and clicking is not the real issue anyway. What really matters is accomplishing what you want to accomplish. "We want to be able to project various benefits scenarios for the individuals, for departments, and for the company," you might say, "and we want to know, for each, the costs we will encounter and the special considerations we face from each vendor." That might be a tall order, perhaps months of work if you were to track it down by old-fashioned telephone. Even if your software nicely tracks benefits, you may not know how to do what you really want to do with it.

You have to be trained in both using the system and in accomplishing your business objectives. Trying to figure things out on your own can be time-consuming and sometimes hopeless. Learning how to do things from an expert who is a skilled trainer can launch you into using your program successfully.

If you have employee self-service or some other program that places your system at the hands of the general population of your company, you have to train not just the HR users but that general population. Even in an era of computer-savvy people, you can take nothing for granted. You have to make sure that people can do what you expect them to do with the system. In other words, you have to train them.

ALIGNING YOUR BUSINESS PROCESSES

It is often tempting early in the process to assume that your business processes neatly fit those of the software. Are you tracking applicants? Well, perhaps you already take the names and addresses of those who apply, and you keep those in the computer somewhere. Your software, though, may ask for much more information than you currently keep. "What was the 'time to hire'?" "What was the 'time to interview'?" "Where did the interview take place?" "Who did it?" "Was it a first interview or a second interview?"

Your software may be working with a process that does not map particularly well to your own. Perhaps the software allows for an approval process, but, again, does it match yours? Your company may require manager approval for a salary recommendation after the second interview. But does the software actually allow for such an approval? Does it require that you enter the approval or simply allow that you do so if you wish. (And which way do you want it to happen?)

No two companies work the same way. Software, for all the best intentions of the programmers, cannot be flexible enough to fit everything that you do or may want to do. Sometimes you may change the software to suit your company. Sometimes you may want to change the company to suit the software, and changing business processes is almost never as easy as you might wish. People like to do things the way they have been doing them so far.

Software currently features "workflow" capabilities. The software will send out alerts to the right managers when certain things happen. When a requisition is approved, a higher up manager may be notified of it. The workflow concept is popular, and with good reason. But if the workflow is not your workflow, then you have to adjust either the software or your process.

During implementation you may have to add business processes, change existing ones, or eliminate them. You have to take the time and the care to see that the software matches what you do, or you will have problems. If you are going to change the way people do things, plan on putting the training in place to assure that the change happens smoothly.

TESTING THE SYSTEM

Once you have your system in place and have tailored it to your company, you do not have to "throw it to the dogs" immediately by letting the entire company get their hands on it. You may think you have adapted it successfully, but you cannot be sure. There could be glitches in any of the steps mentioned so far—hardware, software, training, business processes, or some other consideration that does not fall neatly into any of the categories. The unexpected is the rule when implementing new systems.

Just as NASA conducts private tests before publicly launching a rocket, you may want to plan on testing out your system with an agreeable group of "guinea pig" users. You will find out whether the hardware performs well in the heat of battle, whether people can accomplish tasks you want them to accomplish, whether the training is adequate, and whether the software is yielding the kind of results you expected in the time you expected. You will almost certainly discover a few things that you can smooth out before your general launch.

ROLLING IT OUT

Once you've gone through the steps outlined in the chapter, review them a few more times . . . at least in your head. Get buyoff from your entire team and from management that all is ready. Inform your users of what to expect and of what you expect from them. Let them know where to turn if they have difficulties with the system.

Having systematically stepped through your implementation plan, roll out the system. You are ready. Now make it work.

CHECKING OUT A SAMPLE IMPLEMENTATION PLAN

As you design your own implementation plan, you may benefit from reviewing a plan designed by one company. You may have different requirements and different steps, but this sample can be a template you can use to design your own implementation plan. On the CD-ROM you can see a complete implementation plan developed through years of experience at HRSoft, LLC, for ExecuTRACK, a succession-planning and talent-management product for larger companies.

Here are key ingredients of the HRSoft plan that would apply to almost any organization.

Target Dates

A plan depends on dates—meaningful dates. Discuss with the vendor, IT, and all parties involved. Sit down with a calendar and project appropriate dates for all stages in the process, from beta test to training to final rollout. For each date, also enumerate the features of the software that apply for that date. If you are planning to have "full system administration capability available," then you have to have the system administration feature up and working by that date with access available for the appropriate users.

Project Roles

You may think you know all the people involved in the process. Take the time to list them. Some of the roles you may want would be the following:

- Project leader;
- Data management specialist;
- Training leader;
- IT tech support;
- Network specialist; and
- Report specialist.

For each person, list basic information such as e-mail address and telephone number. Describe the person's responsibilities, and obtain buyoff from all parties as to the percentage of the person's time to be devoted to the implementation.

Systems

The vendor will provide standard requirements for the system. You have had your own requirements in mind as you made your selection. Now you should be sure that the vendor requirements do in fact fit the systems you have in place. Consider the following:

- PCs, kiosks, or other appropriate access for users;
- Internet service as appropriate for the users;
- Database and database security; and
- Hardware systems in place.

Customization

Plan for customization, the step that transforms a "plain vanilla" product into one that suits and satisfies your company. Look over the screens on the product and make sure the fields on the product fit your company. Concerns may be quite basic. Perhaps you use first name, last name, and middle initial for all employees. Make certain the data fields on the screens fit the way you do business. Look over the reporting. If you use standard EEO reports, for example, make certain those reports are available. The more the system fits your company right from the outset, the more your HR users will welcome and appreciate it.

CONCLUSION

Implementation is perhaps a bigger step than selection, no matter how carefully you have done the selection. Your product is nothing until people actually use it and love it. And implementation is the process that turns a product from an abstract theory into a daily reality at your company. Do not slight the implementation process, and encourage all the experts on hand to contribute generously to the undertaking. A well-implemented HR software product is a well-launched product. The essence of selecting software is looking over actual products. In the remaining two sections of the book you look over specific products, beginning in the next chapter with low-cost products.

PART
FOUR

Looking Over
the Low-End Market

Evaluating software is ultimately about selecting software. To select software, you look over a number of candidates to find the one that suits you best. In this section, you look over a number of specific players in the low-end marketplace, see their strengths and weaknesses, and begin to get a feel for what is really available in the marketplace. The first chapter in the section is a review of criteria for selecting any low-end HRIS package. The second chapter contains a discussion of the three most high-profile providers of low-end HRIS. The final chapter in the section ventures into the uncharted waters of less-famous players, which often are fresh, innovative, and dedicated.

CHAPTER

13

Selecting a Small HRIS Package

You're ready for HR software. You are, for sure. You have reached the one-hundred-employee plateau (or maybe as few as fifty or even twenty-five). You have to track all the same things that the big companies do—employee name and job title, time and attendance, benefits packages, training, EEO information, salaries, maybe even employee skills.

You would like to take the plunge, but there is one big problem. What do you plunge into? You are not going to purchase PeopleSoft for some figure such as a cool million. You probably are not even going to invest $100,000. You want to spend a small amount ($10,000) or even a really, really small amount ($1,000) or even less if you can get away with it.

If you purchase a low-cost package, say something for $500, do you really have to worry that much about what it is? It will track your people, won't it? It will let you report on who has what benefits. It will address the basics that you need. And if you don't like it, at that price you can just throw it out and buy another one.

For low-end software, you don't need a complete evaluation, do you? Just the needs analysis would cost more than the software. Vendors would not even respond to a lengthy RFP. If you plan to script the demo, you are likely to find that the vendor has one, fixed demo—and you should view it on the Net. Negotiating? How much lower can they go? This sounds almost like a commodity purchase. Buy the software, and just forget about it. Implementation planning? Read a brochure from the vendor, and call the support line once or twice if you have trouble.

Low end, low-cost software may seem as if it ought to be "no brain" software as well. Buy it; use it; forget about everything else. But the issue may not be quite so simple, not if you are educated about the marketplace. Although a number of vendors, particularly Abra, claim that there is a simple answer to the need for low-cost HR software, you still have to face a number of questions. You can make a mistake.

Besides, shopping for low-end software is fun. I envy those who choose to do it. If you just purchase a package and make it work, you miss out on a great opportunity. First of all, in evaluating the software, you evaluate your department and your business processes. You have an opportunity to put your processes in order. Second, in looking over a number of packages and seeing what they do, you come to understand how you can truly exploit HR software to your own advantage. You see what the products offer, which gives you a good idea of what you ought to do. If you look at five packages, all of which offer training support, and you do not have a very systematic training program, the message is clear: "We should look into our training support."

In shopping for low-cost software, you are hardly betting the farm as you go ahead. You do not want to make a mistake, but it is not the end of the world if you do. You can enjoy all the benefits of going through the kind of evaluation process described in this book without the risks that companies take when they select the high-end, multimillion-dollar software packages.

If you have done a needs analysis, even a preliminary one, you are well-positioned to determine whether or not a low-end software offering meets your needs. There are definitely issues to consider, and one or more of them can be "deal breakers" for you. That is, if the software does not meet certain requirements, it will not be right for you, no matter how little it costs. In the following sections, I have listed potential issues more or less in the order of importance as we see them, although at your company one or another issue may matter much more than the others.

PRICE

Say what you might, price is a significant factor at the low end. Some "low-end" products come in at $10,000 or higher once you factor in various modules, support options, or whatever. Others are shrink-wrapped off-the-shelf products you can throw onto your machine for $150. There is a difference between $10,000 and $150, or, there was the last time I looked.

You can have all good intentions of finding the right functionality, planning for scalability, providing compatibility with existing databases, and so on. The fact still remains: Cheap is cheap and not-so-cheap is not-so-cheap. You may not list price first when asking vendors to provide descriptions of their products. It does not always feel polite to do so. When push comes to shove, though, price matters. It matters a lot.

VENDOR LONGEVITY

When you are looking at these low-priced offerings, you really have to ask, "Who are these guys providing the software?" When you are buying from Microsoft, for example, you can expect that the company will be around to provide support and upgrades, and you will have just the quiet confidence that you are now working with something that is not obsolete.

These low-end HR packages may have begun as a glint in someone's eye. They may have been a quick, money-making scheme based on a premise that soon changed (such as the idea that people were dying to have low-cost or free Internet HR software). I believe that all of the products listed in subsequent chapters have some longevity to them. But you should do your best to make sure. Small companies, like smaller animals, often have shorter life spans than larger ones.

SUPPORT

Will the vendor be able to take care of you as you use the product? As you progress, you may find yourself surprisingly adept at creating reports. Maybe you will find yourself ready to take on Boolean operators. Maybe you will want to import data from some crazy but nevertheless valuable source. Maybe you will lose your data somewhere but know that it still exists in the system. You can have all kinds of support needs.

Your vendor may have phone support, but does he answer the phone? He may have onsite support. He may discourage any support after the first few days, which may be fine if the price is low enough. But you want to find out what kind of support he does have and to go into the bargain with your eyes open.

WEB OR WINDOWS

Some company cultures these days really cry out for a Web product—technical companies, some advertising or media companies with many young employees, or companies where speed matters (such as some forms of stock trading). Other companies are more than content with a Microsoft Windows-based product residing on a desktop or a few desktops. Perhaps those who need the product can get to it just fine within the office. And the Windows product may have a friendlier, more familiar interface and more functionality than the Web product. (The Web companies are getting better, but it is taking some time for Web-based products to take on all the functionality of Windows products.)

RENT OR PURCHASE

Application service provider (ASP) was a positive rage in HR software when the capability first appeared. You could rent your software and use it over the Web. There were obvious advantages, including:

- You did not have to worry about upgrades. They happened automatically on the main software system and were transparent to you.

- You did not have to use your own IT department. The vendor's IT department would take care of the product.

The model can be effective. Something called the economic downturn, however, dealt it a blow early in the decade. Companies found that they might prefer to purchase their software for the same reason they preferred purchasing a car rather than leasing it. Purchase it, and you pay a fixed rate that has an end date. Lease it, and you pay out of pocket forever. Also, many companies are capable of doing the IT maintenance on their own software, particularly small software such as the packages discussed here.

CLIENT/SERVER, PC/LAN, OR STANDALONE

Even a small software package may have to consider the neighborhood it will be living in. Will you just use the product by itself? Will you use it as part of a modest PC/LAN network? Or will you want to operate it, low cost or not, in a sophisticated client/server network where the software resides on a server and is available to multiple users? You may have to pay a little more for advanced networking capabilities, but it may well be worth it.

EASE OF USE

Small does not have to mean easy. In fact, often just the opposite can be the case. Yes, a smaller program may have less programming code than a large one. Some of that missing code, though, might have been the very software to make your program easy to use.

Small does not mean easy, but the makers of the small HRIS packages know that their success depends on the product being easy to use. People who pay $1,000 for software do not want to spend $2,000 on training so that they can use it. In fact, they probably do not want to spend anything on training.

The best way to see whether a program is easy to use is to try it out, and many of the low-cost HR software vendors allow you to try the product free for thirty days. Find out how easy it is to put information in. See whether you can get out the data in the ways that you want. If you can get started, you can learn the rest as you grow with the product. Help files will be useful, although not always essential in a low-end product. If the "help" is there, try it out. If it is not, make sure the product has good phone support to help you start and keep you going.

FLEXIBILITY

A small product is not necessarily a flexible product. If it is small, it may have a limited number of pre-set fields where you enter your data. Will it accommodate the data that you want to put in? (If you have done your needs analysis, you probably know what fields you need to put in.)

As for reporting, you want to be able to generate the reports that you need. You find out something by seeing the list of built-in reports that come with the product. (The more it has, the more the maker has invested in the reporting function.) You find out more by looking over the ad hoc report writer (if it has one) and trying it out. An easy-to-use ad hoc report writer is a great plus for a low-cost HRIS.

SCALABILITY

How much does your business plan to grow? Do you have multiple offices now, and are you likely to want to allow access to the program from those offices? For just a one-location company that does not plan to open multiple offices, a program for a standalone PC may be enough. If you have a client/server network in-house, you may be able to install the software there and use it. Make sure you can, and be sure that the program will function well on multiple PCs.

Perhaps you are a small company now, but your business plan calls for you to grow explosively. Perhaps you have the business formula and the financial backing to do just that. In such a case, you do not want to load all your data into a program that is tied into a standalone PC or a PC/LAN. You would be being short-sighted, even with low-cost software, to fail to plan for expansion.

COMPATIBILITY WITH PAYROLL

Compatibility can mean a number of things. Ideally, you would like the payroll program and your HRIS system to contain the same data in a common database. Or you would like to be able to import data from the payroll program directly into your HRIS program on a regular basis, and vice versa.

Most of the low-cost HR packages provide compatibility with ADP's payroll offering and often with Ceridian's as well. They may or may not be compatible with other offerings, such as Paychex. If you have your own in-house payroll system, as many do, you should check with the vendor about compatibility with what you have.

REFERENCE ACCOUNTS

No one would make a high-end purchase without talking with other users of the system, often by going onto the site of the user. For a low-end purchase, such opportunities may not be as readily available. If you ask, you can probably find some real users to talk with. The company may have some quotations from real users on the website, but such canned information is only partially useful. (It does indicate that the third-party company was willing to allow the implied endorsement, which many will not.)

You learn the most, though, if you can talk directly with real users. People not affiliated with the vendor are surprisingly frank. Particularly at the low end, however, they are not always knowledgeable. You should not take anyone's suggestions as the last word, but you should gather reference information if at all possible.

FUNCTIONALITY

You do not expect all the functionality in a low-cost product that you would in a high-end product. If you did have all the functionality of, say, PeopleSoft, you would likely find it overkill for your smaller company. You should probably not make functionality alone the basis for your purchase. Price and ease of use may come first.

Still, you should compare the functionality of the product with your own "wish list." Look for a fit. If tracking benefits is key to you and the package de-emphasizes it, keep looking. Likewise, if OSHA matters to you but it is not strong in the product, look for another product where it is strong.

Also, you may be surprised at how much functionality you can find in some of the lower priced products. Sometimes the vendors have been working at their product for some time, and they have found that it is just as easy to add capabilities as not. For comparison, look at all the functionality you can find these days in a Microsoft Windows operating system, all for under $500 in some cases. With HR software also, you may be able to get more functionality than you expected. If other considerations are equal and the product does have the base functionality that you need, then more is better. You may find yourself wanting to do more down the road than you anticipated in your needs analysis.

CONCLUSION

Even for a low-end purchase, you should not just take the leap and hope for the best. There are enough vendors out there to create a spirit of free competition, and you can get the benefit of researching the multiple players. Look over the players, and check off their offerings against your list of needs. Even for a small purchase, if you are armed with what you have learned in this book, you can be a sophisticated buyer.

The next two chapters look over some of the products you may consider as you look for low-end HRIS software, first the "Big Three" of the low end and then a number of challengers you may also find worthy of attention.

The Big Three in Low-End HR Software

Three companies above all seem to attract clients in the low end: Abra, People-Trak, and !Trak-It. Their products have matured since their inception ten to fifteen years ago, and in some instances they are viable for midsize companies as well (companies from five hundred to five thousand employees).

COMMON TRAITS

Others might offer other candidates in place of one or another of these three, but I doubt that many would maintain that these are not major players. What goes into giving a low-end vendor serious longevity? No one can really know in advance, as you can tell from the number of companies that have come and gone over the years. However, all three of these big players seem to have certain things in common:

A Sense of the User. Marketing is at the heart of any business success, I suppose. Marketing means knowing the needs of the marketplace, addressing them, and not scaring off the market in the process. Abra, above all, has made an art of understanding the low-end market. If that market needs something, Abra is there to supply it. If it does not necessarily need something, Abra does not burden them with it.

Ease of Use. The smallest roadblock, these providers understand, can cause a tentative, new HRIS user to lay his system aside . . . for good. The user has to get meaningful results right away, and the results have to continue. These people do not want to become HRIS experts. They just want answers without obstacles.

A Sense of Humor. You do not break out in laughter as you use these products. They are, after all, business products. However, !Trak-It HR, in particular, seems to appreciate the lighter side of life. Although its current sellers might be just as happy if you would forget about it, the name Abra is short for "Abracadabra." There is lightness in the heart of someone who supplies such a name.

Price, Price, Price. Do your research on price, and you may find that these are no longer the least expensive products in the low end. These products have survived, and to survive, companies must make money. As their reputations have grown solid and they have proven themselves in the marketplace, they have had the basis for somewhat higher fees than they had initially (although they are still highly affordable).

Support, Support, Support. As we said in the previous point on "ease of use," beginning, low-end users have no patience with failure. They sometimes take a small impasse as a sign that they just are not cut out for this, and they move on to something that does suit them. Provide prompt, skilled support, though, and you can build confidence in the users. A low-end product without some formula for viable support is a dead low-end product.

The Right Functionality. No matter how nice you are, you have to produce. If the question "Where's the beef?" comes up very often with respect to a software product, that product cannot endure for long. Those who are naïve, low-end users transform, sometimes in days, into confident, demanding users. They want the results that were promised when they purchased the system. These three companies have a track record of producing real results, and all have a stable customer base.

Now let's take a look at the big three in detail:

!TRAK-IT HR

!Trak-It began in 1988 as software for the Mac. Resourceful, it moved to the PC and has remained there happily. The Mac roots show through, however. The product is friendly and nice. It loves icons. It takes the user to heart. (A Mac version is still available.) This product does what HRIS products do: it tracks information about employees. A sister product tracks applicants.

If you look at the main screen, shown in Figure 14.1, you get a sense of the personality of this product (and !Trak-It HR is all about personality).

Figure 14.1. Main Employee Screen for !Trak-It

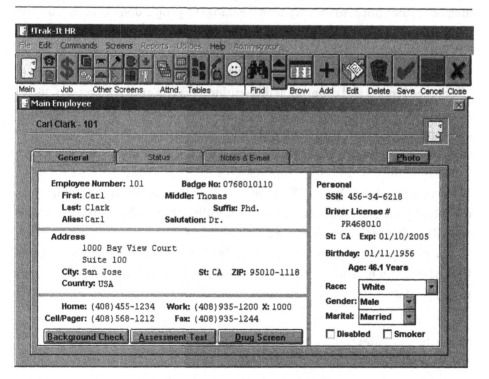

"The icons and pictures are distinctive and appear on both the toolbar and respective screen to quickly and clearly connect you to the right information," the company explains of its interface.

People-First, People-Oriented

The product has notable pluses. This offering has the potential even to be a cult product. One user, for instance, says that she used it without training: "I really just kind of went in and did it." This is a people-first, people-oriented, up-with-people product. Says a technical user, "I don't know of any better software out there, but if there were, and I saw it in a software store, I would pass it up." How's that for loyalty?

Whereas some low-end providers neglect documentation, saying that people truly do not miss it, !Trak-It HR takes its documentation seriously. Says company president and founder John Enyedy, "We've had people call us just to say, 'You've got great manuals.' We put a lot into the manuals." The company does not tout its support line. "Programmers do tech support, but they'd rather be programming than be on the phone, so they try to make things so people don't have to call," says the company founder. But the support is there if you do have to call.

Like other good products in this space, !Trak-It HR has continued to evolve throughout its history. It has added more and more pre-designed reports—up to 270 canned reports and counting at this writing. It's great at custom reports, too. "I can whip out a report in nothing flat," says the technical user. "In ten or fifteen minutes, you can get about any report you want." You can readily find out information such as attendance accrual, shown here in the list in Figure 14.2.

It has a cool feature I have not heard of in other products in its space—a "Grievance Tracking Option." Says the company, the option "tracks complaints, disciplinary actions, disputes, and grievances directly, much as it tracks benefits and salary changes." (See Figure 14.3.)

The pricing, too, is a plus, and !Trak-It claims to beat players like the others in this chapter. You have to analyze what you get for what you pay, but price matters to this vendor.

Issues to Consider

An evaluation is not worth much if it is all on the positive side. There must be some things to be reluctant about with this product. Here are a few to consider:

Figure 14.2. !Trak-It Attendance Accrual Screen

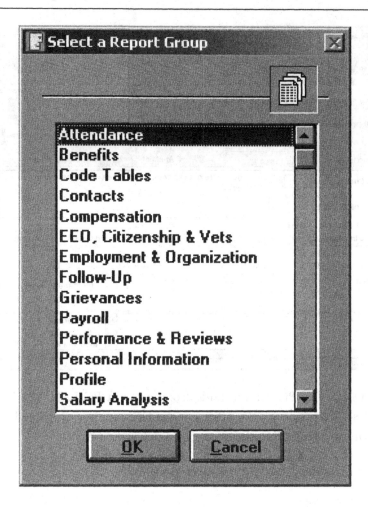

- It does not have much of a Web component. (I love Web things, regardless of the dot-com shakeout.) It does have a link to a Web-based background checking service and another to a service that posts to Web job boards.

- It is written in Microsoft FoxPro. That probably will not matter to you as an end user. But if you are big enough to have your IT department involved, you might ask their opinion. (You're likely to find that others in this end of the marketplace also use the Microsoft offering.)

Figure 14.3. !Trak-It Grievance Tracking Screen

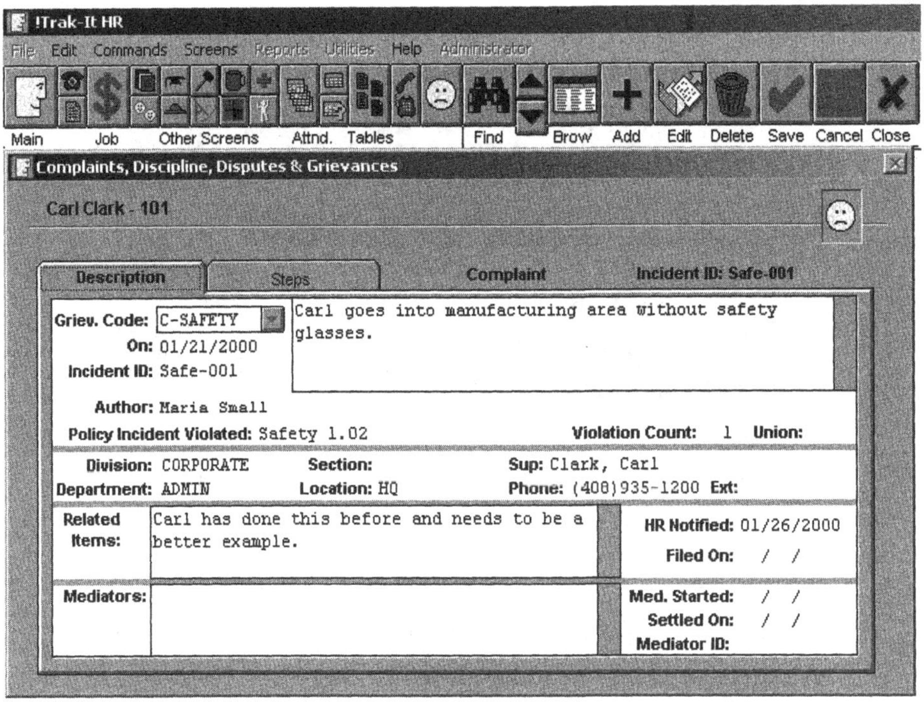

- It is a Mac and PC version and also runs on a PC/LAN, but it is not a client/server product. "We often get the HR people real excited," says the company president, "but the IS people like client/server."

Table 14.1 shows a quick summary of !Trak-It HR.

PEOPLE-TRAK

People-Trak is, of course, a tracker. It does what the other HRIS packages do, which is to let you find stuff on the computer screen instead of fumbling around through dusty, old file folders. It does not pretend to do anything grandiose. Company founder and president Jim Witschger attacks the popular myth that HRMS software is complex, and says instead, "*Reality*—HRMS software is not complex at all when compared to, say, accounting software. The key factor in HRMS software is width. HRMS software tracks a vast array of data for employees, applicants, and jobs. However, that vast array of data is simply stored, reported on, and used for a few basic calculations."

Table 14.1. Summary of !Trak-It HR

Company	!Trak-It Solutions, Inc. 8421 Auburn Boulevard, Suite 140 Citrus Heights, CA 95610 916–728–4880 www.trak-it.com
Product	!Trak-It HR
Product Use	Comprehensive HR system, aimed at small-to mid-sized companies
System Requirements	PC or Mac PC: Windows 95, 98, NT, ME, 2000, XP Mac: OS/8 and above
Release Date	v. 9.52, 02/2002; next general release in Q1 2003
Installed Base	2000 licenses, 500 companies
List Price	*Small Business Edition* Single user $495; multi-user $895 *Standard Edition* Single User Multi-User Up to 100 employees $995 $1,590 Unlimited employees $4,695 $5,990 $695 a user, up to 75 employees; $2,395 for unlimited employees; 1-Platform Multi-User Network, $220

Figure 14.4 shows the main personal screen of the People-Trak program, where you can begin to see its breadth.

Layers of the Onion

While People-Trak may not promise to do anything grandiose, it does promise to do its basic task in a technically elegant way. What is in this technically different product? All kinds of HRMS activities—applicant tracking, compensation analysis, training, attendance, and more. The program has become content-rich in the

Figure 14.4. Main Personnel Screen for People-Trak

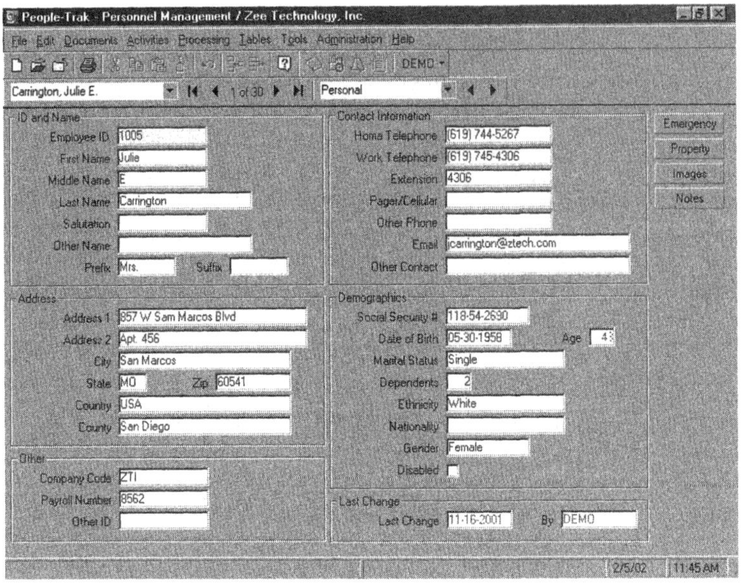

several years of its history. "It's taking months for our customers to understand what we've done," explains Witschger, whose new product, he says, contains four times as much as was in the previous version. "They haven't seen the layers of this onion that go down and down and down."

Figure 14.5 shows the main personal menu of the Applicants Module, another nice capability in the system (for which there is an additional charge).

Technically rich though the program may be, it was written with the full understanding that a low-end program has to be falling-off-a-log simple. It is that, too. Attests one user, "It comes with so many pre-programmed reports, and you can pull them up and tweak them a little bit. I didn't even have to program them from scratch." Figure 14.6 shows a neat screen from the compensation analysis capability—a feature you can not always expect when you pay less than $1,000.

In all respects, People-Trak admires simplicity. It does not have a field salesforce, but it has strong phone sales. It does not have a field support office, either, but it has good support. And the company does not try to nickel and dime you with additional costs every year or so. "It's what I call 'very low maintenance,'" attests a user. "You don't have to keep calling, updating, getting new training. It's powerful enough to do what we need." Maintains Witschger, "We don't create codependent relationships."

Figure 14.5. People-Trak Main Applicant Screen

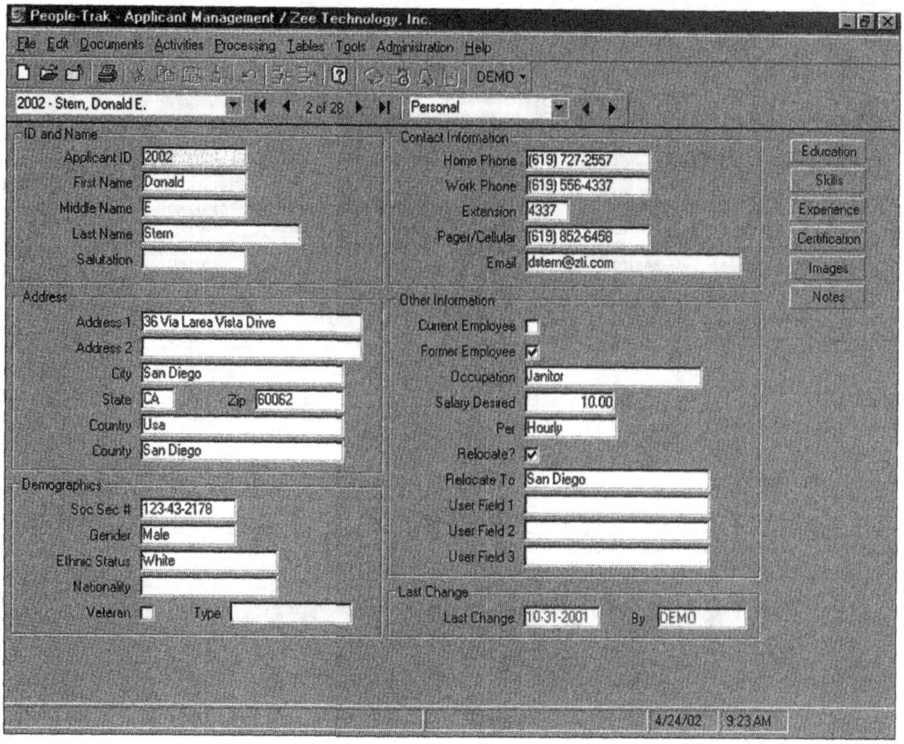

Issues to Consider

Where's the rub, then? If you like manuals, you'll notice that People-Trak does not. "I've never opened their manual. I call them instead," says a user. Likewise, if you are that rare low-end user who pores over help files, you will not find a lot to pore over in the People-Trak system.

Maybe you want to have a detailed, personalized response to your RFP. You may coerce a bit extra out of Technical Difference, Inc. (the company that produces People-Trak), but basically the company sends out one RFP response for everyone. "In responding to your request for a proposal, you will notice that we have not tailored this RFP to your specific company," their company RFP begins. "In general, we like to let our product do the talking for us, so in addition to the general RFP that you have in your hand, we have included a live demo CD of our software."

Finally, although this product is indeed simple to use, you won't be able to exploit its power unless you have a little training. Says Technical Difference

Figure 14.6. Compensation Analysis Screen for People-Trak

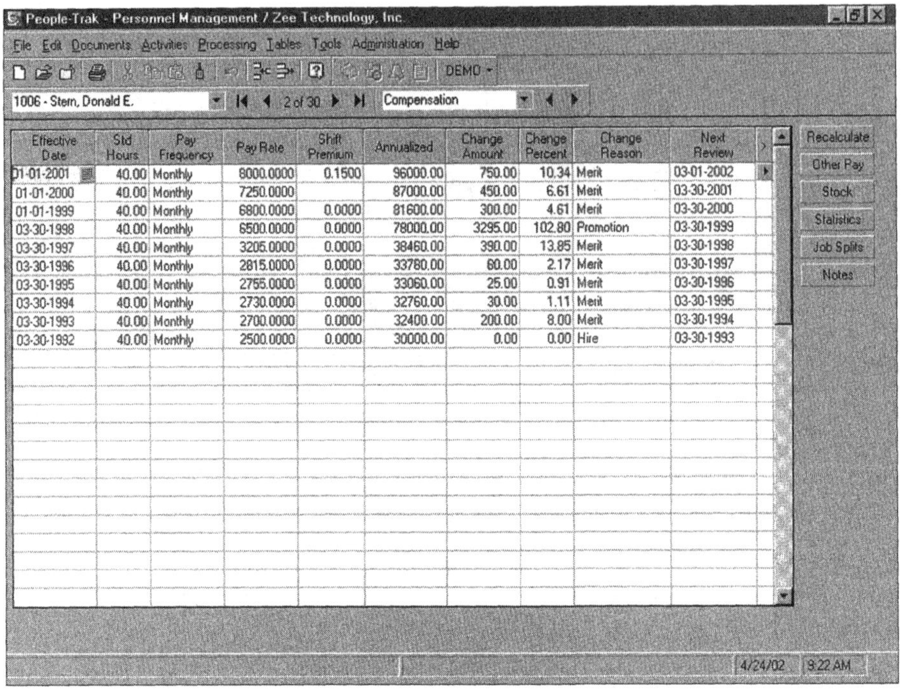

Effective Date	Std Hours	Pay Frequency	Pay Rate	Shift Premium	Annualized	Change Amount	Change Percent	Change Reason	Next Review
01-01-2001	40.00	Monthly	8000.0000	0.1500	96000.00	750.00	10.34	Merit	03-01-2002
01-01-2000	40.00	Monthly	7250.0000		87000.00	450.00	6.61	Merit	03-30-2001
01-01-1999	40.00	Monthly	6800.0000	0.0000	81600.00	300.00	4.61	Merit	03-30-2000
03-30-1998	40.00	Monthly	6500.0000	0.0000	78000.00	3295.00	102.80	Promotion	03-30-1999
03-30-1997	40.00	Monthly	3205.0000	0.0000	38460.00	390.00	13.85	Merit	03-30-1998
03-30-1996	40.00	Monthly	2815.0000	0.0000	33780.00	60.00	2.17	Merit	03-30-1997
03-30-1995	40.00	Monthly	2755.0000	0.0000	33060.00	25.00	0.91	Merit	03-30-1996
03-30-1994	40.00	Monthly	2730.0000	0.0000	32760.00	30.00	1.11	Merit	03-30-1995
03-30-1993	40.00	Monthly	2700.0000	0.0000	32400.00	200.00	8.00	Merit	03-30-1994
03-30-1992	40.00	Monthly	2500.0000	0.0000	30000.00	0.00	0.00	Hire	03-30-1993

vice president of business development Bret Schanzenbach, "We don't say any more, 'You don't need training.' Now we say, 'It's user friendly once you know how to do it.' We recommend one or two days training or an hour a week on the phone with your support rep." Table 14.2 shows a summary for People-Trak.

ABRA

And then there was Abra. Not everyone has heard of People-Trak. !Trak-It is not a household word. Abra, in the tight, little world of low-end HRMS software, is the one everyone else has to contend with. Any software selection at the low end generally includes Abra and someone else. But it just about always includes Abra.

Abra, like its competitors, automates your HR tracking. It tracks HR, payroll, attendance, applicant tracking, training management, and more. It offers local tax

Table 14.2. People-Trak Summary

Company	Technical Difference, Inc. 5256 S. Mission Road, Suite 802 Bonsall, CA 92003 800–809–5731 www.people-trak.com
Product	People-Trak, v. 7.1
Product Use	Comprehensive, Windows-based HRIS designed to be cutting-edge technology at affordable price
Equipment Requirements	PC: Win 95, 98, 2000, NT, XP Minimum: Pentium 166 MHz, 32 MB, Preferred: Pentium II, 350 MHz, 64 MB RAM ESS: Internet Explorer 5+, Netscape 4+ For ESS: Win NT4, Win 2000 (IIS 4+, ASP 2+) LAN: Win NT or Novell Network Also runs on WAN
Release Date	May 15, 2001
Installed Base	6,500 copies sold, 2,000 active users at this time
List Price	From $1,000 up to $10,000, based on number of active employees to track as well as modules or features. Training, implementation, and employee self-service/manager self-service add to cost.

support for payroll compliance, benefits administration, and resume scanning and searching. What has given it such an entrenched position in the marketplace? No one can say for sure, but its solid market presence has helped it to maintain that very thing—a solid market presence over time.

Large Market Share

The first plus about this program? Longevity. Or to use other words for it: momentum, size, experience. Others have begun to challenge Abra with respect to experience, but Abra has been the low-end leader for a long time. It has proved itself on the HR industry front lines. It knows how people work in HR and how to help them do that work successfully.

It has a broad, loyal customer base. "I really believe in Abra. It's just awesome. It's everything that anybody could want," effuses one user, who also does consulting on Abra.

It has a network of resellers around the country. You do not have to count on phone support from the main office. According to Frank Dicicca, Abra product manager, "We distribute primarily through VARs, and they truly do provide value-added. They help in installation and setup and provide ongoing consultative services."

Momentum? Resellers? Loyalty? These may all seem like left-handed compliments. What about the product itself? It has a great interface, as shown in Figure 14.7. Click on a button on the left, and see a choice of activities on the right. It's cool, and it truly seems to place the daily tasks of the HR person at your fingertips.

Figure 14.7. Abra's Interface

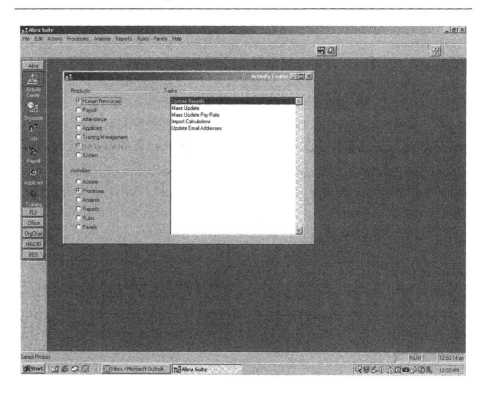

"It's usually very, very easy for someone to get up to speed once they understand how it all works together," explains one user/consultant. If you're the type who turns to documentation, Abra makes sure to cover that base as well. Contends the consultant, "Abra's documentation is really awesome."

With a finger firmly on the pulse of HR, Abra comes forward with modules as the need becomes apparent. As HR has begun to turn to employee self-service as a way to allow employees to answer their own questions, Abra has added employee self-service and manager self-service over the Web. Figure 14.8 shows the Abra self-service module.

For all that HR software brings to an enterprise, payroll remains a mainstay of almost every company. Many may not even have HR software, but most have automated their payroll in one way or another. Not surrendering payroll to companies like ADP and Ceridian, Abra offers its own payroll module (with the strong integration you can expect when HR and payroll modules come from the same provider). Figure 14.9 shows the main screen for Abra payroll reports. "The payroll deposit reports are a tidy package," the consultant relates. "A lot of people refer to that as their Bible."

Figure 14.8. Abra Self-Service Module

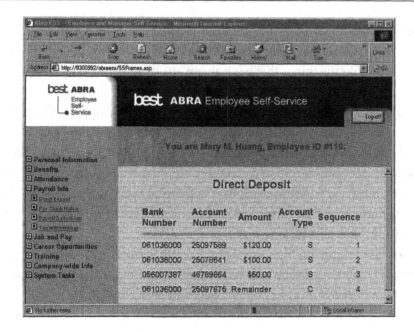

Figure 14.9. Abra's Payroll Module

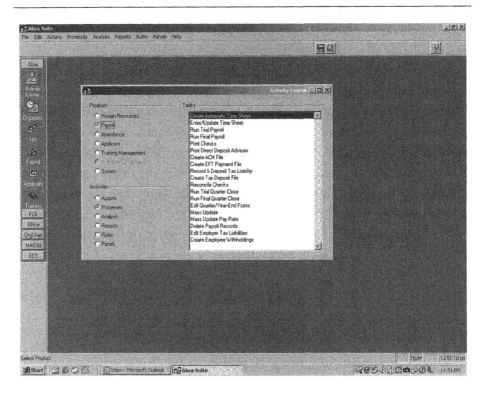

Issues to Consider

With so much momentum on its side, Abra continually faces the question, "Can it continue to do the things that got it there?" Its competitors often see signs that the leader is wavering in one way or another. As a buyer, you may choose to pay some attention to such contentions from the competition. Whereas the other two products in this chapter still have their product visionary at the company helm, Abra has gone through two acquisitions—first by Best software, then by British-based Sage. Acquisitions can add clout to a product, or they can sap momentum. It is not always easy to know which has happened. I think anyone looking at Abra ought to check into the company as well as the product to see whether it still has the spirit that got it where it is.

What else might you look for? Abra, like other smaller products, resides on Microsoft FoxPro—the vehicle so unpopular with IT departments. And for all its glory, it is a PC/LAN product and not a client/server product.

Even the highly touted support network of third-party resellers can be a mixed benefit. Yes, you are likely to receive aggressive, on-site support. But some say that the network of resellers is uneven. If you find a good one, you are golden. But do some checking before you buy to make sure that you do have a good one in your area.

Finally, as to price, Abra still competes in the low end. You can find a nice solution for under $10,000. Listed base price is under $1,000. Chances are, though, you will not get away for so little.

Abra has long been the darling of the low end of HR software. Many may be surprised to learn that it has competitors, even numerous competitors. It satisfies basic HR needs, and many with Abra in place are simply doing their HR business online without much concern that others might serve their needs as well. Abra is good enough.

Table 14.3 shows a quick summary of Abra.

Table 14.3. Abra Suite Summary

Company	Best Software, Inc. 11413 Isaac Newton Square Reston, VA 20190 703–709–5200 www.bestsoftware.com
Product	Abra Suite v. 6. 3
Product Use	HR and payroll administration, including compensation and benefits, government compliance, personnel time and attendance, recruiting, and training
Equipment Requirements	Pentium processor, Win 95/98/NT Runs on Novell or NT LAN
Release Date	September 2001
Installed Base	15,000
List Price	Abra HR: $985 (for up to seventy-five employees); Full suite, including payroll, starts at $4,090

CONCLUSION

Abra, People-Trak, and !Trak-It. The three names often come up together, except for the times when Abra comes up all by itself. All have been around long enough that any one of them is a safe bet. Each has its risks as well. Any one of them can power up your people processes. Even with these safe choices, however, you probably ought to do a thorough evaluation and a careful comparison before plunging ahead.

In addition to these three, others bring vigor, creativity, and solutions to the low end. Still others bring, at least, solidity and predictability. You can read about challengers to the Big Three in the next chapter.

Other Low-End Players

How many low-end products could there possibly be? The more you research them, the more you can begin to confuse yourself with the multitude of choices. If you simply look up official listings in reference works like *The 2000 Personnel Software Census*, you begin to feel about the way you did when you read a catalog of colleges to help you select a college. They all sound alike. The good ones do not sound that much better than the so-so ones, and the so-so ones sometimes put such a great spin on themselves that they sound like the good ones. Eventually, all the listings just become a blur.

Nothing can really substitute for your own needs analysis, your own demos, your own evaluation matrix. Do the work, and eventually the truth emerges quite clearly. However, in this chapter I will attempt to help make some sense out of the seeming chaos of products out there beyond the Big Three mentioned in the previous chapter. Who would think there would be so many products in this seemingly specialized niche of human resources information systems—so many products at a time when, truth be known, many companies simply do not automate at all.

In this chapter, I briefly mention some products that attract many users, realizing that many users know about these products and have come to use them through their payroll vendors. I describe the stripped-down versions you can purchase from those noted for selling to the mid-market. I give a tip of the hat to the energetic, new Internet players, especially Employease (who might just as well be a mid-market combatant). Finally, I look at some players that I like to think of as "really cheap products." These are companies that compete on the basis of price, yet their functionality does not seem bad either.

HRIS FROM PAYROLL VENDORS

Most companies use automated payroll solutions, usually an outside vendor to whom a company outsources the payroll. The benefits in accuracy and speed are so immediate and downright necessary that companies automate payroll one way or another. It is natural to look into HRIS offerings from the same provider, and many companies do so—with, at best, mixed results. Here are two of the payroll providers who also offer low-end HRIS software.

ADP

The company that controls the largest market share for low-end payroll processing is ADP of Roseland, New Jersey. "We're the business behind business," reads the company theme. ADP offers several products that you can use to automate your human resources as well. One that it has been touting recently is CSS HRIZON.

In many instances, ADP is simply the default solution for HRIS, often suggested by the company higher ups, as in, "We are using ADP for payroll. So for simplicity and compatibility, we will use it for HR as well." If your payroll is outsourced to ADP, check into a similar option for the HRIS. Of course, you do have the choice of using ADP for payroll and another solution for your HRIS software—which may allow you to implement an HRIS solution designed and written purely with HR in mind.

In my experience, I have not detected a lot of outright enthusiasm for ADP's HRIS package or the one available from Ceridian. Some people have told me that they found them harder to use than other packages. ADP and Ceridian continue to address that need, and you may come back to them at a time when they have solved the problems.

You probably owe it to yourself to check ADP out. If it does get the HRIS end of things right, and the pricing is competitive, ADP offers the advantage of being a single provider for both payroll and HRIS.

Ceridian

Ceridian of Bloomington, Minnesota, like ADP, tends to ride into an installation on the coattails of its payroll solution. "Working with a single source for all your employment-related needs, you can reduce your costs by eliminating redundancy and wasted effort," the company says on its website. Later, it summarizes the sentiment in these words, "One company. One source."

Unless you do your research and come up with good reasons to use an alternative product, you just may find yourself using Ceridian.

SMALLER VERSIONS FROM MID-MARKET HRIS PROVIDERS

There is no official line of demarcation between low-end and mid-sized software for HRIS. Indeed, some people make no demarcation between any of the offerings. As one vendor related to me, the vendor will sometimes say to an HR person, "What vendors are you considering?" to which the software seeker may reply "Abra [a product in the thousand-dollar range] and PeopleSoft [a product in the million-dollar range.]"

For our purposes, we will define mid-market providers as targeting companies with five hundred employees or more. Mid-market providers will do their best to serve a smaller company and generally will not simply turn away the business. You can, therefore, consider for your smaller company any of the companies discussed in the section on mid-market companies. Following are a few sometime mid-market players you may want to look at, in addition to those discussed in Chapter 16.

HROffice from Ascentis

This product is not the everyday word that Abra may be, and it has not been around as long as People-Trak. It has not surged onto the Internet like Employease. And I have not seen it grab many headlines. Founded by some veteran Microsoft people, it does do an awfully nice job of tracking HR software . . . with some particular specialties of its own.

You can start using it for a basic price of $495, which is why I discuss it here. On the other hand, you can go all out with it for a price of $25,000 to serve your entire company.

Figure 15.1. HROffice Main Screen

As you can see from its main screen, shown in Figure 15.1, it is simple and downright attractive to use. According to Dwight Matheny, a founder and vice president and general manager with Ascentis, "HROffice was designed from the beginning to be configured and used by non-technical HR and benefits personnel." Attack the program properly, and you can end up with a lot for a little.

Ascentis prides itself on helping you solve one of the tough problems for anyone ramping up with HR software: HROffice has a QuickStart utility for importing data, shown in Figure 15.2. "Many of our competitors charge for that," says Matheny.

Attendance is another product specialty. Almost every product these days tracks attendance, but HROffice makes that function a priority.

Figure 15.2. QuickStart Utility for Importing Data in HROffice

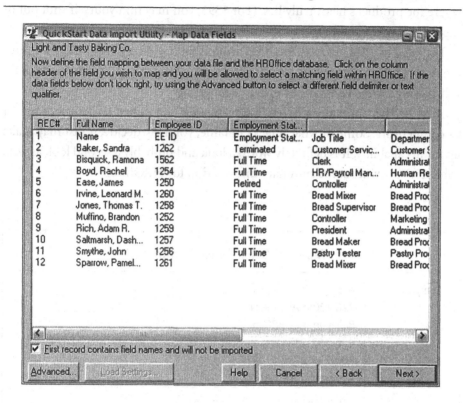

Benefits, which does not even appear on the main screen of Abra, has a prominent place in HROffice. If benefits are your "bag," Ascentis may be your provider. The benefits module is outstanding. One user, for instance, is vice president at a benefits outsourcing company; people pay him to do their benefits tracking, and he uses HROffice. "It is powerful enough in the ability to do all the data warehousing that it will allow you to track unlimited amounts of employees," he attests, "and at the same time be flexible enough to allow you to subject those employees to a multiple array of benefit rules." It is advanced in its ability to handle FMLA and COBRA, offering functionality that Matheny says you can otherwise find only in standalone, specialty products.

Issues to Consider
The product hasn't made the move to the Internet, which may matter to you.

Although the pricing starts at $595, the top pricing of $40,000 may indicate where the product's heart truly lies. (For $595, you may find yourself shut out of capabilities you want.)

Founded in 1994, Ascentis has been around for a while by HRIS standards, but it has not been around as long as Abra and some of the others. Some observers are still waiting for the company to prove its longevity.

Ascentis, then, provides a sweet product that has not gained the fame of some of its competitors. Some of what it lacks in fame, you may decide, it just may make up for in capability. It is definitely worth a look and probably a second look as well. Table 15.1 provides some summary information for HROffice.

Table 15.1. HROffice Summary

Company	Ascentis Software Corporation 220 120th Avenue NE Bellevue, WA 98005 425-462-7171 800-229-2713 www.ascentis.com
Product	HROffice & HROffice Enterprise
Product Use	Comprehensive human resources information system that automates and manages human resource and employee benefits administration. HROffice is designed for small to mid-sized organizations.
Equipment Requirements	Microsoft Windows 98, 2000, NT, or XP Requires Microsoft SQL Server 7, 2000 or later, which must be purchased separately.
Release Date	Version 4.0 in Q2 of 2002
Installed Base	Over five hundred
List Price	$595 for up to twenty-five employees; top-end license: $40,000

HRIS-Pro from HR Microsystems

Founded in 1983, HR Microsystems is an old-timer in the HRIS marketplace—an old standby that has never truly become a market force. Its founder, Don Helt, is respected in the industry and continues to lead the company. Following are some of the product strengths of its HR software offering, HRIS-Pro:

- The interface is nice—clean, simple, logical, as you can see in Figure 15.3.

- The training programs are good. They will get you ready.

- The support gets it done for you, too. "Their support is tremendous," says one user. "How I want to use the system can be very complex," she explains. She wanted to create reports showing "who's going to have an increase next year, the percentage for the increase, and the real dollar cost to the company based

Figure 15.3. HRIS-Pro Interface

Figure 15.4. Employee Time Off Module in HRIS-Pro

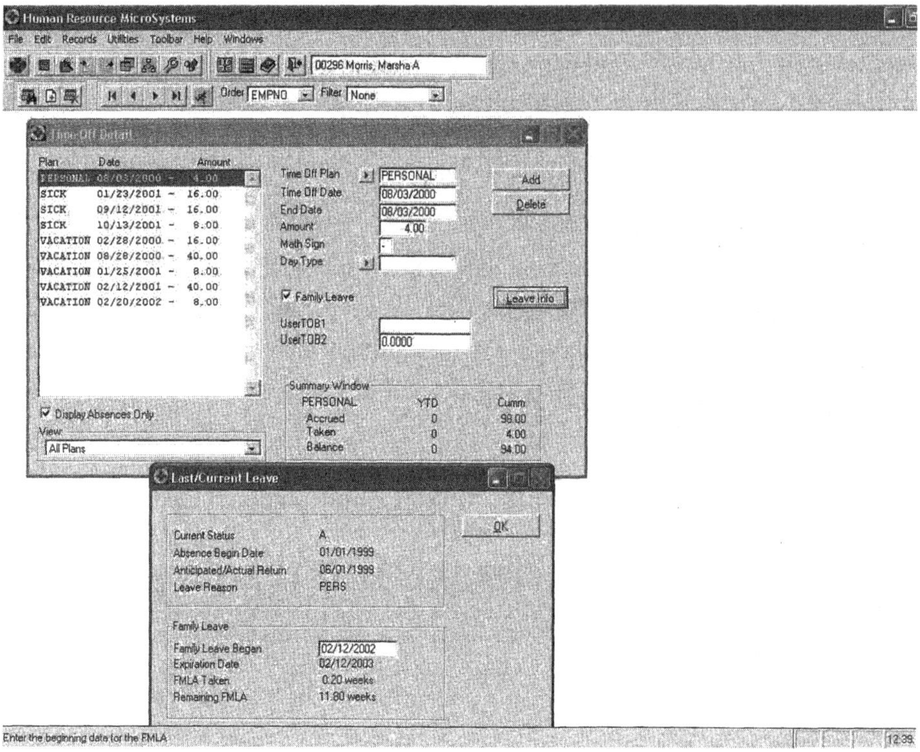

on the anniversary for the increase." Company support folks made sure she could do the task.

- The program offers useful optional modules, like "Training Administration" and a very nice "Employee Time Off" module, shown in Figure 15.4.

- You can take advantage of a Web-based self-service application, HRIS-Pro Net, shown in Figure 15.5.

Issues to Consider

This is a PC/LAN offering. It is for smaller companies—no more than about 1,000 employees. Also, the program runs on Visual FoxPro. That may be fine. It allows you nicely to launch other desktop applications from within HRIS-Pro. You probably will not get much enthusiasm for the Visual FoxPro from your IT department, though.

The company is currently emphasizing its mid-market offering—HR Entré. HRIS-Pro tends to be something of a dark horse candidate at the low end. With a

Figure 15.5. HRIS-Pro Net's Web-Based Employee Self-Service

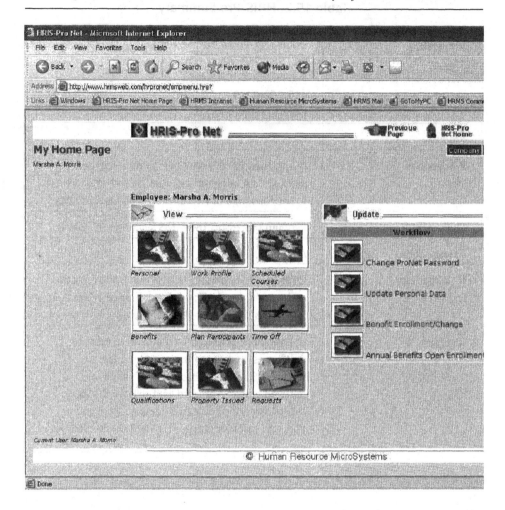

base price of $2,500, it may be a mid-range product right out of the gate. It does not tend to dazzle anyone but, on the other hand, it consistently does the job, provides solid support, and continues to be a contender year after year. Table 15.2 provides summary information for HRIS-Pro.

WEB-BASED "RENTAL" SOLUTIONS

The Web brought a spate of new providers to the HR software marketplace. The formula seemed promising—HR services over the Web for a small fee. Providers developed the ASP (application service provider) model, which allows a company

Other Low-End Players **241**

Table 15.2. HRIS-Pro Summary

Company	Human Resource MicroSystems 160 Sansome Street San Francisco, CA 94104 415-362-8400 www.hrms.com
Product	HRIS-Pro, v. 5.8
Product Use	Comprehensive PC/LAN human resource management system bringing organization and effectiveness to the full range of HR functions and responsibilities
Equipment Requirements	Pentium processor, 166+, MS Windows 95/98/NT
Release Date	April 2002
Installed Base	Over seven hundred installations in United States and around the world; companies range in size from seventy to six thousand employees
List Price	License pricing based on a matrix of number of employees, number of users, and number of modules. Standalone base system with a one hundred employee record limit sells for $2,500. Typical sales (including maintenance, implementation, and software) range from $12,000 to $65,000.

to have a customized HR software installation on the Web hosted by another provider. The biggest advantage of the ASP model is that the end-user company does not have to have hardware and IT support in-house but can rely on that provided by the vendor. Also, at a price of $6 or $7 per employee per month (or even less), the model promised to be low cost for user companies.

Numerous vendors besides those mentioned in this section also offer software by the ASP model as well as by purchase—notably Spectrum, NuView, Best Software, and others. One company, Employease, stands out as a company developed specifically to provide software for "rental only."

Employease

Employease came bursting onto the scene about the time of the Internet boom at the turn of the century. With strong funding, founders with roots in industry-leading PeopleSoft, and the panache of the Web at its heart, it became a market presence almost overnight. Here are some of its strengths:

Employease has a very nice little interface, shown in Figure 15.6. Beyond the interface, the product nicely understands how you work and the paths you are likely to follow as you work. "The beauty of Employease is that it captures the right kind of information and allows a usability that is unparalleled," insists one user.

It has all kinds of power for the price. The product makes "Fortune 500 functionality available to small to mid-sized companies for the very first time," maintains Mike Seckler, Employease co-founder and vice president of marketing and business development.

Figure 15.6. Employease Main Screen

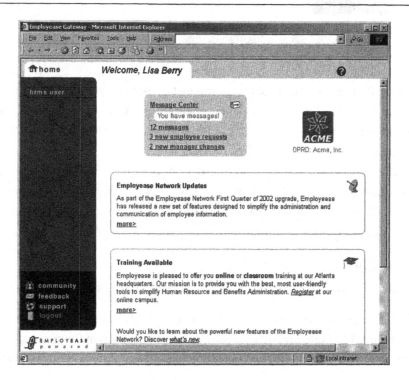

Figure 15.7. Reconciling Benefits Billings with Employease

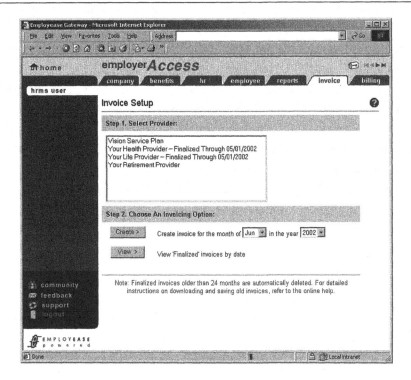

The product does some cool things you just do not come across every day, such as reconcile your billings from benefits providers, as shown in Figure 15.7. Of this capability and others, says Employease Product Manager Dara Brenner, "Nobody else provides the depth that we do."

Not relying on an "industry-standard" report writer like Crystal Reports, as many companies do, Employease steps up to the plate with a nice, friendly report writer of its own (see Figure 15.8). "If I want to ask, for instance, 'What's the number of employees at one of our locations?' I can do it in two minutes," attests a user.

Issues to Consider

What should you be careful about? Here are a few thoughts:

• Employease has an innovative design by which it uses one database for everyone. The "one-size-fits-all" design can be restrictive for some advanced activities you want to do. Cautions one user, "Definitely do your homework.

Figure 15.8. Employease Report Writer

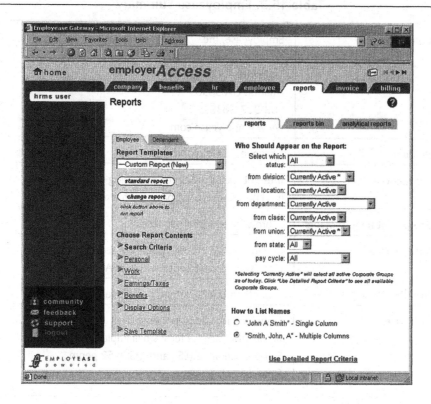

Make sure the applications are what you want. Employease probably isn't right for everybody." (Newer versions of Employease are making the product more customizable than early releases were.)

- Realize, too, that Employease is a commitment, not just something you throw onto a PC somewhere and forget about. Cautions a user, "It wasn't like you just go 'poof' and have it happen. We had to change the way managers think, the way we think. We worked to make the system work."

Employease came into the marketplace at a time when the Internet was nothing but glamour. With PeopleSoft expatriates as its founders, it had the right bloodlines. And it has continued to be a market presence. Yet its per employee per month pricing tends to be affordable. Who wouldn't want to check out this guy? Table 15.3 provides a summary of Employease.

Table 15.3. Employease Summary

Company	Employease, Inc. One Piedmont Center, Suite 400 Atlanta, GA 30305 888-327-3638 www.employease.com
Product	Employease Network
Product Use	Internet-based HRIS, for managing and communicating HR, benefits, and payroll information
Equipment Requirements	A browser and Internet access
Release Date	Original version: 1997; manager access appeared in mid-2000; recruitment module in April 2001
Installed Base	More than one thousand companies
List Price	Employer access: $4 per employee per month (pepm); no up-front license fees; small implementation fee Self-Service Suite (ESS and MSS): $2 pepm Recruitment: $2 pepm

Simpata

Employease used to have a competitor with less fame but seemingly equal functionality, Internet-based Simpata, from Simpata, Inc., of Sacramento, California. The company is shifting from a general distribution model to distribution through insurance providers and benefits providers. You may not be able to purchase the software directly from the company any more, or not do so easily. Here are some of its strengths:

- Its ease of use seems to match that of Employease. Figure 15.9 shows its main screen.

- Like Employease, it has its own report writer, and the product seems to bring more capability with less strain than some of the packaged products (such as Crystal Reports). Figure 15.10 shows the report writer.

Figure 15.9. Simpata Main Screen

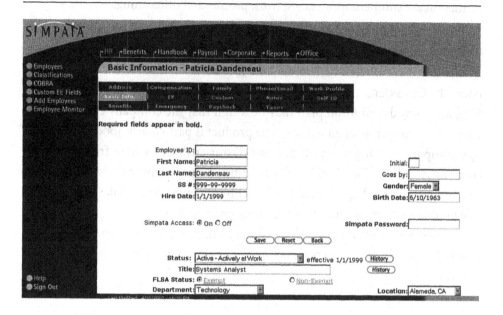

Figure 15.10. Simpata's Report Writer

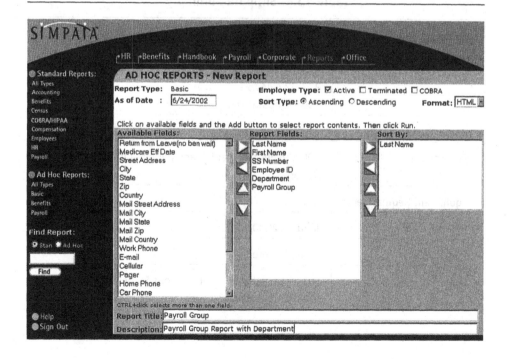

- The product has strong understanding of HR as its basis. Besides basic information are compensation, taxes, work profile, and other things.

- Implementation time is short (often a challenge with Internet-based HR software). Attests one user, "implementation time was one and a half to two weeks."

Issues to Consider

Simpata's new distribution plan may be a sign that the company can no longer compete in the purely open market. The product is particularly good for technology companies. "Originally 80 percent of our customers were from dot-com companies," admits Chuck Moxley, marketing vice president with the company. If you are not a technology company or a technical department, make sure Simpata will be able to meet your needs for training and support.

The best way to get leverage with a company like Employease is to look at a rival that is comparable in many respects. Table 15.4 provides summary information for Simpata.

Table 15.4. Simpata Summary

Company	Simpata, Inc. 80 Iron Point Circle, Suite 100 Folsom, CA 95630 877-477-4675 www.simpata.com
Product	Simpata
Product Use	100 percent Internet HR and benefit administration solution
Equipment Requirements	Browser
Release Date	January 2000
Installed Base	Three hundred
List Price	Subscription based on size, about $5 per employee per month. One-time activation fee of $15 per employee.

"ISN'T THAT NUMBER MISSING A ZERO?"

Low-end software, by the very nature of things, ends up becoming more sophisticated than it was when it started out. A company gradually adds features—an applicant tracking module, Internet-based employee self-service, the ability to reconcile benefits, smoother integration of Microsoft Office capabilities like Microsoft Word, or any number of any capabilities. Products just naturally grow, and that is good. Pricing still may remain quite reasonable, but pricing, too, tends to inch upward.

Someone looking for a first HR tracking package, however, may truly want to spend next to nothing on the product—just to see whether the company would use such a product or would simply neglect it. The risk is obvious with choosing a low-cost product: You might well continue for years to use a more advanced product, complete with training and commitment. If you just pay and "You're on your own," you may never truly implement the product.

Such risk notwithstanding, many companies like the thought of really cheap software—something so low-cost that they do not have to ask for approval from management, they do not have to have IT involved (or only minimally so), and they can just discard the product if it does not work out. Here are three such low-cost products.

Auxillium's HRSource

Many products may have begun with Microsoft Access as their basis but moved on to other engines instead. One product that remains unashamedly a Microsoft Access product is Auxillium West's HRSource, priced nicely under a thousand dollars.

Here are some product pluses:

- No one should have any trouble using the main screen, built on a metaphor of a switchboard, as shown in Figure 15.11.

- Not neglecting the Internet, even though based in a non-Internet vehicle, HRSource allows you to create an intranet site and use it for posting your employee handbook or whatever else you wish. Figure 15.12 shows the HRSource Intranet Solution.

- Just like its competitors, it is great for compiling reports. Says one user, "This allows me to gather reports in a snap, any kind of report that I want." Figure 15.13 shows a sample new hire report.

Figure 15.11. HRSource Main Screen

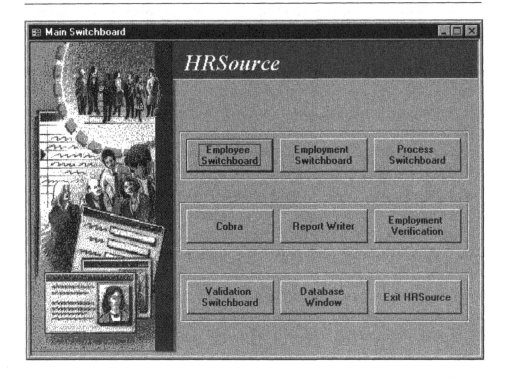

Figure 15.12. HRSource Intranet Solution

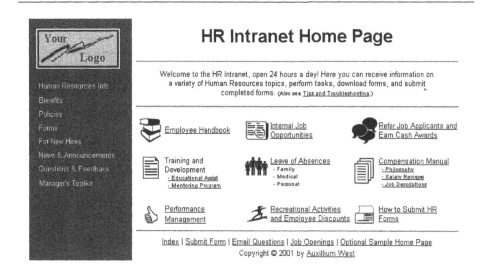

Figure 15.13. HRSource New Hire Report

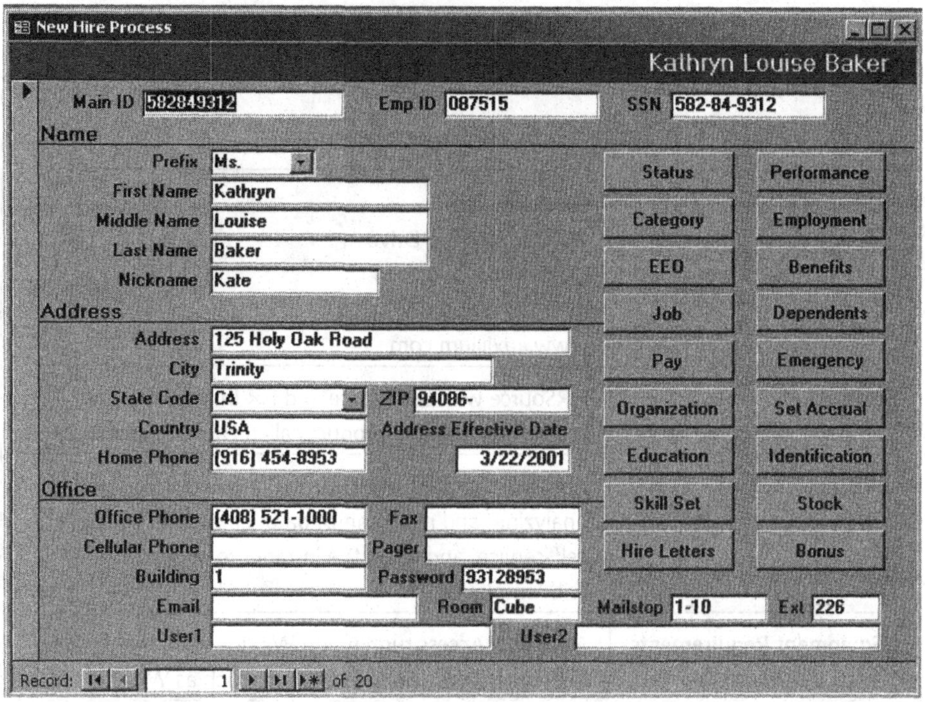

- Given that the power of MS Access is its basis, you can probably use the program to do about anything that an HR database program can do. Says one HR consultant and Auxillium user, "There wasn't anything that I needed, in essence, that wasn't in that package already."

Issues to Consider

You wouldn't want to use this program for a large company, or one that might grow to more than one thousand employees. "I can't see any negatives to this program for a company that's starting out," says an experienced user, but he adds that it does have "shortcomings when employee numbers start to get very large [over 1,000]."

You don't have to know MS Access to use the program. Not at all. But knowing that the capability is there, you might want to develop some Access expertise or befriend a programmer who has it.

All in all, HRSource is a quiet, relatively unknown HRIS program that does the work for you . . . all for under $1,000. A summary of the product is provided in Table 15.5.

Table 15.5. HRSource Summary	
Company	Auxillium West 7560 Waterford Drive Cupertino, CA 95014 408-257-5054 www.auxillium.com
Product	HRSource with SelfSource and HR Intranet Solution (complete, bundled product called HRnetSource v. 2.6)
Product Use	A fully-integrated, HR information system for tracking, analyzing, and reporting of data, employee/manager self-service, and using the intranet to communicate with employees
Equipment Requirements	Microsoft Access running on Windows 95 or above; for SelfSource: Web Server software, such as Windows IIS
Release Date	March 2001
Installed Base	HRSource: 250 companies; Intranet: about 50; SelfSource: about 20
List Price	HRSource HRIS—$895 SelfSource—$1,995 HR Intranet Solution—$1,995

HRmgr from RMS

Does even $895 seem to you to be more than "throwaway" money? How does $295 sound—the base price for HRmgr from RMS Software of Wrightstown, Wisconsin? To use this MS Windows-based program, you click to open the program, then see before you a series of Excel-like columns, shown in Figure 15.14, listing your employee names and such information as education, supervisor, job title, EEO class, and next review date.

Figure 15.14. HRmgr Main Screen

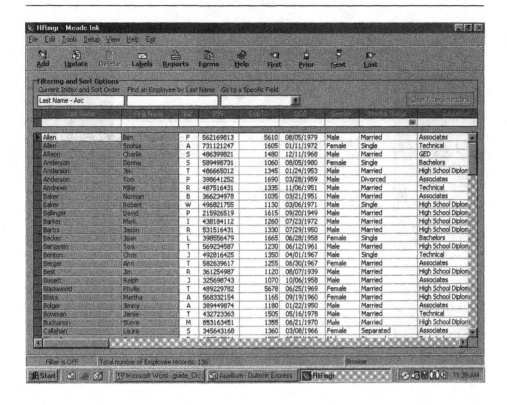

You can even track information such as performance reviews (see Figure 15.15) and attendance (see Figure 15.16), just as you would with a much higher priced program.

The program looks ridiculously simple without sacrificing capability. Says one user, "This is easy-to-use. It doesn't have one hundred options that you're not really going to use anyway."

Issues to Consider

You don't plan to buy a program like this and then use it in a multi-national company. You use it on one workstation. It is not scalable. You do not have a large support staff to turn to. The product's developer is also its support staff. Too much success could overwhelm him.

Figure 15.15. HRmgr Performance Review Tracking

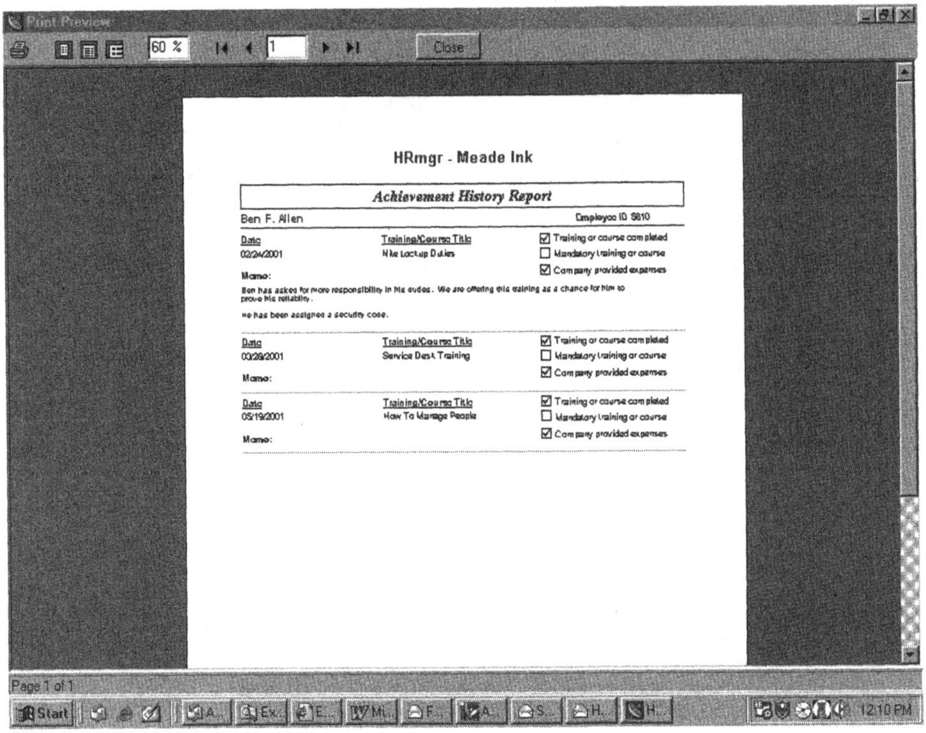

The program does not offer training. "I don't think it's really that complicated anyway," explains company founder Gary Klister. Table 15.6 provides summary information for HRmgr.

People Manager from KnowledgePoint

Founded in 1987, KnowledgePoint is an old-timer in the world of human resource software. Its product line includes the products Policies Now, Descriptions Now, and other products. KnowledgePoint, now a division of CCH Incorporated, has years of accumulated experience in HR and in HR software. It also knows something about low pricing, with such products as Policies Now priced at an affordable $179.

Eyeing the burgeoning market for HRIS programs, KnowledgePoint apparently decided to jump right in there with the old timers like Abra and the upstarts like RMS. Moreover, it seems to have decided to compete on a basis that many

Figure 15.16. HRmgr Attendance Tracking

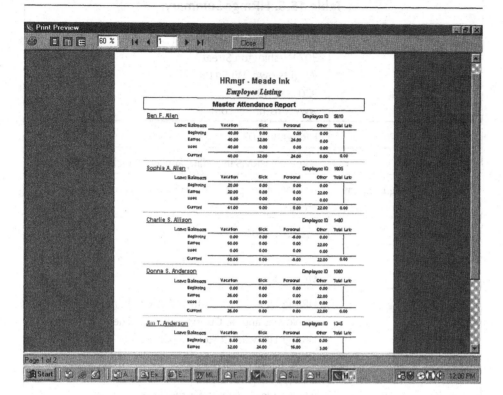

first-time buyers like best—price. People Manager comes in at the pleasantly insignificant cost of $179. It has admirable aspirations of what it will do for your company. Here is KnowledgePoint's summary of what this product will do, from the product's help files:

- Get automatic reminders for benefits eligibility, performance reviews, and other crucial tasks;

- Track attendance and time off benefits;

- Interface with external payroll packages;

- Tap into expert advice on important employment issues;

- Import data for easy set-up;

- Run custom reports by exporting information; and

- Access easy-to-use forms, letters, and checklists.

Table 15.6. HRmgr Summary

Company	RMS, Resource Management Software 307 Washington Street Wrightstown, WI 54180 920-532-4017 www.rms-hrmgr.com
Product	HRmgr, v. 3.03
Product Use	Low-cost HRMS including applicant tracking, benefits
Equipment Requirements	Any Windows platform—Win 95 or Win NT 4.0 or greater
Release Date	April 27, 2001
Installed Base	Twenty-five, ranging in size from five to seven hundred employees
List Price	HRmgr Lite—$295 (restricted to one hundred employees and no Custom Report Builder) HRmgr Lite with Custom Report Builder (Lite CRB)—$395 HRmgr Standard—$495 (unlimited records but does not include Custom Report Builder) HRmgr Professional—$695 (unlimited records and includes Custom Report Builder)

Sound like the main things you tend to do in HR? You may find some gaps, for example, no applicant tracking module. The nifty interface, shown in Figure 15.17, has tabs for your main HR activities.

You can check out time off and even see the information in a nice, graphic format, shown in Figure 15.18.

You of course have built-in reports. If you want to change the report, you can make simple changes right in People Manager. Or you can export the file to your word processor and work on it there. That may sound like an overly simple way to go, but isn't that the way you work much of the time? Figure 15.19 shows the selection screen for a sample report.

Figure 15.17. People Manager Interface

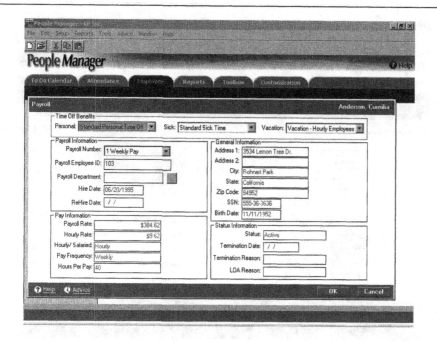

Figure 15.18. Time Off Information on People Manager

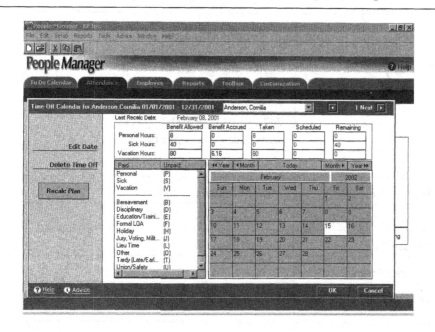

Figure 15.19. Sample People Manager Report

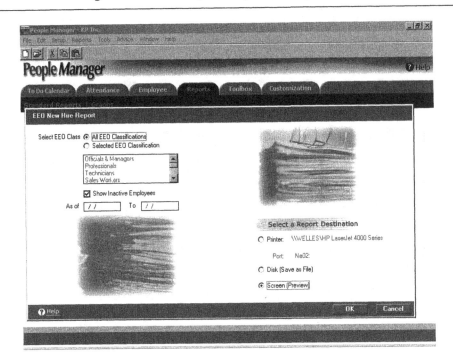

Table 15.7. People Manager Summary

Company	CCHKnowledgePoint 1129 Industrial Avenue Petaluma, CA 94952 707-762-0333 or 800-727-1133 www.cchknowledgepoint.com
Product	People Manager 3.0
Product Use	Manage employee information
Equipment Requirements	Windows 95, 98, 2000, ME, NT
Release Date	October 2001
Installed Base	10,000
List Price	$179

This is a standalone product, not something that you run in a client/server situation. It does not have the visibility that Abra may have. It covers the bases, though. And you cannot overlook the matter of price. A proven company with a strong reputation has stepped forward with a really cheap product. Check the product out against your needs requirements. If it does not fall short, then what is not to like? Table 15.7 summarizes the information for People Manager.

CONCLUSION

The low end is simply a delightful place to shop for HR software. You have to suspect that many purchasers in that space do not do a great deal of research. If you are going to spend $495 on a product, do you really want to spent $4,950 evaluating it? People probably just jump into buying one of these products and take the consequences. Heck, you can jump three or four times and not suffer any bad consequences. Every one of the products I have mentioned in these pages does the basic job of tracking and reporting on your HR data.

Still, there are differences among the products and the companies. Do some comparisons. Do some negotiating. Take some time to reflect. And you can end up with a product particularly well-suited to your needs. Delightful as the low end may be, the rest of the marketplace offers adventures and powerful capabilities for your company as well. Section Five of this book explores software in the mid-market, the high-end, and the specialty niches.

Reviewing the Rest
of the Market

The low end of the HRIS marketplace may offer the most fun. With low-end products, you can readily automate, and you can find some products with amazing "bang for the buck." The mid-market and the high end, though, offer the most functionality and the most staying power. Often, in fact, mid- and high-end products set the trends that low-end products follow.

Besides HRIS products for all segments of the marketplace, there are numerous specialty products aimed at all parts of the marketplace and covering capabilities from recruiting to performance management to time management. This section introduces mid-market products, specialty products, and high-end products.

Mid-Market Main Players

" **M**angled mid-market." "Missing mid-market." "Mid-market madness." It is easy to write headlines about the mid-market for HRIS software, the market for companies with from five hundred to five thousand employees (even ten thousand at times). The headlines are easy; the working solutions are elusive.

Certain HRIS providers do seem to have "solved" the low-end marketplace. Smaller companies simply want to track HR data and prepare simple reports, and they have been having a hard time doing that with paper and file folders. At the other end, high-end providers may have "solved" the problems of that marketplace as well. Giant companies want giant systems in place that contain all the company's data and allow companies to report on the data as well as do sophisticated analysis.

But the solutions from the low end are too trimmed-down for the mid-market. And the solutions from the high end are too ambitious (that is, expensive) for the mid-market. Ergo, vendors fail to penetrate the mid-market, and that market fails to find the solutions it needs.

If you are looking for a place where the competition in HR software gets white hot, look to the mid-market. The stakes are high. Purchases are high enough to make a big difference to any company—from $25,000 to $100,000 and up for the HR software. The market is simply crying out for software solutions, and companies are scrambling to provide them. Larry Munini, president of GENESYS

Software Systems, Inc., of Methuen, Massachusetts, observes, "There is unquestionably a large opportunity in the mid-market for the full gamut of enterprise-style applications, not just HRMS. This is visible through the legion of market initiatives launched by the vendor community. Organizations with between five hundred and two thousand employees have many if not all of the same sophisticated requirements as their larger counterparts."

Jim Spoor, president of SPECTRUM Human Resource Systems Corporation of Denver, concurs. "The mid-market is a very heterogeneous market with a wide range of organizations in a wide range of industries, all with varying needs and expectations, not to mention differing financial and affordability limits," he says. Observes consultant Naomi Bloom, managing partner with Bloom & Wallace, a consulting firm in Ft. Myers, Florida, "This market is awash in possibilities."

Who are the vendors who are competing in the volatile market for mid-sized companies? Of the vendors providing across-the-board HRIS packages, a few companies in particular deserve a close look. Although no company dominates, a number of companies serve the marketplace well. Several seem to come up in any discussion of the mid-market, and I present those here. Others likely will feel that they are at least as deserving as those I have included.

iVANTAGE

Respected consultant Bob Stambaugh, founder and president of Kapa's Associates in Kekaha, Hawaii, nicely summarizes the standing of SPECTRUM Human Resource Systems Corporation, maker of iVantage, in the mid-market. "The company that is probably the bellwether of where the mid-market is going is SPECTRUM," he says. "It's been around since it provided a system on a standalone microcomputer and has continued to be a mainstay in the marketplace through a LAN version and now an ASP offering that provides hosting for small and really, really big companies. Anybody but Fortune 250, anybody looking for a solution ought to look at that system," Stambaugh says, adding that iVantage has "all the options in a fairly small space."

Advantages

SPECTRUM iVantage boasts enough clear pluses that you surely ought to have it on any list of potential HRIS products for the mid-market. Some of the pluses are discussed below.

It is a Web product—pure Web, not requiring any special code on your computer. You can access it from anywhere, even with a wireless, palm-top device. Figure 16.1 shows the menu for this Web-native product.

It truly knows HR inside and out and is not simply a program developed by those who may suddenly see HR as an area of opportunity. "SPECTRUM has focused on a single area," says Nancy Spoor, SPECTRUM senior vice president. "We do HR software."

If reporting is your specialty, as it may come to be for an HR technology buff, iVantage allows you to approach your reporting from many directions. You can access more than one hundred built-in reports. You can use these report generators:

- Seagate Info,
- Seagate Analysis, and
- Microsoft English Query.

Figure 16.1. iVantage Menu

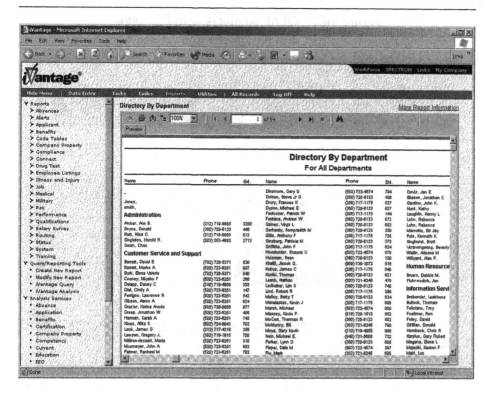

You can even create OLAP cubes, which may not mean much to most folks. If you have worked with Microsoft Excel Pivot Tables, though, you'll appreciate this tool for comparing multiple variables. Figure 16.2 shows a sample OLAP analysis using iVantage.

The product offers about any module you might want, which is particularly valuable in a pure Web format. (Some products using older technologies have been slow in bringing out their capabilities in a pure Web format.) Here are the modules from which you can select:

Absence Tracking   Applicant Tracking
Benefits Administration   Compensation Management
Governmental Compliance   Person Record Finder
Qualification Tracking   Query Tools
Salary Planning   Security Roles
Training History   Unlimited History

Figure 16.2. OLAP Analysis with iVantage

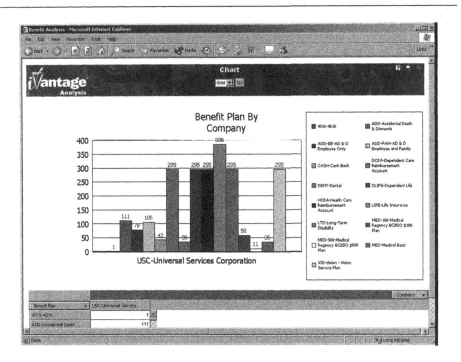

Figure 16.3 shows the salary planning module, which is very attractive to larger companies.

Another advantage is the "rental only" (ASP) option. "What if you don't have the resources to support these technologies?" asks the SPECTRUM website. "SPECTRUM's Remote Hosting Services could be the answer for you."

With a great deal of focus on the client, SPECTRUM has strong training and support. "They have great conferences. You learn tons," attests a user.

iVantage has other strengths as well. The company prides itself on its pure Microsoft basis, including its SQL Server database. Also, the integration allows you to exchange information with widely used products such as Microsoft Word and Microsoft Excel.

Balancing Considerations

What are the cautions when considering such a product? First, although SPECTRUM does scale to suit larger companies, SPECTRUM itself is hardly PeopleSoft or SAP. The small company size may not be an issue for you, but you have to

Figure 16.3. Salary Planning with iVantage

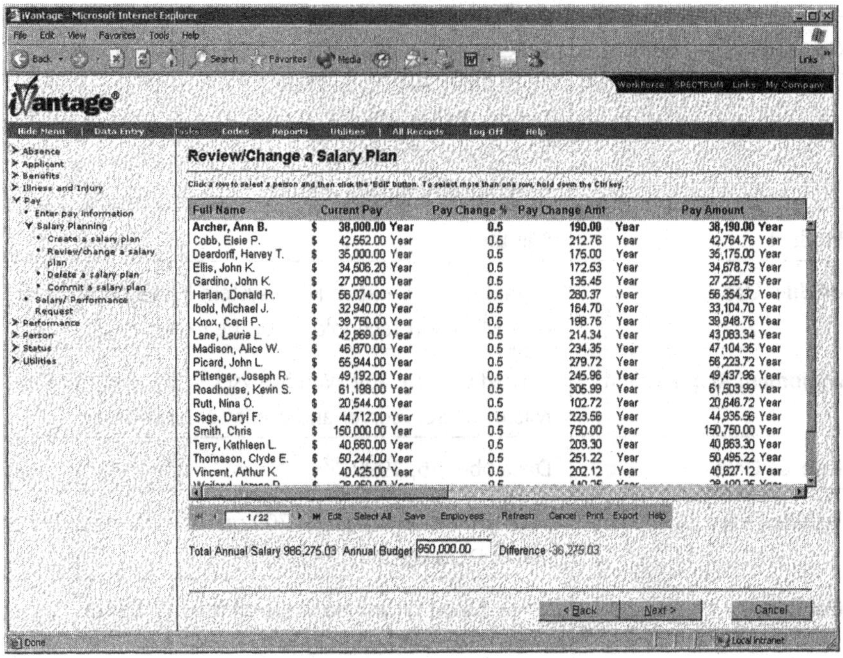

evaluate that if you are a larger company. Can this provider truly respond to the needs of a large company?

Also, the commitment to Microsoft is a strength unless you favor some other infrastructures such as Oracle databases.

Likewise, the commitment to the Internet is not important to everyone, particularly larger companies. (SPECTRUM does have a Microsoft Access product, called HRVantage.)

There is enough to this package that you will almost certainly want training, even though you can start without it. Warns company president Jim Spoor, "If you buy a software package and you don't know how to use it, the package doesn't do you any good. The more training you have, the more value you get out of it."

Finally, a question that sometimes comes up is simply this: SPECTRUM is big, but why isn't it bigger? It has been in this wide-open mid-market as long as anyone. Why has it not become truly dominant? You may not find any good reason for such a lack, and perhaps no such reason exists. But you should ask the question even when contemplating the strengths in this product. Table 16.1 summarizes iVantage.

Table 16.1. iVantage Summary	
Company	SPECTRUM Human Resource Systems Corporation 1525 Broadway, Suite 2600 Denver, CO 80202 303-592-3200 www.spectrumhr.com
Product	iVantage
Product Use	Complete Web-native HRIS system based on 100 percent Microsoft technology for the mid-market
Equipment Requirements	Hosted version: any Web browser; purchased version: Microsoft SQL server and client/server software
Release Date	December 15, 1999
Installed Base	150+ clients on iVantage, 700 on HRVantage, 2,500 on earlier DOS version
List Price	Value-based pricing depends on the number of employees and optional features selected

GENESYS ENTERPRISE SERIES

Looking for outsourcing? Genesys Software Systems, Inc., would love to handle your HR needs using its Genesys Enterprise Series. "We will become their HR and payroll department," explains Larry Munini, Genesis CEO.

Advantages

Looking for a pure Web implementation? If you decide to use Genesys yourself, you enjoy the benefits of pure Web design. Figure 16.4 shows the opening screen of this Web-based product.

Genesys has another gigantic plus not offered by most other HRIS products for the mid-market. It offers its own payroll as well as HRIS. Some may view payroll as simply a secondary matter. Others may see it as too sticky and too purely technical for HR to take on. Genesys does not see payroll that way, but rather takes great pleasure in tackling that and other tough problems. It will work with your mainframe if you wish.

Genesys prides itself on its architecture, which allows it to move in so many different directions—outsourcing, in-house (purchased) version, ASP version,

Figure 16.4. Genesys Main Screen

mainframe compliant. It offers its own database, or it supports Microsoft SQL-server databases and others. "The differentiation point is our primary architecture," explains Mike Hanninen, Genesys' director of strategic systems.

Genesys likes to move ahead of the curve technically, and currently prides itself on its e-learning modules. Maintains Lisa Rowen, Genesys director of marketing, "We offer not only HR and payroll but also benefits, e-learning—everything in employee relations management."

Balancing Considerations

What's to be careful about with this product? It is easy to use, but, because of its abundant tools and rich options, it is particularly attractive to the technically oriented. Urging people to take advantage of the possibilities, "managers should be getting in and working with their people to provide better tools to do their jobs. In doing so, everybody wins," one user says.

To put it another way, Genesys particularly delights the technical user, and its user base tends to be more technical than most, even in the sophisticated midmarket. If you're looking for a powerful, adaptable engine that will do both your payroll and your HRIS process, take a good look at Genesys, a summary of which is provided in Table 16.2.

ULTIPRO

UltiPro from Ultimate Software, a Web-enabled product, also combines both payroll and HRIS. UltiPro takes on the tough problems that some might prefer to ignore. For instance, the Phoenix Suns and Arizona Diamondbacks use the combined HRMS/payroll solution. Deductions can be complicated for highly paid athletes who travel among multiple states and take deductions from multiple states. UltiPro takes on the challenge.

Figure 16.5 shows the opening screen of this point-and-click, browser-based software.

Advantages

Ultimate Software prides itself on its dedication to people—both its own employees and its customers. "We selected [UltiPro] after an extensive process because of what we felt was a corporate philosophy of taking care of people," says Barry Shorten,

Table 16.2. Genesys Summary

Company	Genesys Software Systems, Inc. 5 Branch Street Methuen, MA 01844 800 540-5470 www.genesys-soft.com
Product	Genesys Enterprise Series, v. 5.5
Product Use	Technologically advanced solutions for administering human resources, payroll, and benefits
Equipment Requirements	For client/server—any machine running Windows NT or Windows 2000, works with Win 95, 98, ME; for mainframe, any IBM mainframe running MVS operating system; for the ASP option, IE 5.0 or higher
Release Date	October 1999
Installed Base	Six hundred
List Price	Based on number of employees supported in the master file (target of one thousand employees or more) and whether software is licensed or hosted; licensed (purchase) for 1,000-person company: $100,000 to start; for hosted version: $6.99 per employee including payroll, HR, and ESS

CEO of Alcott Staff Leasing of Farmingdale, New York. "They've been very responsive to our needs."

UltiPro combines many "best of breed" applications within its own offering. If something has become widespread in the marketplace, you are likely to find it available in this offering.

Balancing Considerations

What's to be careful about? As for other sophisticated products, you serve yourself well to have someone technical involved in the implementation. And the implementation is an ambitious undertaking. Advises Shorten, "Don't have any unreal expectations that implementation will be easy. You've got to plan thoroughly and

Figure 16.5. UltiPro Main Screen

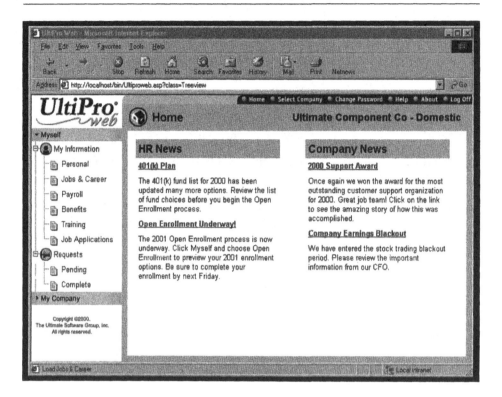

have a realistic end date. If you have a tough date to meet, you can almost guarantee that some problem will come up."

As with almost any mid-market supplier, Ultimate is not large enough to inspire complete confidence. It is a big, serious player, but it is hardly a household name. You can check out its stock price to get a feeling for how the company is doing at any given time. Table 16.3 provides summary information for UltiPro.

ABRA ENTERPRISE

Another mid-market player is Abra Enterprise from Best Software. Where Abra Suite addresses the low-end market, Abra Enterprise addresses the mid-market and up. "It doesn't replicate everything PeopleSoft and SAP systems do," says one user at a large company. "For us it replicates enough of them, though. For the price, they've got a great product."

Table 16.3. UltiPro Summary

Company	Ultimate Software 200 Ultimate Way Weston, FL 33326 954-331-7000 or 800-432-1729 www.ultimatesoftware.com
Product	UltiPro v. 4.4
Product Use	Web-based employee management and payroll with strategic tools for reporting and analysis
Equipment Requirements	For installation in-house in PC environment, Microsoft Windows NT, Microsoft SQL server, MS BackOffice, Microsoft IIS (for ASP option, only a browser required)
Release Date	August 2000
Installed Base	More than one thousand customers
List Price	If purchase, pricing begins at $50,000; ASP based on price per employee per month

Advantages

This is another mid-market player worthy of your attention if you are working up a selection matrix. Here are some strengths:

- One of the earliest to develop a pure Web interface, Abra Enterprise has an attractive interface. Figure 16.6 shows a sample screen.
- Abra Enterprise has its own payroll offering, saving you from compatibility concerns if you are implementing a payroll/HRIS solution;
- Abra Enterprise comes in a hosted version as well, Abra Online; and
- Both versions offer employee self-service and manager self-service.

Balancing Considerations

What's to worry about with this offering? Although Abra spokesmen insist that the product is aggressively holding its own, competitors maintain that they are not so sure about that. Competitors do say such things, so you cannot take that at face

Figure 16.6. Sample Abra Enterprise Screen

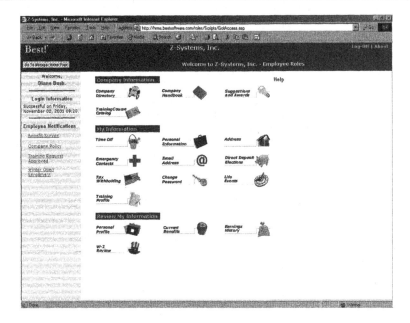

value. Do some checking around the marketplace. Abra Enterprise was an early leader. Only reliable, current sources can tell you if it has maintained that position. Table 16.4 provides a summary of Abra Enterprise.

HRWINDOWS

A strong mid-market player for many years, hrWindows from PerfectSoftware certainly deserves a look. Some of the strengths of this product, shown in Figure 16.7, are described below.

Advantages

First of all, hrWindows is building its strategy around a strong distribution system. If you are looking for a mid-market offering with support in your region, PerfectSoftware may be the provider for you.

Reporting should be all your could ask for, with over 175 standard reports. If applicant tracking is your aim, you can include PerfectSoftware's hrApplicant version. If you are looking for a SQL server version to run in a client/server environment, PerfectSoftware offers that with its hrSQL version.

Table 16.4. Abra Enterprise Summary

Company	Best Software, Inc. 11413 Isaac Newton Square Reston, VA 20190 703-701-5200 www.bestsoftware.com
Product	Abra Enterprise
Product Use	Enterprise-wide HR and payroll solution, browser-based, using advanced Microsoft technology in a client/server environment
Equipment Requirements	Workstation: Pentium processor, running Win 95 or Win NT and Internet Explorer; servers: client/server environment with at least two servers; Microsoft BackOffice; SQL
Release Date	May 15, 1998
Installed Base	Two
List Price	Starts at $20,000; support: 25 percent of total per year; premium support: 35 percent of total per year

Figure 16.7. hrWindows Employee Information Screen Attendance Tab

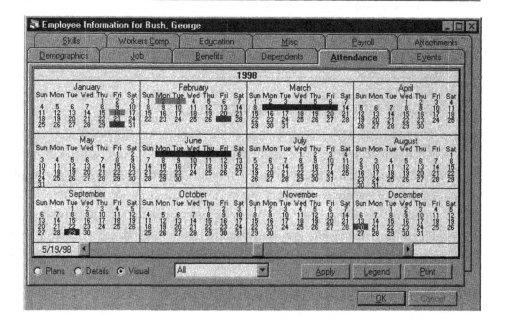

Balancing Considerations

I do not know of extraordinary strengths to distinguish PerfectSoftware from the pack, a problem that most vendors in this space face. But the product has a proven track record of solving mid-market HR needs. Table 16.5 provides a summary of hrWindows.

Table 16.5. hrWindows Summary	
Company	PerfectSoftware, a division of Aspectuck Systems, Inc. 200 Connecticut Avenue Norwalk, CT 06854 203-852-9100 www.perfectsoftware.com
Product	hrWindows 6.0
Product Use	hrWindows automates all the major activities of an HR management function, allowing accurate records and tracking of employee data at every stage. hrWindows is for companies with between two hundred and five thousand employees
Equipment Requirements	IBM Pentium or compatible, any Windows operating system, including 2000, XP, or higher. 64 MB system memory (minimum), 50MB available disk storage. Networks: Novell, Windows, Banyan, and others
Release Date	1990
Installed Base	1,000+
List Price	Call for information

OTHER MID-MARKET PROVIDERS

The five products presented so far in this chapter are not necessarily the first five you will meet when exploring the mid-market. In fact, ADP, which I discuss in just a moment, is likely the provider you will run into the most. A number of other mid-market software vendors might catch your attention, and there are enough vendors that one might easily overlook one or several (and possibly the one that is best for you). If you are motivated to do a thorough search and analysis, the mid-market is for you. If you are trying to make a choice along the lines of

"Nobody ever got fired for choosing IBM," you may be out of luck in this market-place. If you can stretch your budget to fit PeopleSoft, you might be able to consider that a safe choice. If not, you had best just go through the selection process, set up a relationship with a good vendor, and take charge of your installation so that you can make sure that it does meet your needs. Following are a number of other mid-market HRIS vendors, each with notable strengths, each with its cautions (which you cannot always uncover at first blush).

ADP Enterprise HRMS

The prominent payroll provider has a solid foothold in the mid-market. Its mid-market offering is ADP Enterprise HRMS. Contends SPECTRUM president Jim Spoor, who ought to have a good perspective on the question, "Within the mid-market as SPECTRUM defines it, I think it is safe to say that ADP has delivered the most systems. With well over 200,000 mid-size organizations as payroll clients using their services, the enormous ADP salesforce has been very effective in convincing those clients that they also need one of ADP's several HR offerings."

If you think you detect an edge to his words, you are probably right, but the perception is a common one. ADP is not so much selected by end users as it is sold by salespeople and accepted by users. I have found in my own informal surveys the same sentiment that Spoor diplomatically expresses here: "While those [ADP HR] offerings provide a wide range of differing capabilities depending on the product, it is rare to hear users with high expectations really rave about an ADP solution—satisfaction yes—real enthusiasm not that often."

You may often think that company size begets product strength. That often may be the case, but it has not yet proven to be so for ADP. You will encounter it. You may adopt it. You are not likely ever to love it. Table 16.6 provides a summary of ADP Enterprise.

Cyborg's Solution Series/ST

Founded in 1974 and headquartered in Chicago, Cyborg offers many of the features you will be likely to find on your own checklist, such as:

- Career and succession planning;
- Position management;
- Training administration;
- Configurable GUIs (which may sound a bit out-of-date, actually); and
- Online help wizards.

Table 16.6. ADP Enterprise HRMS Summary	
Company	ADP 1 ADP Boulevard Roseland, NJ 07068 973-974-5000 www.adp.com
Product	ADP Enterprise HRMS
Product Use	Best-practice human resources management, benefits administration, and payroll
Equipment Requirements	32-bit Internet technology, offered on an outsourcing model
Release Date	Not available
Installed Base	Not available, but market share is probably the largest of any vendor in the low- and mid-market.
List Price	Information not available because product offered on outsourced basis rather than as direct sale.

Cyborg is well-known in the HRIS space. It has longevity. It has a user base. And it has a reputation for providing the basic capabilities that people need. Does it have a reputation for being exciting, though? You may want to look into that question. Table 16.7 provides a summary of the product.

DynaSuite

Here is a product, not necessarily well-known, that does generate excitement in those who manage to find it. If you are looking for a Web-based HR and payroll solution for the mid-market, you will find something special in DynaSuite on the Web from Performance Software, Inc., of East Hanover, New Jersey.

"We're one of the first transaction processing systems to run on the Internet," proclaims Karen Rusinak, vice president of product marketing at Performance. This product does not just display information using the Web, which is what any program will do. It does not just do simple database searches and then display information. It does complex analysis on the Web. "Most people don't seem to

Table 16.7. Cyborg Solution Series/ST Summary

Company	Cyborg Systems, Inc. 120 South Riverside Plaza, 17th Floor Chicago, IL 60606 312-279-7000 www.cyborg.com
Product	Cyborg Solution Series/ST
Product Use	Comprehensive HRMS
Equipment Requirements	Windows NT® with Microsoft® SQL Server™ or Oracle® database UNIX (AIX®, HP UX, or Solaris ™) with Oracle database OS/400 (AS/400) with DB2® OS/390 (S/390) with DB2®
Release Date	NA
Installed Base	NA
List Price	NA

get it," explains one DynaSuite user. "DynaSuite is built from the ground up to be Web-based. It's built to do what it does."

You may find the product easy enough to use as an end user. Figure 16.8 shows a sample screen. Those who most appreciate the program, though, are techies. Service bureaus sometimes select it for their third-party HR and payroll offerings. Most of us most of the time have no appreciation of what it means to do transaction processing on the Web. If you know someone who does, ask her about the advantages of this system, DynaSuite on the Web. Table 16.8 provides a quick summary.

HR Microsystems' HR Entré

Perhaps it says something about the overall marketplace that HR Microsystems, previously mentioned as a player in the low-end market, has turned its attention to the mid-market. "We are primarily selling our new product, HR Entré, these days," says Len Mayo, vice president of sales and marketing with the company.

Figure 16.8. DynaSuite Screen

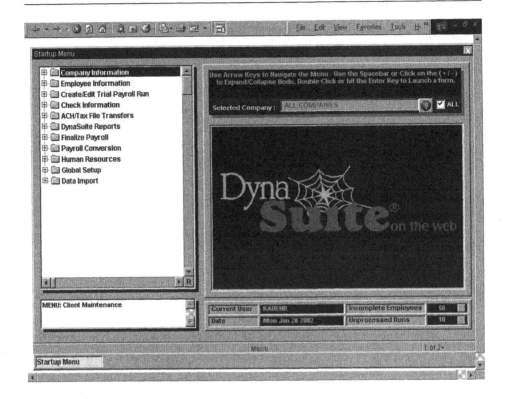

Figure 16.9 shows the main screen for the product.

HR Microsystems, in my experience, is not the first vendor people mention when discussing the mid-market. But the company knows HR, and its users are often satisfied users. Table 16.9 provides a quick summary of what you will find with this product.

NuView's MyHRIS

Looking for the sleeper of the HRIS mid-market? Check out MyHRIS from NuView Systems of Wilmington, Massachusetts. One of the first HRIS programs to go Web-native, if not the very first, MyHRIS has developed rich functionality on the Web.

First, I would say that the product has an intimate understanding of HR. Its makers, if anything, err in the direction of a commitment to HR and to HR technology over a commitment to publicity and sales. (Such an approach is the ideal way to create a sleeper product, just lying there waiting for you to discover it.)

Table 16.8. DynaSuite Summary

Company	Performance Software, Inc. 383 Ridgedale Avenue East Hanover, NJ 07936 800-560-1930 973–739-1780 www.dynasuite.com
Product	DynaSuite on the Web
Product Use	Java/HTML Internet integrated HR, self-service, payroll, and billing
Equipment Requirements	For the end user: only a browser required; for those running the complete system: NT or UNIX, Oracle, Informix, SQL Server, Sybase, DB2
Release Date	September 1, 2000
Installed Base	Clients are service bureaus, which then have their own clients; five service bureaus, each bureau with at least six clients; many thousands of end users
List Price	To purchase: $50,000 to $350,000, depending on the size of the company

Figure 16.10 shows the main information screen for an employee, with the personnel menu on the left.

Here are some of the strengths of MyHRIS:

- All the modules you might want, in Web-native format, including an applicant module and a training module;

- Skills-based analysis of employees for planning training and for succession planning (Figure 16.11 shows a gap analysis of employee skills);

- A robust succession planning module, offering capabilities for filling management positions that you usually find only with higher-priced, specialty programs;

- A nice, click-and-drag org charting capability (shown in Figure 16.12);

Figure 16.9. HR Entré Main Screen

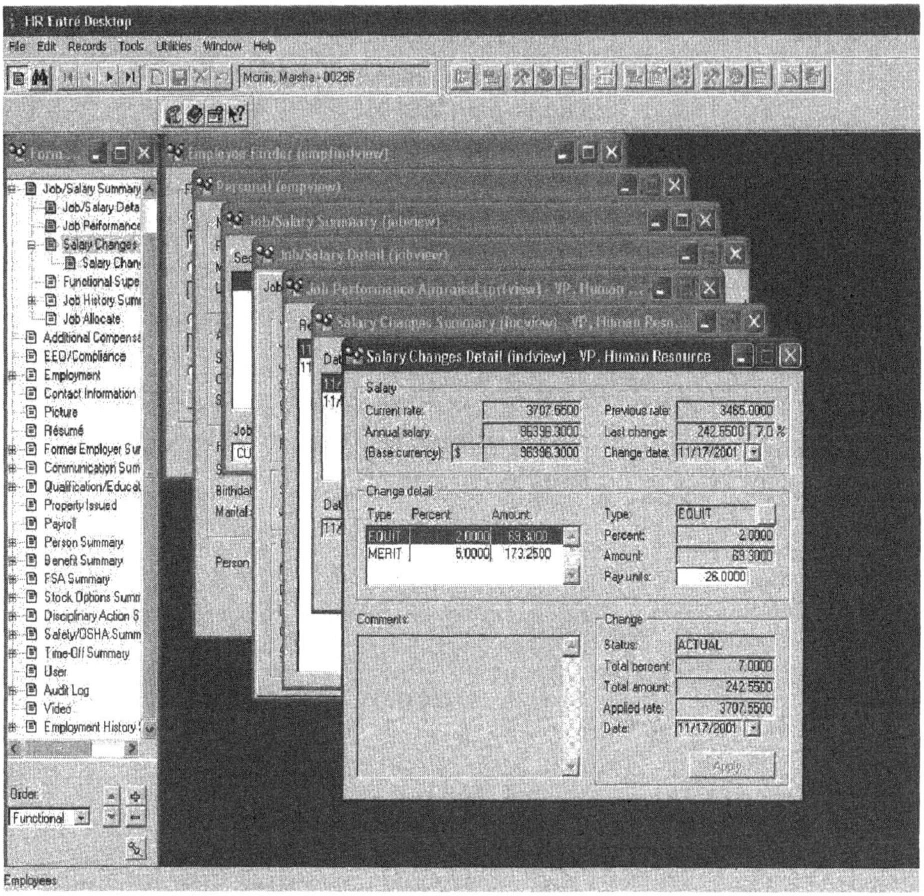

- Strong use of metrics for analytical reports and for human capital management (HCM); and
- Strong reference accounts spanning the whole range of company size and including some high-end companies.

President Shafiq Lokhandwala, with an HR background himself, enjoys using technology to lead HR into the future. Here is his analysis of HR analytics and the role of HR technology in fulfilling the need for analytics, from a company white paper titled, *MyHRIS: The HCM Implementation Tool for the Corporation*:

"Company metrics are made available to line managers, so that they can compare their performance with respect to their peers. Even before

Table 16.9. HR Entré Summary

Company	Human Resource MicroSystems 160 Sansome Street, Suite 1050 San Francisco, CA 94104 415-362-8400 www.hrms.com
Product	HR Entré
Product Use	Comprehensive n-tier HRMS bringing organization and effectiveness to the full range of HR functions and responsibilities, based on .NET framework Web services
Equipment Requirements	Client Workstation: Pentium processor 400+; 50MB hard drive: 128MB memory; MS Windows 98/NT/2000/XP Network Server: Pentium processor 500+; 100MB+5MB/100 employee records hard drive; 256MB memory; NetBIOS compliant (Windows NT Server or Novell) or TCP/IP compliant Web Server: Pentium processor 500+; 100MB hard drive; 256MB memory; Microsoft Internet information server (IIS) and ASP.NET Browser: Microsoft Internet Explorer 4.0+ or Netscape Navigator 4.0+ Databases Supported: Microsoft SQL server, Visual Foxpro, Oracle, or other ODBC-compliant databases
Release Date	October 2000
Installed Base	Over seven hundred installations in United States and around the world; companies range in size from seventy to six thousand
List Price	License pricing based on a matrix of number of employees, number of users, and number of modules. Standalone base system with a 150-employee record limit sells for $5,000; typical sales (including maintenance, implementation, and software) range from $25,000 to $85,000

Figure 16.10. MyHRIS Main Screen

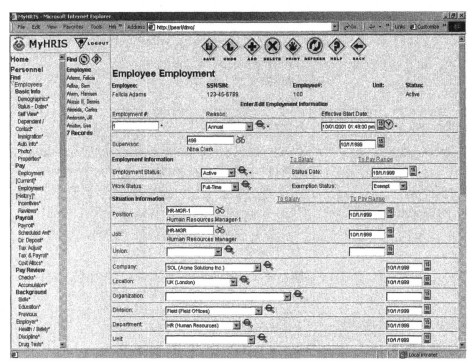

management comes knocking at their door wondering what is wrong, managers have an opportunity to see how they are doing. HR, the strategic business partner, can provide a helping hand in suggesting methods that have succeeded and ways to turn around the trends reported in the metrics. Since everyone is looking at the same metrics, the entire organization can rally around a central set of operating guidelines. This unity of objectives, and a simple yet effective mechanism to communicate them, help the corporation align itself behind the central vision, improving the chances of success dramatically. If compensation plans are devised around goals achieved, every line manager is going to be energized and motivated to succeed."

What's to wonder about, then, with this product? One competitor says this of the product: "NuView remains the most highly regarded and least sold product around." A consultant remarks, similarly, "It's quite a clever product, but it's getting nowhere."

Figure 16.11. Gap Analysis in MyHRIS

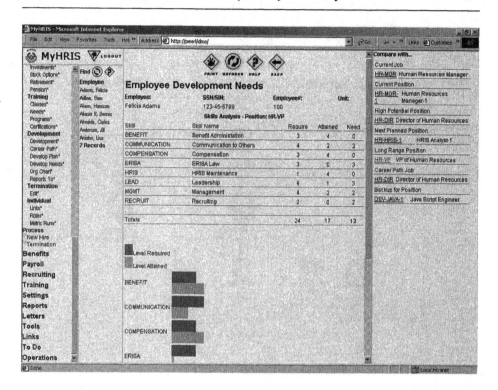

The privately held company has thirty-five employees and an installed base of perhaps one hundred client companies. It has been around long enough to have earned its wings (more than five or six years). Even though it won a Top 10 New Product of the Year award from *Human Resource Executive Magazine* in 2000, it has remained a relatively unknown player in the mid-market.

If Web-native functionality is your priority, you simply cannot overlook this product. It is caught in a kind of Catch-22 trap, though. People want to install a product well-known in the marketplace. But to become well-known in the marketplace, a product has to be installed. Table 16.10 provides a quick summary of MyHRIS.

OPEN4

If you are in the mood for sleepers, here is another. OPEN4 Human Resource Information System from BMH, Inc., in Addison, Texas, is potent stuff. It is not an Internet application. On the other hand, it has integrated payroll of its own right,

Figure 16.12. Organization Charting in MyHRIS

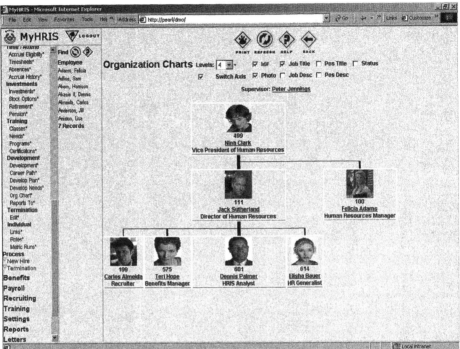

along with the HRIS application. If you decide to mix this one into your selection matrix, you may end up surprising yourself. You just might end up selecting it.

It has an advanced query function. "I use the query function [more than the report writer]," says a user. "I'm too lazy to set up the reports." It's also flexible. Says the user, "[OPEN4] has so much more flexibility than what we were using. Before, we could not run queries easily, and we could not get the reports we wanted without going through a programming process." Figure 16.13 shows the query function for the product.

What's to worry about with this selection? Well, techies developed this product (which is, nevertheless, easy to use). Some people find that the creators got a little carried away. Says the user, "Their systems are almost too flexible. . . . down to the field level. We chose not to implement all the security features that we should." Such a problem—an overabundance of technical riches—is not much of a problem to have. The other problem is the same Catch-22 we noted about NuView. People

Table 16.10. MyHRIS Summary

Company	NuView Systems, Inc. 155 West Street, Suite 7 Wilmington, MA 01887 978-988-7884 www.nuviewinc.com
Product	MyHRIS, both ASP (rental) and purchase versions
Product Use	Web-based comprehensive HRIS—HR, recruiting, succession planning, training administration, employee self-service
Equipment Requirements	Browser v. 4+; any machine, including UNIX, WebTV; Windows NT server
Release Date	2.3 released May 2000; 3.0 October 2000
Installed Base	1,275 users, eighty-five customers
List Price	Rental from as little as $3 per employee per month to $10 per employee per month; purchase from as little as $30,000 to $150,000.

want a product with market presence. To get market presence, people have to be using your product. If you are daring and check this one out, you may find yourself with a winner. Table 16.11 provides a summary for OPEN4 HRIS.

People-Trak

Long a giant of the low-end, People-Trak has tossed its hat into the ring in the mid-market as well by coming out with a client/server version in 2002. It does not have a national distribution or support network. It does have intimate understanding of the HR marketplace and sweet technology. And it has proven staying power in the HR marketplace. For a more detailed discussion of People-Trak, see Chapter 14.

Microsoft Great Plains Business Solutions

Long a sleeper in the mid-market arena, Great Plains Software of Fargo, North Dakota, now has a new name that speaks volumes about its possibilities in the

Figure 16.13. OPEN4 HRIS Query Function

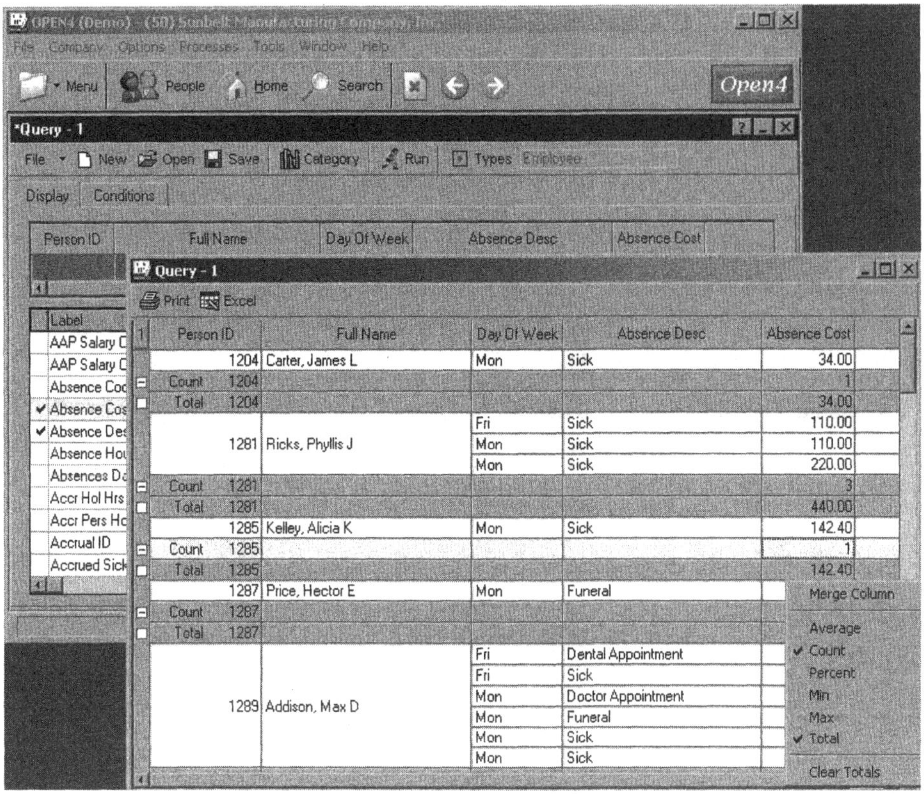

mid-market. Acquired by Microsoft Corporation, Great Plains has now become "Microsoft Great Plains Business Solutions." In the name "Microsoft" resides the magic. According to one scenario, advocated by consultant Naomi Bloom along with others, Great Plains may have the right technology base and the right market clout to become the long-missing force in the HR mid-market. "Many in the mid-market use Microsoft platforms to give a lower-cost IT experience," explains Bloom. "The big news is . . . Microsoft Great Plains Business Solutions."

Using the technology base already in place in mid-market companies, Great Plains is coming to market with an HR solution that, says Bloom, is well-positioned to compete head-to-head with mid-market solutions from the Big Three (PeopleSoft, Oracle, and SAP.) "These guys [Microsoft Great Plains]—it's theirs to lose," says Bloom.

Table 16.11. OPEN4 HRIS Summary

Company	Bonnecaze, McLeroy & Harrison, Inc. 4004 Beltline Road, Suite 125 Addison, TX 75001 972-702-0892 www.open4.com
Product	OPEN4 Human Resources Information System, v. 5.19
Product Use	Integrated HRIS and payroll, full-featured, readily customizable; HRIS includes benefits, compensation, applicant tracking, training, report writer, query
Equipment Requirements	Win 95/98/2000/NT; client/server; can also be UNIX server or ASP option
Release Date	1994
Installed Base	150 licenses
List Price	Price by number of w-2s (employees); low-end pricing per module is $8,450, up to $50,000 per module (modules are HR and payroll, with employee self-service and manager self-service modules priced at about 50 percent of the others)

PerfectSoftware, a competitor to Great Plains, likewise sees the possibility that Microsoft might one day sit atop the mid-market space. Says PerfectSoftware President Mike Gabriele, "Of course, any of the big players can possibly make a strategic acquisition and move into this market. We believe the company with the largest distribution network will have the best chance. While this may sound far-fetched, one of the companies that has the best chance at pulling this off is Microsoft. They have made good acquisitions, such as with Great Plains. They are moving that acquisition to the lower market through their bCentral services. This approach could be very effective in the middle market." A summary of their eEnterprise Human Resources offering is provided in Table 16.12.

PeopleSoft

PeopleSoft is a serious mid-market player with a chance to dominate the marketplace. From the perspective of a competitor, SPECTRUM Human Resource

Table 16.12. eEnterprise Human Resources Summary

Company	Microsoft Great Plains One Lone Tree Road Fargo, ND 58104 701-281-6500 www.greatplains.com
Product	eEnterprise Human Resources and Payroll
Product Use	A comprehensive solution for managing applicant and employee information, paying employees, and tracking payroll information
Equipment Requirements	Operating System: Windows 95, 98, Millennium Edition (Me), NT 4.0 Workstation Sp 6a, Windows 2000 Professional Sp 1 or 2 Processor: Pentium 166 (intel) Hard Disk Space: 175 MB Ram: 64 MB CD-Rom: Optional Network Card: 100 base T
Release Date	May 31, 1994
Installed Base	850 Customers
List Price	$25,000–$28,000, depending on the number of applications selected and number of concurrent users

Systems Corporation, here's a summary that you might hear from any number of other players in the mid-market: "PeopleSoft is expensive. If it ever does solve the mid-market, stand back."

PeopleSoft is not shy about proclaiming its own viability in the mid-market. "We have gone from five hundred mid-market customers a year and a half ago to eleven hundred by early 2002," proclaims Jeff Read, vice president and general manager of PeopleSoft Mid-Market Solutions. "About a quarter of the total PeopleSoft customers are mid-market," he adds, expressing some question from his point of view that no company has established dominance in the mid-market. PeopleSoft, he implies, may either have done so or be well on the way to doing so.

PeopleSoft's approach is to adapt its successful high-end product to the mid-market. Among the features PeopleSoft is bringing to the mid-market are these, according to Read:

- An unlimited user license (allowing companies to place unlimited users on the system for a single fee);

- Fixed price with no hidden fees (which counteracts the longtime objection to high-end products that the list price does not match the ultimate real price);

- Accelerated solutions (in the past, companies have been concerned about the long time required to implement the high-end products); and

- Modular design (companies can select just the modules they need).

With modular design combined with accelerated installation, companies can implement solutions quickly, says Read. For instance, he says, a company could, in three and a half months, go from purchasing a PeopleSoft system for open benefits enrollment to having completed the first such open enrollment.

For more information on PeopleSoft, see Chapter 19.

CONCLUSION

The mid-market in HRIS software has a multitude of players, and they have invested heavily over quite a few years to create their product offerings. The net effect of all the attention is powerful products with a good bit of differentiation. Some are more technically oriented. Some are strong in payroll. Some specialize in understanding the HR business process. Some are proud, above all, of their complete Internet capability. All are looking for an edge. The software evaluator in the mid-market faces a challenge because of the sheer amount of information to evaluate. It can be tempting simply to reach a conclusion early, but a shortcut is probably not the best idea. Sift through these rich products carefully, and you will begin to see the product best suited for your company.

Specialty products in HR are also rich and technically solid. The next chapter introduces some of the more notable specialty products.

Exploring Specialty Software

Throughout this book I have discussed primarily comprehensive HRIS systems, because it seems to me that most of the time people would begin with an across-the-board system. Once you have such a system, you might bring in specialty software to go with your base system. However, you might just as well decide to go directly with specialty software to address a particular need, whether you have a main HRIS or not.

Listings of HRIS products may go to one hundred or one hundred fifty items. Specialty products number from fifteen hundred to two thousand. If you include fringe products that are not exactly HR but not exactly "not HR" (such as room scheduling or psychological profiling), you might well end up with almost the entire software landscape to review and analyze.

In this chapter I look at a few of the software products you are most likely to want to consider as you plan your HR system. Certain problems, such as compensation planning, seem to invite the idea of a specialized solution. The premise would be that a special tool does a better job than an all-around tool. That premise, however, may not be accurate, as comprehensive packages sometimes have capabilities that fully match the specialized packages. Sometimes, in fact, the HRIS packages include capabilities that literally are the specialized packages. Following a "best of breed" approach, they simply subsume market-leading capabilities like org charting within their own packages.

Specialized packages, then, can truly be a maze for you to wander through. Here are some of the areas where you may particularly want to consider specialty packages and some of the packages you may want to examine.

TIME AND ATTENDANCE

Some products are raising time tracking to new levels, making it a tool for measuring the effectiveness of human capital. Companies including Synygy, Incentive Systems, Workbrain, Replicon, and Performaworks are making a science of understanding employee time and which employees are using time best and accomplishing most while they are doing it.

Most HRIS packages include some kind of tracking for time and attendance. The packages track accrued vacation and sick leave and allow you to report on it in a number of ways. Some specialize in it more than others. Ascentis, for instance, is particularly proud of its attendance tracking in HR Office.

Some kinds of industries place more emphasis on time and attendance than others. Manufacturing environments where workers check in and out with time clocks place particular emphasis on it. Others such as legal firms and consultancies track their billed time. The entire undertaking can be quite challenging.

Workforce Central

One product above all has established a leading name in time and attendance tracking, and that is Web-based Workforce Central 4.0 from Kronos Incorporated. Workforce Central, shown in Figure 17.1, helps you manage your labor. You use the product to check vacation balances, leave information, and any other time-related items you may track.

According to the company, Kronos is the market leader, with about 60 percent market share. A specialty tool, Workforce Central can handle about any kind of time tracking you can think of—days, hours, evening, night, overtime, vacation, sick time, and whatever variations on it you may happen to have at your company. Attests a user, "We haven't found any pay rule the thing can't handle . . . overtime, shift differentials, anything."

Figure 17.1. Workforce Central Main Screen

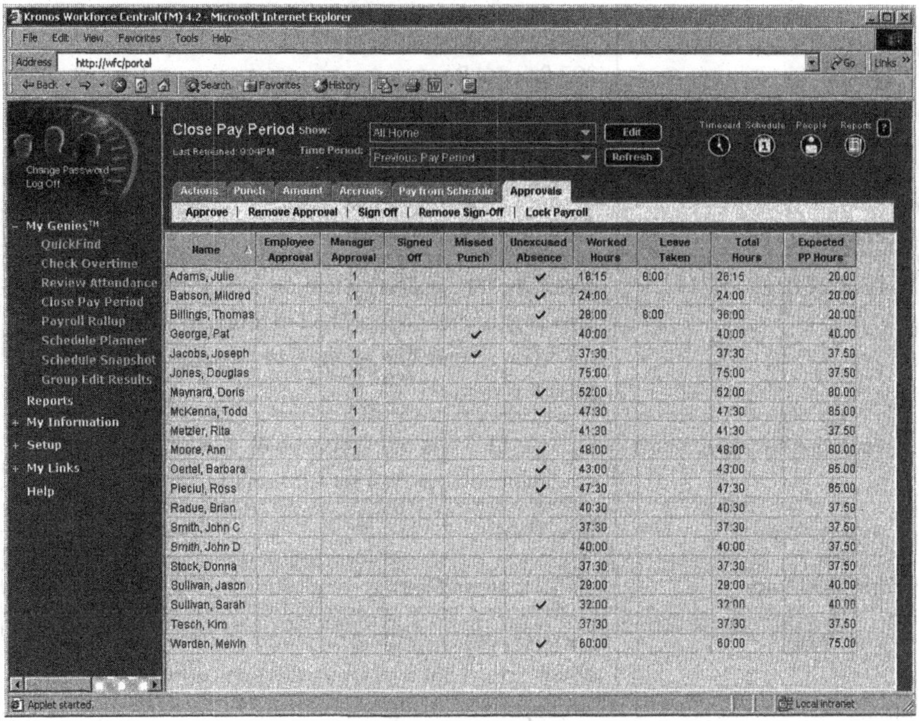

Certain federal laws require you to track time properly, including FMLA (Family and Medical Leave Act) and FLSA (Fair Labor Standards Act). This specialty product is equal to the task.

Considerations

First of all, you may not need this much power for the time and attendance tracking you do at your company. Second, keep in mind that, while the program implements the complex rules you have in effect at your company, you have to take the time and trouble to implement those rules accurately in the system. Table 17.1 shows a quick summary of the product.

COMPENSATION PLANNING

Salary planning really ought to be consistent and scientific. After all, when push comes to shove, what matters more than salary to the average employee? What creates greater dissatisfaction than unfair compensation? The matter is critical

Table 17.1. Workforce Central Summary	
Company	Kronos Incorporated 297 Billerica Road Chelmsford, MA 01824 978-250-9800 www.kronos.com
Product	Workforce Central Suite, v. 4
Product Use	Automates the collecting and processing of labor data. One very popular use of the product is to automate the collection of time and attendance information to feed a payroll system
Equipment Requirements	Browser (IE 5 and 5.5; Netscape 6); a database (Oracle or comparable); a Web server; Kronos provides all else
Release Date	June 2001
Installed Base	Thirty thousand customers worldwide
List Price	Pricing varies depending on number of employees and other factors, but average cost is approximately $85 per employee

enough that the automation in a simple HRIS may not be enough (if your HRIS even has the capability).

Kadiri TotalComp

One nice compensation packages is Web-based Kadiri TotalComp from Kadiri Inc. It allows you to work on a single screen, shown in Figure 17.2, where you can look at performance review information, salary recommendations, guidelines from a compensation manager, and a running total of how your salary recommendations are affecting the budget.

Twenty built-in reports show you such information as salary plan by employee or how much projected compensation varies from a budget.

Figure 17.2. Kadiri TotalComp Screen

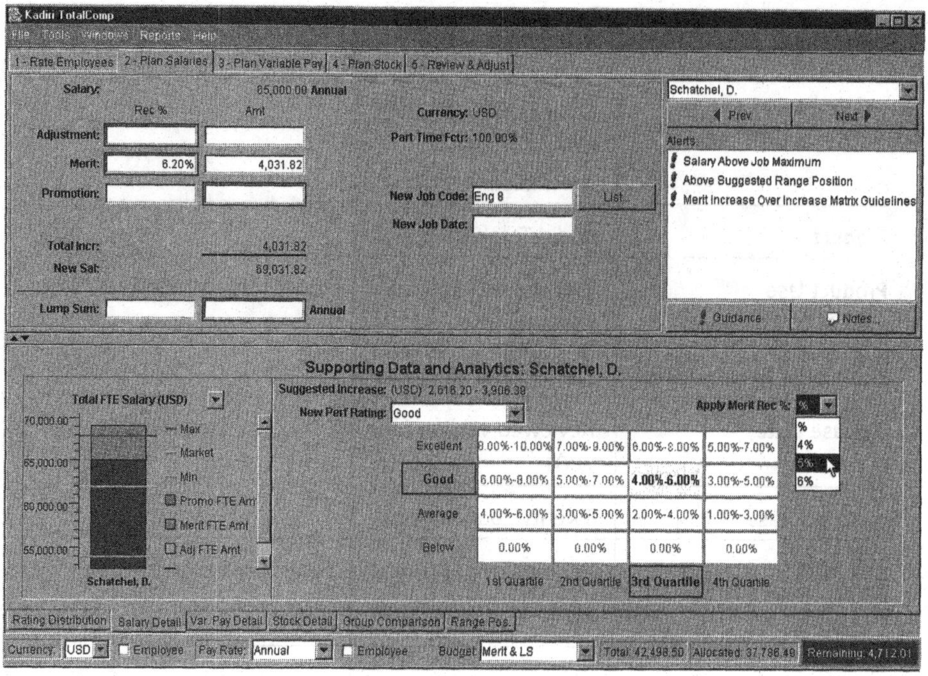

Considerations

As was true with time and attendance software, the biggest caution here is probably that you have to take the time to set up the program properly if you truly want it to be useful. "Make sure you know what your business rules are going into this," remarks one compensation manager who uses the TotalComp program. "If you're not set as to how you're going to go forward, that's really going to slow you down." Table 17. 2 shows a quick summary of Kadiri TotalComp.

SUCCESSION PLANNING

Choosing successors often seems to be more an art than a science. Those in power make their selections, often mystifying others, who wonder, "Why on earth did they choose that person?" In smaller companies, or within a single division,

Table 17.2. Kadiri Summary

Company	Kadiri, Inc. 1350 Old Bayshore Highway, Suite 650 Burlingame, CA 94010 877-642-2299 www.kadiri.com
Product	Kadiri TotalComp, v. 3.5
Product Use	Web-based application for total compensation management
Equipment Requirements	ASP (rental): any browser
Release Date	Reviewed version June 2001; new version October 1, 2001
Installed Base	Twenty-four customers
List Price	Per employee planned for; sliding scale: as company grows larger, there are volume discounts

decision makers may know their people well enough to know the logical candidate to succeed someone who is leaving the company. In larger companies, though, managers find it impossible to know all the possible candidates and their qualifications.

ExecuTRACK Enterprise

ExecuTRACK Enterprise from HRSoft allows you to pull together data from multiple databases and plan for succession, manage your talent in other ways such as evaluating your own "bench strength," and in general make decisions in hiring and promotions.

You can readily display the positions in the company to see which have people in line for them and which need further planning. Figure 17.3 shows a sample succession planning report from ExecuTRACK.

With this product, you can take a lot of the guess work out of promotions. Says one director of talent management, "We are rarely surprised. We're able

Figure 17.3. ExecuTRACK Enterprise's Succession Planning Report

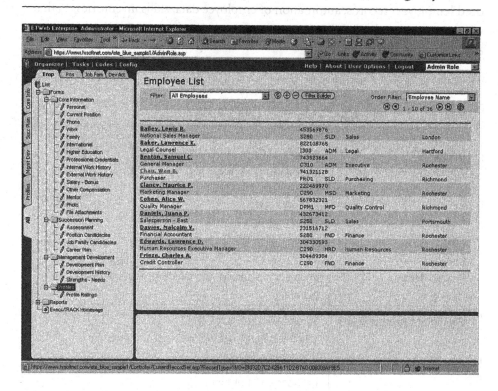

to predict areas where we will have needs, and deal with those changes in the workforce."

Considerations

The biggest caution with this specialty package, as with many others, is that you have to understand it if you are to get the benefit of putting it into place. According to a talent management director, "You have to put the infrastructure in place so that it becomes a systematic organizational process, just a normal part of doing business, not something extra. SPOTS—succession plans on the shelf—don't do anybody any good."

Although anyone might want to automate succession planning, ExecuTRACK is really only for larger companies. Says Chris Mueller, vice president of business development at HRSoft, "As a rule of thumb, you really need to have some sort of measurable volume of data to require software to support the process. If you're a twenty-man company, you don't buy ExecuTRACK. When you have several hundred [employee] records, automation of employee data, skills inventories . . . that's when you start to look for software to support the process." Table 17.3 shows a quick summary of the product.

Table 17.3. ExecuTRACK Summary	
Company	HRSoft, LLC 10 Madison Avenue, Third Floor Morristown, NJ 07962 800-437-6781 www.hrsoft.com
Product	ExecuTRACK Enterprise, v. 9.0
Product Use	Succession planning and talent management, HR planning
Equipment Requirements	Server—Windows NT, IIS Client—Win 95, 98, NT, or 2000 and Internet Information Server Browser—IE 4 or higher HRSoft also offers a hosting service but not a rental (ASP) option
Release Date	July 2001
Installed Base	One hundred+ companies in North America; several hundred worldwide
List Price	For ExecuTRACK Enterprise, license fees are between $30,000 and $125,000, depending on your configuration

Workforce Vision

Another product for managing your workforce is Workforce Vision from Criterion Incorporated, which automates everything in the process of career planning, succession planning, and training. The program implements a set of skills and competencies that you define. Figure 17.4 shows a screen for this Web-based planning product.

In the words of Bruce Kile, Criterion vice president of client services, "You can look at skills and competency assessments on the [Workforce Vision] screen and come up with a plan for your people just as you would do a financial plan for a company." Table 17.4 shows a quick summary of the product.

PERFORMANCE REVIEW

You may turn to performance review information when doing salary planning or succession planning. At times, though, you choose to focus closely on the performance reviews themselves.

Figure 17.4. Workforce Vision Gap Analysis

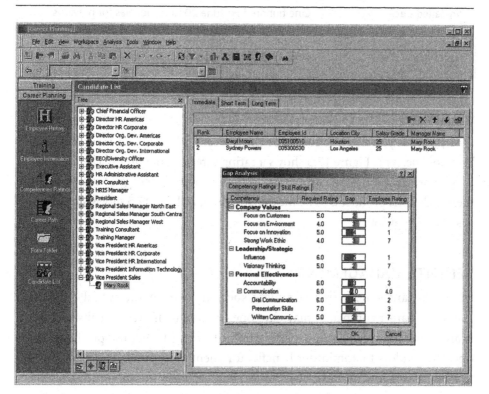

Table 17.4. Workforce Vision Summary

Company	Peopleclick 2 Hannover Square, 7th Floor Raleigh, NC 27612 877-820-4400 www.peopleclick.com
Product	clickEM (formerly Workforce Vision)
Product Use	Enterprise-wide, analytical people-planning tool. Used for succession/career planning, competency management, performance management, development plans, training administration
Equipment Requirements	Any Windows platform (95, 98, 2000, NT); Web browser for Internet version
Release Date	October 1, 2000
Installed Base	One hundred Fortune 2000 companies for previous version, named Blueprint
List Price	Starts at $50,000 for enterprise-wide rollout

Visual 360

One product you might choose for the process is Visual 360 from MindSolve Technologies, Inc. Figure 17.5 shows a rating screen in the product.

The product relies on competencies being entered, and you have to develop them well if the product is to be meaningful for you. Table 17.5 shows a quick summary of Visual 360.

BENEFITS MANAGEMENT

Benefits management is a complete specialty within the world of human resources. Larger companies may have one or more dedicated benefits specialists. Many companies, called third-party administrators (TPAs), use products developed by vendors to administer benefits for client companies. The field of benefits even has its own trade magazines dealing with just the subject of benefits.

Figure 17.5. Visual 360 Rating Screen

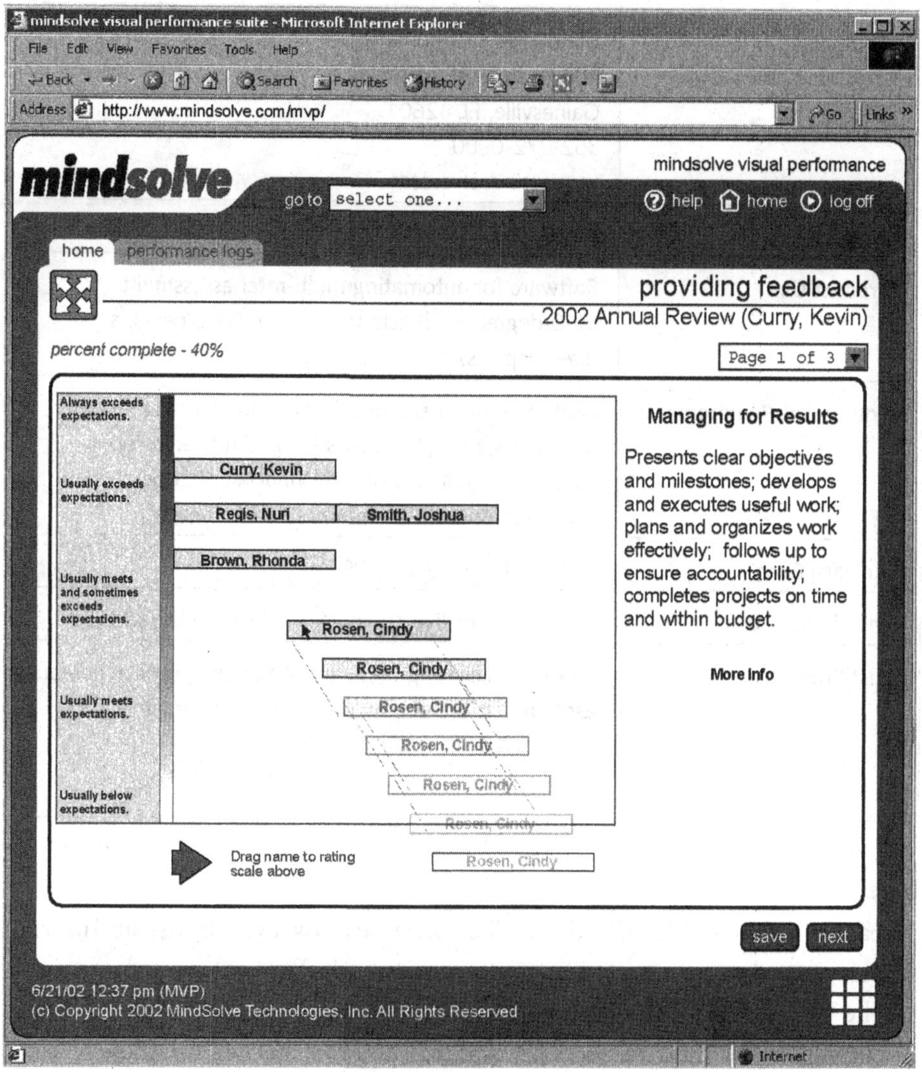

PRE-EMPLOYMENT SCREENING

Social trends can bring products unexpectedly to the fore. Workplace violence and world terrorism have brought fresh attention to pre-employment screening products that validate a job candidate's resume, check for brushes with the law, and otherwise screen potential candidates.

Table 17.5. Visual 360 Summary

Company	MindSolve Technologies, Inc. 203 Southwest 3rd Avenue Gainesville, FL 32601 352-372-0000 www.mindsolve.com
Product	Visual 360
Product Use	Software for automating multi-rater assessment (360-degree feedback, from supervisors, peers, and direct reports)
Equipment Requirements	No special requirements. Runs on Intel 486 and higher processors, using Windows 3.1 and higher versions, including Windows NT and Windows 98; operates on various networks, the Internet, and intranets
Release Date	Version 3.7: May 1, 1999
Installed Base	About twenty-five companies have used the software
List Price	One-time licensing fees start at $25,000; service bureau assessments are also available for approximately $200 per user Fixed price (no extra charge for customization)

HireRight

A leader in the field is HireRight. The software allows you to use an Internet interface to do some pretty nifty detective work. You put in your requests on the Web, and information comes back on the Web after a HireRight employee or contractor has done the necessary research. You can choose from these services:

- Verify employment and education;
- Check criminal records; and
- Check credit, SSN, and motor vehicle records.

Figure 17.6 shows the results of background screening reports in HireRight. Table 17.6 shows a quick summary of the product.

Figure 17.6. HireRight Results Screen

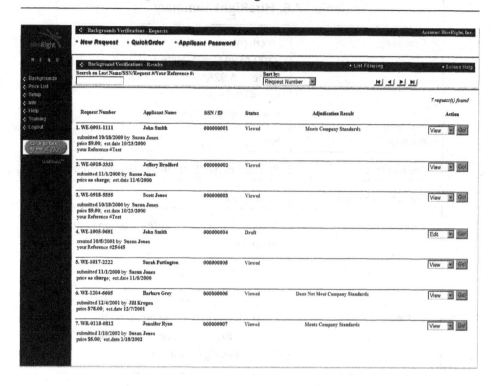

SKILLS MANAGEMENT

Human resources is supposed to do so much more than track how many employees are at the company and who is due for a performance review (not that companies find it so easy to stay on top of even such limited information). Human resources would love to be able to understand employees well, train them for what they need, guide them nicely on a career path, and keep them happy so they will stay with the company.

SkillView

Some specialized software providers offer just such in-depth analysis of the workforce. SkillView Technologies allows employees to assess their own skills as a basis for career planning and a basis for training. Figure 17.7 shows an

Table 17.6. HireRight Summary

Company	HireRight 2100 Main Street, Suite 400 Irvine, CA 92614 949-428-5800 www.hireright.com
Product	HireRight
Product Use	Pre-employment screening over the Web
Equipment Requirements	Web browser
Release Date	First release—1997. Hosted solution with frequent updates
Installed Base	More than 600 customers, including many large enterprise accounts
List Price	From $40 to $100, depending on the scope of the verification; Package and a la carte pricing is available

analysis page from the SkillView program, showing career planning for a candidate.

Not every company does skills analysis. But if you do make such analysis part of the company culture, you help HR fulfill its mission of not just tracking people but actually helping them. Table 17.7 shows a quick summary of the SkillView offering.

EMPLOYEE SELF-SERVICE

When a concept like employee self-service begins to come into its own, it has the promise to become universal. The concept is simple enough: Let employees go online to answer for themselves all those questions they used to have to ask their HR person. Lines outside the HR office can disappear, and maybe you can even keep the size of your HR staff to a minimum.

Figure 17.7. SkillView Analysis Page

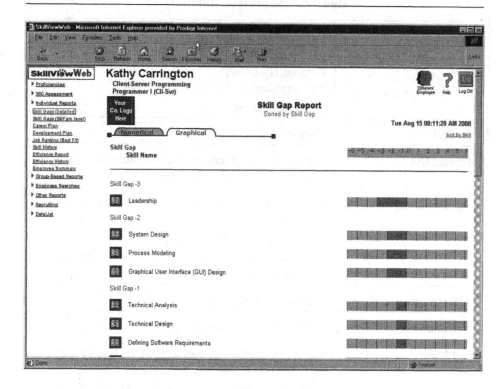

Authoria's HR Suite

Some companies take the employee self-service concept to new heights. Using what it calls a "knowledgebase" (as opposed to a simple database), Authoria provides in-depth answers to employees. Here is the company's own summary of what it does:

> "Human Resources is perhaps the most sought-after department in any organization," says the Authoria company website. "Questions range from 'How much vacation time do I have left?' to 'Do we have Columbus Day off?' to 'How much have I contributed to my 401(k)?'
>
> "Authoria HR Suite allows you to deliver intelligent, personalized, Web-based answers to these and thousands of other benefits and HR policy questions. It instantly and dynamically generates answers to

Table 17.7. SkillView Summary

Company	SkillView Technologies, Inc. 95 Plaistow Road Plaistow, NH 03865 603–382–9882 www.skillview.com
Product	SkillView
Product Use	Self-assessment of skills, as a basis to manage those skills, plan career paths, and plan training
Equipment Requirements	Works with any midsize, SQL-based database, using either Windows-based systems for the client/server environment or, for the Web product, any browser; Client/server version uses PowerBuilder from Sybase, Inc., on the front (user) side
Release Date	Version 3.1: January 2000
Installed Base	Thirty-five to forty companies
List Price	For in-house solution, depending on size of enterprise, from $30,000 to $60,000. For application service provider solution, approximately $10,000 setup fee and monthly fee of $2 to $8 dollars per person

employee questions based on their individual needs. Twenty-four hours a day. Seven days a week. Try to do that with a static-text website."

Table 17.8 provides a summary of HR Suite.

Link2HR

A few years back, some enterprising engineers developed a wonderful, innovative Internet-based product for employee self-service and manager self-service at a time when those concepts were new to most people. The product, named Seeker software at the time, attracted almost a cult following. This product led the world in employee and manager self-service.

Table 17.8. HR Suite Summary

Company	Authoria, Inc. 300 Fifth Avenue Waltham, MA 02451 781-530-2000 www.authoria.com
Product	Authoria HR Suite
Product Use	Employers and HR outsourcers use the technology to communicate benefits and HR policy information to employees
System Requirements	Web browser
Release Date	First in 1997, latest release 3.5 July'02
Installed Base	Over 100 customers
List Price	Varies, based on employees served. Six figure sale; Average sale price is $350,000.00

Charmed at the possibilities, another company acquired Seeker and renamed it Concur HR. The product stopped soaring, and another company acquired it and renamed it Link2HR. In its newest incarnation, it again holds great promise. Figure 17.8 shows an employee self-service screen from Link2HR.

A major technology company like Dell uses the product for its HRIS product, even though it was initially designed for its ESS and MSS capabilities. If ESS and MSS are as much the wave of the future as people think, Link2HR just may be the product to be the backbone of their HR system. Table 17.9 shows a quick summary of the product.

OTHER SPECIALIZED HR NEEDS

Begin to explore HR specialty packages, and a world of possibilities opens before you. You begin to find solutions to problems you did not even know you had

Figure 17.8. Link2HR Employee Self-Service Screen

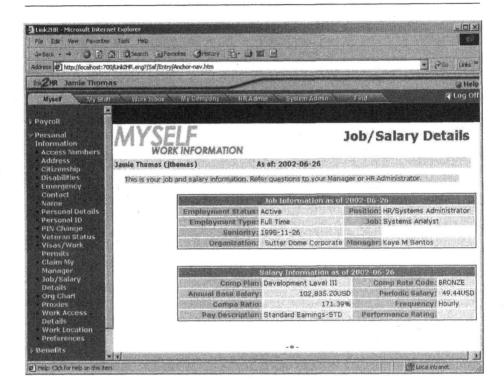

(although you may well have had them anyway). Aside from those categories discussed above, there is HR software for the following:

- Compliance;
- Employee ID badges;
- Health;
- Instructional design;
- Relocation management;
- Safety; and
- Surveys and survey processing.

Look at any of the products meant for these purposes, and see how they would help you. If your company is in the trades, for instance, you might see immediate value in SafetyPlanBuilder from Jian, Inc. It helps you create a written plan for

Table 17.9. Link2HR Summary

Company	MBH Solutions Glenpointe Centre East 300 Frank W. Burr Boulevard, 2nd Floor Teaneck, NJ 07666 201-287-0901 www.mbhsolutions.com
Product	Link2HR
Product Use	Prepackaged workplace Web applications to automate HR transactions and workflow
Equipment Requirements	Web servers: Microsoft IIS; Netscape Enterprise server Databases: Oracle; Sybase Adaptive server; Microsoft SQL server Web server operating systems: Microsoft Windows NT; Sun Solaris Web browsers: Microsoft IE; Netscape Navigator
Release Date	Version 7.0 released March 2002
Installed Base	Twenty customers with 100,000+ users
List Price	$30,000—$100,000 per module, depending on the size of a company; ten application modules currently available

preventing illness and injury and, not incidentally, protecting yourself against lawsuits under OSHA. "Don't let OSHA and lawyers tear your business apart with fines and lawsuits," says the company literature. "Create a custom written illness and injury prevention plan to quickly and easily comply with OSHA, avoid lawsuits, and provide a healthy workplace."

CONCLUSION

The possibilities are extensive. Specialized HR software is abundant enough to be a bit overwhelming at first. On the other hand, it is quite inspiring. If you want to automate something that your HR department does, the chances are excellent that you can find one, two, or ten products out there, whatever you need it for—training, compensation management, succession planning, vacation time tracking, or just about anything. You have to decide, but in many cases the specialty package may do the function better than your comprehensive HRIS. At least the idea is that specialists ought to know more than the generalists, although the general HRIS packages may surprise you with the strength of their offerings in specialized areas. One form of specialty software enjoyed a major explosion at the turn of the century—Web-based hiring software. The next chapter looks at such software.

The E-Recruiting Revolution

Human resources and HR technology at times have had a reputation for something approaching stodginess. They are solid, reliable, and useful. But they are not the topic generating the buzz around the company water cooler. Enter the e-recruiting revolution. Suddenly, one technology changed everything. E-recruiting became the buzz around the water cooler.

E-recruiting is at the heart of everything a business does. Business is about competing. Competing depends on talent. And e-recruiting is at the heart of the talent war. Two technologies above all made e-recruiting a reality. First, Internet job boards like Monster.com became not only the preferred method of advertising for jobs and locating jobs, but they virtually displaced the print-based newspaper ads that had been at the heart of the industry for so long. Second, Internet applications within organizations (e-recruiting) allowed companies to screen candidates from those job boards and walk them through a complete recruiting process . . . all from the computer desktop.

The process of selecting e-recruiting software is the same as for selecting any other HR software. You prepare a needs analysis. You analyze vendors. And so on. What is different? First, the buzz is so much greater. Probably never before had so much happened so fast in the HR technology arena as happened with e-recruiting. Second, the risks are greater in some respects. Powerful companies sprang up overnight, funded by venture capital, and came storming into the marketplace. Their pitches were almost irresistible, and the business plans matched. To be kind, they were not yet established. You could end up losing your investment (which did happen on occasion) or even your precious recruiting database (which happened with a company named iSearch and possibly others).

E-recruiting is not, at this writing, the white hot topic it was in 2000 and 2001. An economic downturn has slowed the attention on hiring. A backlash has set in, and once-glamorous companies are finding that they are now ordinary technology providers. Nevertheless, the powerful e-recruiting companies—a blend of methodical HR and the more sales-oriented hiring department—have established a permanent beachhead in the HR technology arena. You cannot ignore them any more. And you may be able to use them to raise the competitive quality of your entire company.

This chapter provides a look at some applicant tracking and e-recruiting companies to give a flavor of the marketplace. But the marketplace is so volatile that you will also have to conduct your own firsthand research if you want to find reliable information on current products. The selections I have chosen do not purport to be the best, certainly not the best selection for your company. The companies discussed here are simply a sampling of the marketplace and of what you might find there.

APPLICANT TRACKING AND AUTOMATED RECRUITING

Yearn for simplicity sometimes as you contemplate the market for applicant tracking and recruiting? You can fall back on the old-style systems, which performed a pretty simple function. They helped you keep track of the candidates for jobs at your company. What were the candidates' names and addresses? Where did they live? What jobs did they want to interview for? Where were they in the process? Reports would allow you to go to the data you had compiled and put together such information as the number of applicants you had interviewed, the number of positions filled, and other basics. Such packages have now moved to the Internet, perhaps giving you the best of both worlds—connectivity to the world through the Internet and familiar processing on your company's computer system.

Old-Style Applicant Tracking: iGreentree Employment System

iGreentree Employment System from Greentree Systems, Inc., automates the process as you prepare requisitions, manage and approve them, post them to job boards and your corporate website, bring in applicants, send out materials to the hiring manager, conduct interviews, and send offers. Figure 18.1 shows a typical menu that an HR person would see when using this product.

Greentree Systems offers a number of advantages, not the least of which is that the company has been a stalwart in providing applicant tracking for some years. It has over four hundred installations in forty states, Canada, and Europe. Following are some other product strengths:

- Although it could just as easily be aimed at recruiters, this product focuses on HR. "We've made a strategic decision not to sell to agencies," says company marketing director Doug Rodgers. "It's hard to do a good job of both [agencies and HR]."

- The company has had time to develop an easy-to-use product, and customers find it that way. "It's easy, very easy to use," says one HR secretary and Greentree System administrator.

Figure 18.1. iGreentree Employment System Menu

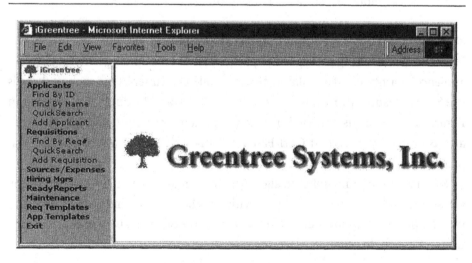

Table 18.1. iGreentree Summary

Company	Greentree Systems, Inc. 3131 South Bascom Avenue, Suite 200 Campbell, CA 95008 408-879-1410 or 800-348-8845 www.greentreesystems.com
Product	iGreentree Employment System, v. 7.1
Product Use	Web-based employment management
Equipment Requirements	For HR users, Internet Explorer (IE) 5 or 5.5; for hiring managers, IE or Netscape; recommended—at least Pentium 300 with 128 MB memory
Release Date	January 2001
Installed Base	Four hundred
List Price	$75,000 to $250,000 based on number of concurrent HR users

What's not to like? The biggest question might be whether you want this proven applicant tracking system or one of the glamorous new Internet hiring management systems. Table 18.1 shows a quick summary of iGreentree.

Headhunting with a Computer: Safari Headhunting System

Where some recruiting packages aim particularly at HR, others go after a different audience—fast-paced, fast-talking, pressure-filled recruiters. One such package is the Safari Headhunting System from Safari Software Products, Inc., shown in Figure 18.2. "Safari is designed from my experience as a professional recruiter," attests company president Carl Fausett. "It is written the way a professional recruiter works best."

Safari is proud of its ability to allow for strong searches, not just by code but by keywords. And the screen is designed with one thought in mind—quick access to information with a minimum of keystrokes. (You can quickly type shortcuts for things that you do often.)

Figure 18.2. Safari Headhunting System

What cautions should you observe? If you are an HR person and not a recruiter, make sure the product meets your HR needs. Does it have EEO information you may want? Does it help with benefits planning or training in ways that you may want your applicant tracking system to work?

If your department is all about the fast-paced business of landing new recruits, this may be the software for you. Table 18.2 provides a quick summary.

Cute, Cheap, Effective Applicant Tracking—HR Tools

Does the number $195 mean anything to you? If you've been contemplating applicant tracking software in the range from $25,000 to $100,000 and up, you just might like the idea of laying down a mere $195 for the simple job of keeping track of those who have applied for jobs at your company.

HR Tools from Archer Software keeps track of applicant information. Period. "You put the data down electronically, and you are able to refer back to it later," explains company founder Ed Carson.

Simplicity is the goal. You key information into the system. When you want it later, you type in a search criterion and get the information out. Figure 18.3 shows the result of one HR Tools search.

Table 18.2. Safari Headhunting System Summary

Company	Safari Software Products, Inc. 604 East Maple Street Horicon, WI 53032 920 485–4100 www.safarisoftproducts.com
Product Name	The Safari Headhunting System
Product Use	Windows-based staffing and recruiting software
Equipment Requirements	Win 95/98/NT
Release Date	Version 4.1: January 1999
Installed Base	More than six hundred users across U.S., Canada, Great Britain
List Price	Basic system: $4995 site license Tracker module: $1,295 Deluxe communication module: $1,995 Additional modules, priced separately—dedicated document server, management and multi-office module, automated candidate entry system, billing and invoicing, back office (accounting) Safari On-Line: $399.00/month (three users)

Biggest strength of the system? Unbelievable price. Second biggest strength—elegant design that gets the job done.

Biggest weakness? If your company is gigantic, you may not want this software. (Then again, you might want it within your department for simple tracking.) Or if your needs are quite small, maybe you will not have to bother with any software. "If you only have thirty applicants a year, don't waste your money," advises one experienced user of the system.

If you want just to try out applicant tracking to see if it works for you, a system like this is a good place to start. Table 18.3 shows a summary.

Overall, perhaps the single biggest drawback of applicant tracking software is the need to input all the information in the first place before you can get anything

Figure 18.3. HR Tools Search Result

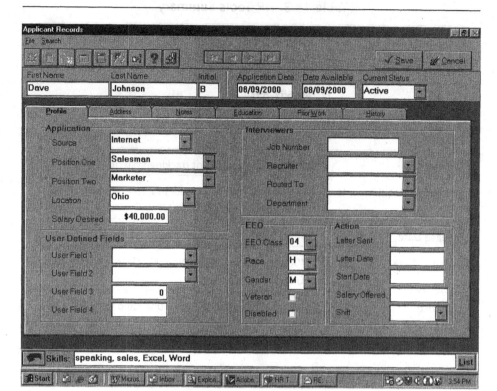

back out of the system. The Internet and online job boards have revolutionized everything, though.

RISE OF E-RECRUITING

If you do not know how to recruit off the Internet, you are left standing at the gate when the rest of the competitors have launched into the race. For a company of any size, neglecting Internet recruiting is close to unthinkable. E-recruiting begins with electronic applications fed directly from the Internet, either from job boards or from a company's own website. It does not start with information that your HR people key into an applicant tracking system. E-recruiting does not simply track applicants, allowing you to see where they are in the hiring cycle, as did the older applicant tracking packages. It manages the hiring process, allowing you to find applicants quickly, move them through the process, analyze how well you are doing, manage

Table 18.3. HR Tools Summary

Company	Archer Software 2062 Parklawn Drive Lewis Center, OH 43035 740-657-8934 www.archersoftware.com
Product	HR Tools, v. 6.03
Product Use	Really low-cost applicant tracking system
Equipment Requirements	Any Windows PC; any standard PC network, such as Novell Netware or Windows NT
Release Date	January 1997
Installed Base	1,400 over the life of the product; 750 registered users; 500 to 600 active users
List Price	$195 for single user; $495 for unlimited network license

the interview process, and make your deal. Whereas the old systems put the emphasis on tracking, the new Internet programs put the emphasis on hiring.

Consultants Rick Fletcher (vice president and founder of HRchitect, Inc.) and Ron Hanscome (principal of REH Consulting) explain in a presentation (2002) just how quickly the Internet recruiting revolution came about. During 1997–2001, they say, the Internet and Web changed the game. Dot-coms and high-tech, high-growth companies expanded staff rapidly. On-line job boards proliferated. The Web provided the capability to involve managers in a collaborative on-line hiring process. And the corporate website became a recruiting tool.

Fletcher and Hanscome (2002) also offer their own expert summary of the top e-recruiting vendors. They offer this list of *best-in-class* Web-based hiring vendors offering the basic features:

- BrassRing
- Deploy
- Icarian

- RecruitSoft
- WebHire

The two consultants also offer a list of major *new generation* ATS (applicant tracking system) vendors. (Some companies appear on both lists, indicating that they are both new and best-in-class.) Here are the companies:

- Alexus
- BrassRing
- Deploy Solutions
- Icarian
- PeopleClick
- RecruitSoft
- VirtualEdge
- WetFeet
- Workstream (formerly e-Cruiter)

The marketplace has seen many Internet-based recruiting companies come—and some have gone as well. But the productivity tools they offer have brought excitement to HR technology and promise to continue to be a shaping influence on the way companies do business. Following is a close look at a few selected providers of Internet recruiting software.

Consistent Leader: Hiresystems

You would have difficulty checking out Internet-based hiring systems without encountering BrassRing systems. Formerly Hiresystems, with a product still named Hiresystems, BrassRing's product automates the business process of locating and hiring candidates. Here are some of the processes it handles: manage requisitions; post to job boards; handle applications; screen and sort applicants; search candidates; and market to candidates and establish a relationship.

The product (shown in Figure 18.4) is an Internet application that is meant for hiring purposes. It is a powerful tool in a competitive game. Testifies a user, "We do it to be effective, efficient. That overwhelms everything else."

If you work with a product that will become a big part of your business process, be ready to put a good deal of planning into your implementation. "Put a lot into

Figure 18.4. Hiresystems Screen

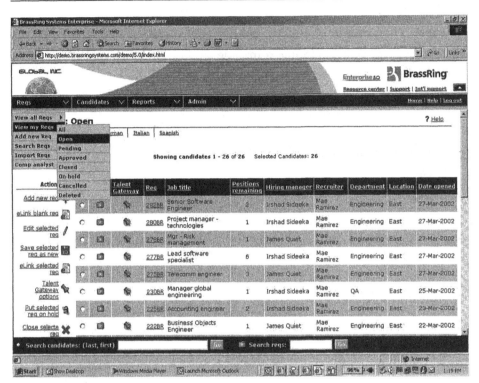

the implementation team to do it right the first time. Get a group together that includes recruiters, recruiter assistants, some IT—and senior management," advises another user. Table 18.4 shows a product summary.

Another Top Contender: RecruitSoft

Many of the best-known products offer similar features and capabilities. Recruiting, after all, is recruiting. You prepare and track requisitions, interview candidates, make offers, and manage the responses. One company, RecruitSoft, offers a study done by Electronic Recruiting Exchange comparing all the top vendors. (Other vendors in this hotly contested space dispute the methods and results of the study.) Figure 18.5 shows the results of the ERE study—a matrix similar to one that you might prepare yourself in comparing Internet recruiting vendors.

Table 18.5 provides a summary for RecruitSoft.

Table 18.4. Hiresystems Summary

Company	BrassRing Systems A Division of BrassRing, Inc. 170 High Street Waltham, MA 02453 781-736-1000 www.brassringsystems.com
Product	Hiresystems, v. 3.75 with integrated Joboo (for corporate job site hosting)
Product Use	Web-based hiring management System to Manage both internal and external talent
Equipment Requirements	ASP solution (rental only), so only a browser required
Release Date	September 2000
Installed Base	Two hundred companies, several thousand users
List Price	Pricing based on volume of resumes and service level (not number of users), from $45,000 to over $1,000,000; pricing is inclusive—includes all services, customization, implementation, training, upgrades in the future

Well-Designed Newcomer: Employ!

Although the products described here all automate the same set of activities, the companies and products nevertheless differentiate themselves from one another. Strongly endorsed by a number of consultants and industry insiders, Employ! from Deploy Solutions automates not just hiring but deployment and retention as well.

It offers a library of behavioral competencies that companies use to set up their criteria for success. It can then screen candidates based on those competencies, helping get the right fit (thereby deploying people well and helping assure that people enter into jobs that suit them well). And it goes the extra mile to be sure that a company automates its own processes and does not simply install a cold

Figure 18.5. ERE Internet Recruiters Study Results

System Performance	Recruitsoft	Alexus	Brassring	Resumix/SS	Icarian	Peopleclick	Personic	RezLogic	Webhire
Ease of use	4.71	2.43	3.79	3.46	3.86	4.00	3.14	3.89	3.44
Overall functionality	4.29	2.57	3.43	3.62	3.71	3.53	3.00	3.72	3.28
Customized functionality	4.14	2.86	3.19	3.67	3.38	3.35	3.14	3.61	2.62
System reliability	4.71	3.43	3.32	3.75	4.13	3.12	3.29	4.56	3.16
Data security	4.57	4.20	3.81	4.33	4.50	3.93	3.86	4.61	3.80
System scalability	4.43	4.00	3.83	4.18	3.75	3.60	2.71	4.00	3.16
Integration with HRIS	3.80	3.00	2.95	3.36	3.43	2.77	3.25	3.00	2.50
Average Score	4.38	3.21	3.47	3.77	3.82	3.47	3.20	3.91	3.14
Rank	1	6	5	4	3	5	7	2	8

Vendor Performance	Recruitsoft	Alexus	Brassring	Resumix/SS	Icarian	Peopleclick	Personic	RezLogic	Webhire
Customer service/tech support	4.86	3.14	3.50	3.45	3.00	3.06	2.29	4.39	2.90
Training	4.29	2.57	3.18	3.17	3.25	3.59	3.29	3.61	3.12
System delivered or installed on budget	4.86	3.75	3.68	4.00	3.00	3.19	3.57	4.67	3.47
On-time/timely installation of system	4.71	3.33	3.79	3.71	3.13	2.71	3.43	4.59	3.56
Upgrades or new capabilities	4.71	3.00	3.50	3.27	3.71	3.27	3.29	3.94	3.00
Average Score	4.69	3.16	3.53	3.52	3.22	3.16	3.17	4.24	3.21
Rank	1	7	3	4	5	7	8	2	6

Functionality Performance	Recruitsoft	Alexus	Brassring	Resumix/SS	Icarian	Peopleclick	Personic	RezLogic	Webhire
Internal job-posting capabilities to corporate website	4.57	2.50	3.73	3.64	3.63	3.81	2.00	4.06	3.00
Resume-scanning capabilities	3.60	3.29	3.82	4.00	3.63	3.25	2.83	4.00	3.17
Search capabilities	4.14	2.71	4.04	4.08	3.50	3.31	3.43	3.78	3.71
Reporting capabilities	4.00	2.71	3.22	2.54	2.38	3.71	2.00	3.00	3.20
Scheduling capabilities	3.80	2.50	2.79	3.00	2.40	2.77	3.14	3.47	3.06
Cost analysis/metrics capabilities	4.17	3.00	2.72	2.89	2.57	3.55	2.29	3.13	2.67
External job posting capabilities to job boards, newsgroups, etc.	4.57	2.00	3.10	3.00	3.57	2.94	1.80	3.50	2.83
Resume- or information-sharing capabilities	4.29	3.00	3.96	3.54	3.86	3.53	3.57	4.17	3.52
Resume sourcing	4.00	2.60	3.23	2.80	3.33	3.27	2.67	3.36	2.62
Automated response to applicants/response-management	4.57	3.00	3.50	3.58	4.14	3.67	3.17	4.06	3.35
Average Score	4.17	2.73	3.41	3.31	3.30	3.38	2.69	3.65	3.11
Rank	1	8	3	5	6	4	9	2	7

	Recruitsoft	Alexus	Brassring	Resumix/SS	Icarian	Peopleclick	Personic	RezLogic	Webhire
Average Score	4.57	2.43	3.46	3.62	3.38	3.24	2.71	4.00	3.35
Overall Rank	1	9	4	3	5	7	8	2	6

Table 18.5. Recruitsoft Summary

Company	Recruitsoft, Inc. 182 Second Street, 5th Floor San Francisco, CA 94105 415-538-9068 or 888-836-3669 www.recruitsoft.com
Product	Recruitsoft Enterprise Staffing Solution
Product Use	Improve staffing process so organizations can find quality candidates faster, increase retention and improve overall performance from the hired workforce
Equipment Requirements	Internet Browser and PC
Release Date	June 20, 2002, original release was Sept 1999
Installed Base	100+ enterprise-wide installations
List Price	Average annual selling price is $500,000

system that does not fit the company. "Our passion is for the employee, the customer," says Deploy president Nicole Stata.

Figure 18.6 shows the main screen of this product, which prides itself on ease of use.

Particularly with a product that automates what you do at your company using behavioral competencies, you make best with Deploy's product if you plan ahead. Advises a user, "Before you go out and start looking at software vendors to be the solution to employment, you really need to map out your current process and what you want to see as a new process." Table 18.6 shows a summary for Employ!

Figure 18.6. Employ! Main Screen

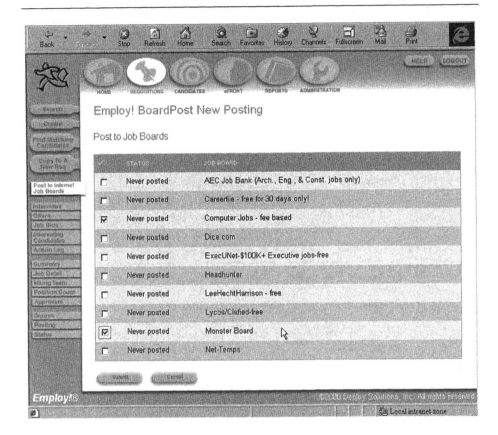

Sourcing, Sorting, Screening: Hire.com

Hire.com, based in Austin, Texas, is in some respects to hiring management systems what Safari is to applicant tracking. That is, it is software for recruiters by recruiters. Figure 18.7 shows the main screen of the product.

Hire.com founder and president Hank Stringer explains that Hire.com facilitates "speed hiring" and "puts companies in touch with candidates who are interested, qualified, and available in minutes rather than days or weeks." It encourages candidates to profile themselves even if they are not actively seeking work, giving companies access to a collection of people who are interested. By evaluating the profiles, you can see whether the candidates are qualified.

Table 18.6. Employ! Summary

Company	Deploy Solutions, Inc. 100 Lowder Brook Drive Westwood, MA 02090 781-461-9024 www.deploy.com
Product	Employ!
Product Use	Internet-based, integrated hiring, deployment, and retention tools to automate and streamline hiring
Equipment Requirements	When used as a service, requires IE 4.0 or higher, Netscape Navigator 4.5–4.75 For purchase, requires a 400 MHz processor 1Gb RAM, UNIX SOLARIS 2.6, 2.7 (Employ! versions before the current 3.0 also run on Windows NT)
Release Date	Version 3.0: May 17, 2001
Installed Base	Eight installed, four ASP (rental only)
List Price	Base pricing starts at $125,000 per year, both rental and purchase

If they have taken the time to profile themselves, they are at least minimally available.

Hire.com specializes in building relationships with candidates by collecting profiles of potential future candidates and keeping in touch with them through periodic communications. Table 18.7 presents a summary of the product.

Screening and Advertising: IdealHire

Another company that sounds a good deal like Hire.com is IdealHire, division of Pentawave, Inc. IdealHire's distinguishing trait may be that it understands media and advertising companies and brings a strong understanding of advertising to the game of Internet recruiting. One of its menu selections on its main screen

Figure 18.7. Hire.com Main Screen

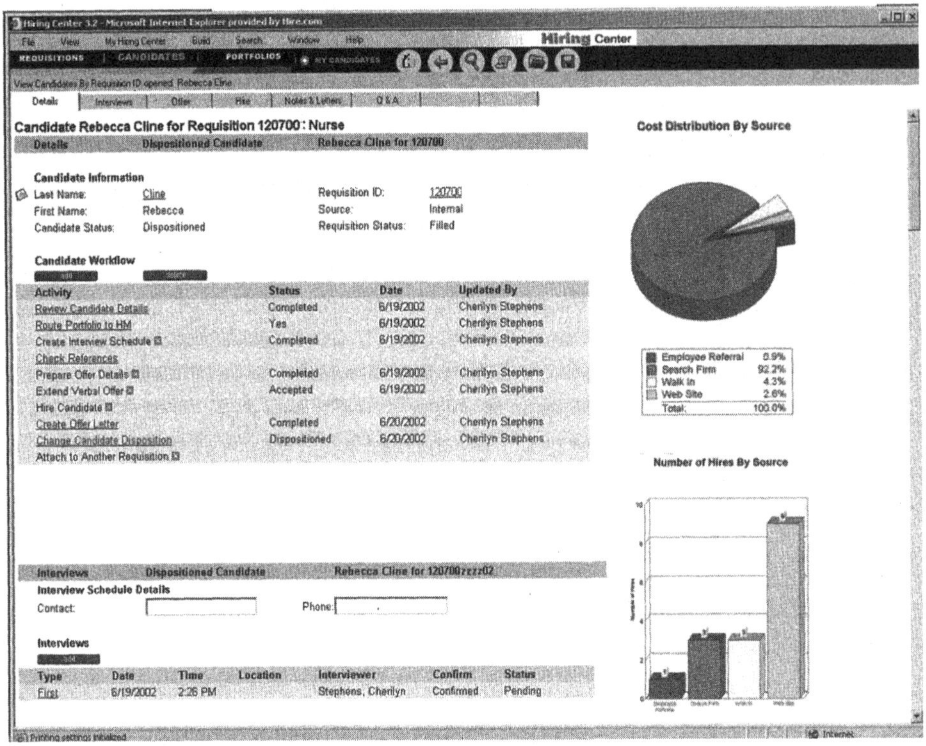

allows you to prepare a hiring ad—not a standard offering with all Web hiring programs but a specialty of IdealHire. It also automatically screens candidates using criteria you have to build into the system. And it prepares a short list of candidates for you. In many ways it attempts, like Hire.com, to aggressively go out and seek candidates for you. If you are looking at one of these products, you might well want to look at the other for comparison. Table 18.8 presents a summary of the product.

Innovator in End-to-End Hiring: Icarian eWorkforce

A true industry darling initially was Icarian, which prided itself on an end-to-end solution that did not stop simply because the company had hired a candidate. Their Icarian eWorkforce product uses a workflow model. Users move from left to right as they follow the choices on their computer screen, and the choices follow the

Table 18.7. Hire.com Summary

Company	Hire.com 200 Academy Drive Austin, TX 78704 512-583-4400 www.hire.com
Product	Hire.com, Including Hire.com Sourcing Center, Hire.com Recruiting Center, Hire.com Hiring Center, and Hire.Analytics
Product Use	Sourcing, recruiting, hiring, and analytics
Equipment Requirements	Either hosted or purchase; for hosted solution, Web Browser; for purchase, Hiring Center has been tested on Windows 98, NT, 2000 and XP
Release Date	The current release of Hiring Center, 3.0, was generally available Q401
Installed Base	over 120 clients
List Price	For a company with between 15,000 and 50,000 employees with up to 150 recruiters, the average monthly fee is: list price is $18,000/month to $100,000/month, depending upon the size of company and the solution set.
	For a company with over 300 recruiters, the average monthly fee is:
	N/A priced by number of employees

chronological flow of a task, such as creating a hiring requisition and sending it off for approval. The product may be even more extensive in its end-to-end design than Employ!, which has similar goals. Following the deployment of the employee, it works with compensation and even performance reviews, which are generally felt to be part of an HRIS package rather than a hiring package.

The biggest question mark for the product after its first couple years had to do with the strength of the company. It went through a number of changes at the top

Table 18.8. IdealHire Summary

Company	IdealHire A division of Pentawave, Inc. 2375 E. Camelback Road Phoenix, AZ 85016 480-281-0300 www.idealhire.com
Product	IdealHire
Product Use	Recruitment software for corporate websites or media companies; automatically generates a matched and ranked pool of candidates to meet user requirements
Equipment Requirements	A browser (Netscape or IE 3.0 or up)
Release Date	March 2000
Installed Base	Thirteen to fifteen sites
List Price	From $2,000 to $15,000 per month for corporations, based on size of company, number of employees, and whether one-year or three-year agreement; additional fee for additional user id's; $2,000 to 8,000 a month for newspapers, based on circulation, viewership

but continued to insist that its best days lay in front of it. Now it has announced plans to merge with Workstream, Inc. If it does prove it can recapture the magic of its early days, you just might find that this industry darling could be your darling as well. Table 18.9 shows a summary.

Integrated High-End: Lawson's e-Recruiting

As the frenzy over Internet hiring systems began to quiet in 2001, Lawson Software, Inc., of St. Paul, Minnesota, made a deliberate move. It incorporated its e-recruiting solution into its overall product offering. That is, users could no longer purchase the product separately. If you do happen to be a Lawson customer already, you might want to look no further than your own HRIS provider for your e-recruiting software. Table 18.10 provides a quick summary of the Lawson e-Recruiting offering,

Table 18.9. Icarian eWorkforce Summary

Company	Icarian, Inc. 333 Moffett Park Drive Sunnyvale, CA 94089 408-743-5700 www.icarian.com
Product	iCarian eWorkforce 2.0
Product Use	End-to-end talent acquisition and retention subscription service designed for staffing organizations and hiring managers
Equipment Requirements	Web browser, Internet connectivity
Release Date	Version 1.0: January 1999; Version 2.0: October 1999
Installed Base	Ten companies
List Price	Subscription, monthly, based on number of employees and options selected; begins at $5,000 per month

Table 18.10. Lawson e-Recruiting Summary

Company	Lawson Software, Inc. 380 St. Peter Street St. Paul, MN 55102 651-767-7000 www.lawson.com
Product	e-Recruiting, v. 5 (part of Lawson's Human Capital Management Solution including HR, Workforce Analytics, and e-Recruiting)
Product Use	Internet recruiting; manages and automates hiring—from sourcing candidates to moving data into the HR system
Equipment Requirements	Internet Explorer 5 for this hosted service
Release Date	2001
Installed Base	Sixty companies have purchased e-Recruiting; forty have now gone live
List Price	Initial charge buys core application plus one year of use, then pricing goes monthly; a one-year subscription for the two services—e-Recruiting and Workforce Analytics—for ten concurrent users ranges from $50,000 to $500,000

which seems to do the same as other electronic recruiting packages but with the full support of a proven, high-end company.

CONCLUSION

In many respects, the e-recruiting marketplace is inspiring for human resources. Where HR may often complain that the corporation reduces it to tracking administrivia, Internet-based hiring has suddenly elevated HR into the spotlight. Power resides with HR, or at least with hiring, which may or may not be a part of HR.

With power, as is always the case, comes responsibility. Software selectors can help set a company on an upward course, or they can bring in a tricky bag of headaches and cultural adjustments. A look at the e-recruiting marketplace, now a bit dormant but still powerful, reveals just how exciting, risky, and valuable the job of the HR software selector can be.

Software evaluators may be able to take a bit of a "wait and see" attitude toward Internet recruiting software during a period of a cooled-off economy. But these are powerful applications, forged during a time of intense creativity. Selecting from among them is an education in itself. If you make a good choice, you strengthen your company—and you strengthen HR. Another area where you should "look before you leap" is high-end HRIS systems, where the costs are high and the price of a mistake could likely be your job. Even if your organization is too small to consider one of the high-end products, it could be worth your while just to see what they offer. The next chapter provides a look at high-end HRIS providers.

The Exclusive High End

In this book, we have indulged in the enjoyable activity of looking over the competing horde of smaller and mid-sized providers in the HR marketplace. Fresh, eager, and ambitious, these providers promise to solve immediate needs and bring immediate return to HR departments. They are manageable in price and easily installed. Another entire world of HR software exists, though, and it has a different personality from the rest of the marketplace. First of all, it is bigger. Produced by large companies, it is aimed at large companies. The software is costly, takes considerable time to install, and remains in place for a considerable time once it is in place.

The high-end marketplace, which overall may well account for more HR users than all other HR companies put together, is dominated by three companies: PeopleSoft, SAP, and Oracle. The three have similar personalities, and their directions tend to dictate the direction of all the rest of the marketplace. Not pretending to offer a comprehensive guide to these providers, in this chapter I provide a quick introduction to the high end of the marketplace.

In many respects, the methods described so far in this book do not entirely apply at the high end. That is, a well-meaning HR person cannot just go out, solicit information from vendors, and introduce one of these HR packages to the company. However, even a book on small and mid-market HR software cannot entirely overlook the high end. Much of what happens there "trickles down" to influence all the rest of the marketplace. And for all segments of the marketplace, a certain degree of overlap takes place. Someone looking for a mid-sized product may decide that a larger sized product is worthy of the investment.

TRENDS AT THE TOP

Trends noted in Chapter 2 in this book are trends across all company sizes in HR:

- Companies are moving into self-service;
- Companies are moving onto the Internet; and
- Companies are becoming strategic.

But for large enterprises, gradual evolution does not seem to be an option. The Internet above all seems to have forced the issue, along with such other pressures as the sudden plunge in popularity of ERP at the end of the previous century. (Enterprise-wide computing, still the style, had to be reinvented in such forms as CRM, customer relationship management.) The Internet meant that a worldwide customer base could be available to a company over its own computers. Those who reached customers over their computers appeared to have a mammoth edge over those who did not. Also, a company's own employees could be instantly reachable thanks to the Internet. Any company that did not capitalize on the Internet seemed to be placing itself at a considerable competitive disadvantage.

Facing a clear situation of "retool or die," HR providers at the high end took steps to modify their offerings drastically. They reinvented themselves. PeopleSoft quite openly "bet the farm" on a pure Internet strategy with its PeopleSoft 8 offering, and the other players were not far behind.

As you look over the marketing descriptions of products from the high-end providers, you may have a great deal of difficulty differentiating among the products. All now claim to be the global leader in these offerings:

- Pure Internet;
- Human capital management (analytics);
- Enterprise-wide integration; and
- Employee and manager self-service.

Because the literature from these players all sounds so much the same, you have to rely on scuttlebutt more than at other levels of the marketplace to tell you the truth about the providers—if even that will work. To really distinguish among products, you need to apply a thorough selection process.

High-end HR software is a world unto itself in comparison with other HR software you might select. You do not really choose it; you "tour" it. You do not really decide; you sign off or perhaps request moderate changes on what someone else has decided. The software, too, is a world unto itself. For you as the HR person, it can be transforming for your department and for the way you work. And, of course, it can be immensely beneficial.

THE BIG THREE

Although some other pretenders might object, essentially three providers have come to dominate the high end of HR software. Conference speakers, members of the profession, and consultants routinely refer to them as "the Big Three," and everyone in the field knows who they are—PeopleSoft, Oracle, and SAP. As mentioned, all have taken similar directions—an Internet application providing self-service and strong analytics. Each company, too, carries with it an image it has created over the years. PeopleSoft, the only one of the three that began as an HR company, has a reputation for understanding HR issues. Oracle, long a world-leading database provider, has a reputation for technical excellence in sophisticated, large-scale database systems. German-based SAP has a longstanding record of solving tracking and reporting problems, particularly for manufacturing companies.

The big three companies may have come to HR from different directions and with differing strengths, but all have adopted overlapping strategies. Without a painstaking analysis, you really cannot easily tell which one might be better for you than the others. Here is a quick look at what the companies say about themselves.

PeopleSoft

Anyone from HR who has a voice in selecting high-end software probably ought to look at PeopleSoft first, for the simple reason that PeopleSoft has its roots in human resources. It has made a business of understanding HR and, on the strength of its understanding of HR grew, from its beginnings in 1987 to its present size as a $500,000,000 company.

Advantages

PeopleSoft's greatest strengths would be these:

- A genuine commitment to HR, as mentioned; and

- A history of both rapid growth and of successfully reinventing itself to adapt to the marketplace.

Two recent PeopleSoft innovations bode well for those who are interested in the company:

1. In 2000, PeopleSoft delivered its PeopleSoft 8 product, a pure Internet product that required PeopleSoft to rebuild its product from the ground up.

2. In 2002, again wanting to stay abreast of changing trends in the business community, PeopleSoft announced its Human Capital Management Solutions. No longer simply directing its products at a self-contained HR department, PeopleSoft was shifting their "narrow views of human capital management from traditional HR support such as benefits, personnel, or payroll, to the delivery of a comprehensive set of enabling services required by employees and managers," according to Kathy Harris, vice president and research director at The Gartner Group. Doug Merritt, vice president and general manager of PeopleSoft's HCM division says, "Organizations are nothing but people going forward. Optimization of those people is a business imperative to success in this new economy." PeopleSoft's new directions empower the entire company, not just HR, in helping a company move forward.

Considerations

What are the cautions with a company like PeopleSoft? To adapt to a rapidly changing business world, PeopleSoft has had to reinvent itself quickly again and again. When successful, such change is a plus. But change brings risk and uncertainty. Check the stock prices and the recent history of the company. Check changes in leadership at the top. Find out the current "word on the street" from unbiased consultants. Do not assume that, because PeopleSoft is PeopleSoft, it remains the leader that it was before. Be sure to look into the question: "What is PeopleSoft doing today?"

Oracle

Long a darling of the technical marketplace, Oracle has dedicated itself to developing strong applications to satisfy those in the end-user marketplace (and not simply providing the database technology that resides behind the scenes).

Advantages

Oracle, like PeopleSoft, wants to leverage the Internet. And the company has been touting its ability to meet genuine needs of HR.

The biggest reason to favor Oracle, I would say, would be the strength of its technology infrastructure. If you are looking for an alternative to giant Microsoft, you can find it in Oracle. Its databases are synonymous with power and reliability.

Considerations

On the other hand, despite its hand waving, Oracle does not have the record of commitment to HR and HR software that PeopleSoft has. I would recommend a "show me" attitude toward the HR component of its offerings. Look at the actual functionality, and make certain that the product in fact provides easy-to-use solutions to your genuine problems.

SAP

SAP, the third member of the big three (or, in its own eyes, the first member), similarly emphasizes e-business (the Internet), analytics, and self-service.

Advantages

Particularly for companies in manufacturing, SAP holds the attraction of its long record of success in manufacturing. It understands the process, and it understands how other enterprise functions interact with manufacturing.

Considerations

Like PeopleSoft, SAP took a nosedive in popularity at the turn of the century and is continuing to prove that it can restore its tarnished image. It seemed to many that it lost touch with its constituency during its glory years of the Nineties. As it retooled for the Internet era, it faced a bigger challenge than even PeopleSoft in building its product into an Internet product from the ground up, a challenge that many regard as ongoing.

Because of its roots in manufacturing, which is more mechanical and less people-oriented than HR, many question whether SAP will ever truly understand and appreciate the human concerns of HR. Look closely at its offerings to make certain that they in fact do address real HR issues at your company.

OTHER ASPIRANTS

No matter how big the big three companies may be, three seems like too limited a number to work with. Following are descriptions of some of the other companies that provide HR software for large companies. In some cases, these companies position themselves as mid-market providers. Truly oversized companies may want to take note. However, they service the high end of the mid-market, and in many instances can meet the needs even of larger companies.

Although none of the companies listed here seem to have the market presence of the big three, they do service large companies and just may provide the energy, personal attention, pricing, or other features that your company is looking for.

J.D. Edwards

With J.D. Edwards, the song is the same as that of the larger companies.

Advantages

Particular strengths it may bring to the table include the fact that it is smaller than the big three (and therefore possibly more maneuverable) and that it is *not* one of the big three (and therefore possibly "hungrier" and more eager to compete on price, service, and other matters). Here is J.D. Edwards' summary of itself, from its website:

> "With J.D. Edwards human resources solutions, you can easily bring e-business functionality to your HR department. E-business and workflow technologies are transforming the way HR departments operate by allowing you to push data collection and maintenance to the source—employees and managers. With our employee self-service and manager self-service applications, your HR staff can focus on strategic tasks such as workforce planning and employee development. And your employees and managers experience a higher degree of

workplace satisfaction when more information and tools are available to them. Given the tight labor market that exists today, increased employee satisfaction is a critical factor in retaining your valuable employees.

"J.D. Edwards' HR solutions are designed to meet the constantly changing needs of HR departments in medium to large-sized organizations. You know the drill—employee master information, applicant tracking, requisition management, position control, headcount budgeting, EEO, OSHA, etc. But in addition to traditional functionality, we have added exciting new technologies that transform the world of HR. Recognized as the market leader for enterprise solutions in the middle market, J.D. Edwards understands the business problems, budget limitations, and cultural environments you work in every day—and has developed solutions that work for you."

Lawson Software

Another attractive company that can boast that it is not one of the big three is Lawson Software, based in St. Paul, Minnesota.

Advantages

The company prides itself on the attention and service it provides to its customers, and it specializes in particular vertical markets, namely: healthcare, professional services, financial services, and retail. Here is the company's quick description of itself:

> "The Lawson suite of human resources applications helps automate the core functions of the HR department, such as payroll and benefits administration. The HR department can use the Lawson Recruiting Service to build a strong database of candidates, and Workforce Analytics Service helps you analyze your organization's effectiveness within your industry in areas such as revenue per employee, time to hire, and turnover rate."

Offering e-business, self-services, and analytics, Lawson is particularly proud of its benchmarking, which, it says, "Allows organizations to measure themselves with industry benchmark data to realize the true value of HR."

Considerations

Lawson has a reputation for taking excellent care of its customers. According to a former executive at one of the big three providers, Lawson "kills the opposition" when it competes on price. What you may not find at Lawson, however, is industry-leading innovation. Look more to PeopleSoft or Microsoft or small players like NuView for that. Lawson is not particularly an early implementer of technologies, and you have to consider the tradeoffs when looking at a company that specializes in vertical markets. Yes, Lawson serves healthcare well. But what if you are in manufacturing? Lawson would help you, but perhaps not with the expertise of SAP.

Big companies are a big marketplace. They have admirable budgets, which means, inevitably, that vendors seek them out. A big three may predominate in the HR market for large-sized companies, and two or three others may deserve mention along with the three, but others can also operate on a large scale. They may have only one of the pieces of the popular puzzle in large-scale HR—for example, primarily analytics or primarily self-service. But large companies themselves, they aspire to serve the large market and, given the opportunity, can do it well—particularly in their areas of specialization. Here is a look at two such players, although such a brief listing makes no pretense of being exhaustive.

SAS

SAS Institute Inc., of Cary, North Carolina, has become synonymous with statistical analysis. With analytics becoming one of the main pillars of HR for large companies, how could the world leader in analytics resist the temptation to bring its offering to the marketplace? In truth, SAS has not been able to resist the temptation.

Advantages

Here is what SAS says on its website about its offering:

> "HR Vision gives you organizational insights that enable you to plan effective human capital strategies and measure and compare your company's best practices. It's the only solution that combines award-winning data warehousing technology with Web-based, HR-specific decision support. And it's designed by HR professionals—not statisticians."

What is the HR technology selector to make of a company like SAS? First of all, take with a grain of salt the notion that SAS is "designed by HR professionals—not the statisticians." SAS is known worldwide for its statistics or, in other words, its analytics, the trend that is taking over HR these days in the form of human capital management. The first reason to take an interest in SAS, I would say, would be its expertise not in HR but in analytics. As HR begins to move into the area of SAS's traditional strength, why not look to SAS for leadership in statistical analysis? Just as you might look to Oracle for strength in databases (and not necessarily in HR per se) or to Microsoft for leadership in its strength (integrated and standardized solutions that control a market segment), why not look to SAS for its strength—statistics.

Considerations

Take a hard look at the product's ease of use. Evaluate whether or not its statistical capabilities overpower the average HR user. Consider whether or not it understands HR. Decide, in general, whether it has become a genuine HR product or is a statistical program in HR clothing. Although only careful evaluation can decide the issue, one might expect SAS to excel in analytics. At the same time, one might wonder if it can compete with the PeopleSofts of the world in understanding HR overall. SAS has yet to prove that it is more than a statistical package adapted to the burgeoning HR marketplace. Perhaps it is an overall solution, however, and an alternative to the dominant presence of others in the marketplace.

Computer Associates—interBiz

Known as a company that has grown primarily through acquisition, Computer Associates International, Inc., has acquired an HR provider as part of its overall suite.

Advantages

Here is the company's description of its HR product:

> "interBiz is proud to announce general availability of Masterpiece/Net HRMS, part of the ongoing interBiz commitment to provide our clients with innovative business software that meets their changing business needs. Masterpiece/Net HRMS incorporates new functionality and enhancements across the main feature areas, human resources, benefits, and payroll, but is much more than just an update

to our existing HRMS solution, CAHRISMA. Just a sampling of the improvements:

- Web-enabled, operating across multiple platforms, and on multiple databases;
- Employee self-service option to empower employees at their desktop or via kiosks, reduce data processing time, and improve data accuracy;
- Fully integrated with Masterpiece/Net financials for smooth back-office integration;
- Available alone or with the added power of BizWorks, the eBusiness Process Management Suite;
- Pre-packaged or custom-built key performance indicators (KPIs) offered with BizWorks, to help boost your company's bottom line; and
- Choice of delivery models—traditional or managed hosting through interBiz Online."

Considerations

interBiz, like SAS, does not seem to have the complete HR savvy of some of the leading players. It emphasizes its technology behind the scenes, it appears to me, even more than its solutions in the forefront. Nevertheless, it is a large company and it targets large companies. It is an HR provider, and just may be a company for you to include on your checklist of candidate companies.

A CAUTIOUS PERSPECTIVE

The sheer size of the high end defines what takes place there. Whereas you might manhandle a $500 HR software package to your heart's content, you might find yourself manhandled by your $500,000 high-end package. At the same time, if you harness the power of the high end effectively, you may perform well, not just with the software, but with your job function and in your overall contribution to the company. Small and mid-sized companies may have reservations about using the high-end providers, however.

Following is some information you should keep in mind if you are considering asking management to invest in software from companies specializing in high-end products.

High-End Software: HR's Limited Say

To be frank, if you are looking for high-end human resources software—software for a company of more than ten thousand people and perhaps a lot more than that—you may have a fairly limited say in the software that will be selected anyway. You might want to go after smaller versions of HR software for the simple reason that such software might empower you rather than dominate you.

Perhaps someone in a large company would want to select software for a small portion of the company—a division or a department—in which case the suggestions from the previous chapters of this book would apply. If, however, a company is selecting software for its entire enterprise, then—as just noted—an individual or small group would likely have limited say.

Although HR may have limited say in what software will be in place, HR software is likely to be in place in these corporations. The small say that you may have just may be timely and influential, making a large difference in corporate direction. Certainly time you spend researching HR software and helping with the decision is time well spent for two reasons.

1. You may influence the decision in a positive direction.

2. You learn a great deal from the process about what you can expect from your HR software and about how to get the most out of it, whatever product you end up using.

Be aware, though, that some truths of the marketplace no longer seem to apply at the high end, such as these:

The RFP Is No Longer in Vogue. The RFP may not be in vogue when evaluating software of a manageable size, including mid-market software. However, the RFP is a *must* for larger companies. Whether you choose to call the document an RFP, an RFI (request for information), or simply an inquiry, you have to spell out your requirements systematically for the vendors and ask them to respond systematically as well.

Script the Demo for Your Vendors. You can certainly indicate to vendors what you want to see in a sales demo. The principle still applies. But high-end HR vendors have such ambitious offerings that, truth be told, you face challenge enough in simply beginning to understand what they offer.

A Team Approach Has Only Limited Value. For evaluating smaller packages, one informed HR person can take a good deal of initiative and generally force the issue in reaching a decision. IT may provide a quick set of requirements and a quick appraisal of HR's recommendation. Finance and upper management may want to have some involvement. For all the commitment involved in a high-end package, though, HR is genuinely dependent on other departments for assistance. You need a thorough review from IT, careful evaluation from other departments that may use the software (which may include all departments in the company), and in-depth analysis by the management that has to take responsibility for the decision.

"Conflicted Consultants" and Other Cautions

High-end HR systems tend to be so impressive that they can in fact be overwhelming. They say so much about themselves that, to many observers, they end up saying almost nothing that they can truly "take home with them." A note of realism may be worthwhile before taking a look at the offerings from this end of the marketplace. Such realism may bring you down to earth a bit and make you feel bolder as you evaluate the offerings. They are so large as to seem almost unreal and impenetrable. In truth, they are quite real. If you do not see past the impressive surface, you do not give yourself a fair chance of adopting a system that will be meaningful to you. Realism, too, helps you be fair to the vendors. When they appear too perfect and unreachable, people tend to feel, "Since they are so great, I will not go near them. We are a human company."

Here are a few of the cautions about problems often associated with high-end HR software providers:

Long Implementation Times (and High Costs). The high-end HR providers have been addressing the issues, but skepticism remains in the marketplace. Implementation of ERP systems could take many months, even years. I heard of one company that simply decided to consider implementation an open-ended, never-ending process. Worse, sometimes the implementations can be so far from the desired result that companies invest millions in the software, then simply cancel.

Conflicted Consultants. High-end consultants and high-end HR software companies often have a close relationship. Accounting firms have raised eyebrows by earning lucrative consulting contracts from the same firms they audit. In what may be a parallel situation, HR consulting firms earn lucrative implementation contracts from the very companies they have recommended during the selection process. Some of the success of the high-end providers, says mid-market vendor Jim Spoor, "is also attributable to the very close alliances they have formed with the consulting firms that assist large employers in their evaluation and selection of software. Once the selection is done, these consulting firms then continue to provide consulting services in the implementation process. This is how many of those system implementations end up well into the seven-figure range of costs."

Sometimes consulting firms openly engage in formal partnerships with vendors. Unless you know of the relationship, you can mistake a "competitive analysis" of the marketplace funded by one of the vendors for an objective study from the consulting firm. If the study is funded by one of the vendors being studied, how much value does it have? "Quite a bit," some may aver. As I reflect on the process from a distance and consider the veto power exercised by the company holding the purse strings, I again come back to the question: "How much value could it have?" At a minimum, you should be sure to find out what ties exist between consultants and vendors so that you can discount consultant reports accordingly.

More Sizzle Than Steak. The high-end products promise to revolutionize your company. Rarely do you hear any more about solving the classic problem of the Nineties—too much paper, too much data. The high-end products launch right into the strategic analysis of complex information—a function hardly commonplace for most HR folks in the past. Human resources finds itself needing training to utilize the capabilities in the new system or simply taking advantage of some small, fairly pedestrian capability of a big, impressive system.

Computerphobia. No one is afraid to jump in and use a one-person HR system. If you make mistakes or crash the computer, you can just buy another piece of software. You do not bring the company to its knees. Log onto a system that is interconnected with satellite offices around the globe as well as with all departments in your location, and you can develop a case of computerphobia. Crash that system, and people will come storming into your office in a hurry. Enter inaccurate information, and you may throw off calculations in departments you do not even know exist. You probably will not. The fear is probably unfounded. But large systems nevertheless do instill a certain reluctance on the part of some HR users.

Challenging Migration to the Net. All the large Internet providers have adopted an Internet strategy, which means that they are rewriting millions of lines of computer code in a completely new language. Saying so is one thing; carrying it out is another. Sweet, intricate applications already existed in the old medium. Could the providers bring up those same applications in the new medium without leaving things out or without having things break? Of course not. The more realistic question for you to ask as you evaluate the software would be, "Have they now gotten far enough along in development to leave the initial problems behind?"

Such cautions are not a reason to stay away from high ends systems. They are merely a sobering influence in what can become a runaway race to implementation. If your company is large enough, you should certainly proceed with selecting HR software. But you may want to proceed deliberately and with caution.

CONCLUSION

Like every other part of the HR marketplace, then, the high end is quite fascinating. It seems to have rules of its own, rules dictated above all by sheer size, but it nevertheless has some of the characteristics of the rest of the market. Companies ultimately have to provide real solutions to real users. And companies have to compete successfully with one another. As an HR department, you cannot go into the high end and expect to make a choice with the same freedom you can with low-end and mid-market software. At the high end, you can witness the trends that are likely to influence all the rest of the marketplace. In examining such software, you can decide whether it will genuinely meet your needs or whether you would like to adopt HR software from an independent HR vendor to use in conjunction with enterprise-wide software at the company.

Closing Thoughts

To the uninitiated, buying HR software might appear to be little more than reaching out and accepting one of the possibilities out there. To those who have surveyed the field, though, HR software is a world unto itself. The choices are many, the potential rewards are great, and the risks are numerous. Throughout this book, chapter by chapter, you have seen the steps in successful software selection. In this chapter, you take a final look at HR software selection and review the stakes, the process, and the risks.

AMBITIOUS UNDERTAKING

You can start your search for HR software without knowing a great deal about the software or about the process. I see little wrong with just getting started however you can. As the old saying goes, even the longest journey begins with a single step. Nevertheless, you will quickly find out that there is much more to the process of selecting HR software than you imagined. Here are some of the things you have to consider:

- *The large number of vendors.* The number of vendors is in the thousands, and almost all of them are credible and valuable in some way.

- *The tiers of the marketplace.* Unless you know about the tiers, you might think of the marketplace as one homogeneous place. Most companies benefit by matching their company size to one or another tier of the marketplace—low-end, high-end, or middle.

- *The flavors of the products being offered.* Thanks to a nicely competitive marketplace, providers are looking for an edge. One will be strong in its benefits offerings, another in its overall training and support, another in price, and another in technical design. The variety gives you leverage as a buyer but also requires that you do your homework.

- *The value in doing the work yourself.* Working with a consultant is a viable choice, but doing the selection yourself allows you to become intimately familiar with both your own business processes and the solutions the software provides.

- *The need to move through the process efficiently.* Vendors are busy people who make choices about how to use their time. You, likewise, have much to do and limited time. If you move through the process effectively with such tools as an effective RFP and a good demo script, you are most likely to find the results you are looking for.

Human resources software selection can hardly be a "toss off" any more. If there was a time when the choices were few, that time has passed. Selecting HR software is a complete business process, I hasten to add, a process that can be enjoyable from start to finish.

HIGH STAKES

Human resources software is not a side issue or a form of amusement. Much is at stake, and software impacts HR in the following areas:

- *Effectiveness of the HR department.* With automation, you can find answers for your people on everything from benefits to compensation to their career path and their training. Without it, those answers may not be so readily available.

- *Efficiency of HR.* Perhaps I should have listed this one first. Automation saves time and gets rid of paper. A report on "the number of people who used cafeteria style benefits" might take an instant to compile with software but several weeks to compile from mere paper sources.

- *Competitiveness of the company.* Often HR is concerned primarily with keeping the existing workforce running smoothly, which in itself contributes to competitiveness. Human resources can also contribute to timely, effective hiring and to such matters as competitive compensation or overall strategic planning.

- *Retention.* Dissatisfied employees may point to some other cause than HR as a reason for leaving a company, but HR can often eliminate issues before they turn into problems. Smooth handling of performance reviews, benefits, compensation, leave taking, and compliance matters can help keep the workforce satisfied.

- *Viability of the HR department.* Today's workplace is simply too streamlined and too competitive to carry much dead wood. An HR department that is not forward-looking and viable is making itself into an "endangered species." Automation is one of the best ways for a department to be a valuable contributor to the enterprise.

STREAMLINED SELECTION PROCESS

Like the technology that results, the evaluation process has become increasingly streamlined over recent years. A bit of a lumbering process in its infancy, HR software selection has become nimble while also gaining force. The most prominent example is likely the decreased importance of the RFP, which used to be a primary document in software selection and could be painstakingly thorough.

Unfortunately, both the process of creating the RFP and the process of completing it could bog people down. Companies were looking for ways to get around the RFP, often compromising the effectiveness of the search as they did so. Now many who select HR software use a shortened RFP to gather information quickly without scaring off vendors. Here are some of the other steps that are becoming streamlined and modern:

- *Needs assessment.* First, companies had to learn the importance of doing the needs assessment. The step was often overlooked, with the unfortunate consequence that companies began looking for software without knowing what they wanted the software to do. Once the value of the needs assessment became established, companies sometimes tended to look at it as an end in itself. Now on a middle ground, companies are tending to see the needs analysis as a quick way to set forth the genuine business needs that the new software is to address.

- *Scripted demo.* Software demonstrations used to be vendor-controlled circuses, for the most part. Uninformed HR folks were captive audiences for vendors who told them what they ought to look for, then informed them that the vendor's software best met those needs. Now users are gaining the ability to spell out exactly what they need to see when the vendors demonstrate their wares.

- *Selection matrix.* A selection matrix can become so complex as to be almost unreadable. Evaluators can put all the information from their evaluation onto a collection of worksheet pages, impressing everyone without truly providing answers. A well-done selection matrix displays the strengths and weaknesses of a number of products in a form that allows you to compare them readily.

- *Negotiations.* Some of the "rules of engagement" are beginning to be understood by both sides. Software evaluators are doing more than simply holding out for the right price. Vendors, for their part, are providing multiple options to purchasers, such as multiple modules. Also, the competitive marketplace can help keep vendors honest.

- *Implementation planning.* Even the best evaluation process comes up short if implementation is not successful. More and more, savvy HR departments are learning to keep implementation in mind almost from the beginning of the selection process. The point of selection, after all, is not to make a good choice. It is to solve business problems. Only good implementation of the right software truly solves problems.

RISKS

Human resources software selection is fraught with risks from the very beginning. The purpose of this book is to protect you against some of them. No one can protect against acts of God, such as the well-respected company that suddenly closes its doors, causing you to lose your data. Such cataclysms are rare, but the steps of software selection do have their "gotchas." Here are some of the risks of which to be aware:

- *Overdoing the needs analysis.* You may face some inertia as you look to begin the needs analysis. Get started, though, and the process can be fun . . . altogether too much fun. You can get bogged down in tracking every possible bit of data and every possible report you have made or would like to make. You can waste time reviewing needs of other companies that have little to do with your own. Create a needs analysis that defines your business needs, and get on with the process.

- *Deciding whether to employ a consultant.* You can err by having a consultant or by not having one. If you do not have one, you lose out on valuable expertise and experience. If you have one, make sure he or she is qualified. An unqualified software consultant brings you the worst of both worlds—the expense of hiring a consultant but an unqualified person doing the work.

- *Overloading the RFP.* You have heard enough in earlier chapters to know the risks with the RFP. Request information from vendors, but do not overload them with requests for information you do not truly need.

- *Engaging in power struggles.* Selecting software is a people process, and the same people problems can arise during the process as arise in other business processes at the company. If a person makes a premature commitment to a supplier or makes up his or her mind too quickly, the process does not play out fully.

- *Lacking management support.* All your research is for naught if management does not approve your recommendation. You can use thorough software selection as a tool to persuade management. You are best off, though, if you have management's support from the beginning.

- *Implementing poorly.* If you focus too much on selection, you may overlook the fact that the best software still has to meet your needs on your equipment with your employee population and your HR people using the system.

ONGOING REWARDS

Human resources technology strengthens your department and the company. Here are some other examples where technology helps HR address modern needs:

- *Hiring.* The whole process of hiring has undergone a transformation. Technology helps assure that the HR department functions as an aggressive recruiter, a relentless tracker, a systematic and fair interviewer, and more.

- *Training.* Human resources software helps on multiple fronts. It helps track the training needs of the workforce. It helps schedule the training. It helps assess the results of the training, often by using skills and competencies to provide scientific results.

- *Compliance.* Simply keeping up-to-date with federal regulations is a demanding task. Technology often places the latest regulations at your fingertips.

- *Benefits administration.* Benefits are a complete field of study. Even specialists have difficulty keeping track of the possibilities. Thanks to technology, HR departments can administer rich, varied benefits programs for the workforce.

- *Strategic analysis.* Human capital management is becoming a way of life in modern business. Companies want to analyze the workforce and deploy it effectively. The HR department is at the center of the process.

The reason to purchase HR software is for the results the software brings, nothing less. Human resources software brings powerful, compelling results, and the results are becoming stronger day by day.

Human resources software is a world unto itself—a rich and rewarding world. The process of selecting software can itself become a specialty within the world of HR. The technically strong user of HR software can be a valuable member of any HR department. And almost any member of an HR department these days benefits by knowing at least the rudiments of an HR software system. Selecting the right HR software for your company is one of the most valuable contributions one can make to the company, right up there with designing an effective business process or coming up with a valuable product or service for the company to provide.

This book has shown you how to go through the process of choosing technology that strengthens your HR department and your company. As an HR person, you can make one of your most significant contributions to your company and to the people you serve by providing yourself with well-designed HR software that addresses the present and future needs of the company.

Appendix

Software Products Profiled in the Book

Product	Company	Contact Information
ADP Enterprise HRMS	ADP	Roseland, NJ www.adp.com (973) 974-5000
Abra Suite	Abra Enterprise	Best Software, Inc. Reston, VA www.bestsoftware.com (703) 709-5200
Authoria HR Suite	Authoria, Inc.	Waltham, MA www.authoria.com (781) 530-2000
CSS HRIZON	Automatic Data Processing (ADP)	Roseland, NJ www.adp.com (973) 974-5000
Cyborg Solution Series/ST	Cyborg Systems, Inc.	Chicago, IL www.cyborg.com (312) 279-7000

Product	Company	Contact Information
DynaSuite	Performance Software, Inc.	East Hanover, NJ www.dynasuite.com (973) 739-1780
eEnterprise Human Resources	Microsoft Great Plains	Fargo, ND www.greatplains.com (701) 281-6500
Employ!	Deploy Solutions, Inc.	Westwood, MA www.deploy.com (781) 461-9024
Employease Network	Employease, Inc.	Atlanta, GA www.employease.com (888) 327-3638
e-Recruiting	Lawson Software, Inc.	St. Paul, MN www.lawson.com (651) 767-7000
ExecuTRACK Enterprise	HRSoft, LLC	Morristown, NJ www.hrsoft.com (800) 437-6781
Genesys Enterprise Series	Genesys Software Systems, Inc.	Methuen, MA www.genesys-soft.com (800) 540-5470
Hire.com	Hire.com	Austin, TX www.hire.com (512) 583-4400
HireRight	HireRight, Inc.	Irvine, CA www.hireright.com (949) 428-5800
Hiresystems	BrassRing Systems, a division of BrassRing, Inc.	Waltham, MA www.brassringsystems.com (781) 736-1000

Product	Company	Contact Information
HR Suite	Authoria, Inc.	Waltham, MA www.authoria.com (781) 530-2000
HR Tools	Archer Software	Lewis Center, OH www.archersoftware.com (740) 657-8934
HR Vision	SAS Institute, Inc.	Cary, NC www.sas.com (919) 677-8000
HRIS-Pro, HR Entre	Human Resource MicroSystems	San Francisco, CA www.hrms.com (415) 362-8400
HRmgr	RMS, Resource Management Software	Wrightstown, WI www.rms-hrmgr.com (920) 532-4017
HROffice & HROffice Enterprise	Ascentis Software Corporation	Bellevue, WA www.ascentis.com (425) 462-7171
HRSource	Auxillium West	Cupertino, CA www.auxillium.com (408) 257-5054
hrWindows	PerfectSoftware	Norwalk, CT www.perfectsoftware.com (203) 852-9100
Icarian eWorkforce	Icarian, Inc.	Sunnyvale, CA www.icarian.com (408) 743-5700
IdealHire	Pentawave, Inc.	Phoenix, AZ www.idealhire.com (480) 281-0300

Product	Company	Contact Information
iGreentree Employment System	Greentree Systems, Inc.	Campbell, CA www.greentreesystems.com (408) 879-1410 or (800) 348-8845
iVantage	SPECTRUM Human Resource Systems Corporation	Denver, CO www.spectrumhr.com (303) 592-3200
Kadiri TotalComp	Kadiri, Inc.	Burlingame, CA www.kadiri.com (877) 642-2299
link2HR	MBH Solutions, Inc.	Teaneck, NJ www.mbhsolutions.com (201) 287-0901
Masterpiece/Net HRMS	Computer Associates	Chicago, IL interbiz.cai.com (312) 258-6000
Microsoft, Inc.	Microsoft Great Plains Solutions	Fargo, ND www.greatplains.com (701) 281-6500
MyHRIS	NuView Systems, Inc.	Wilmington, MA www.nuviewinc.com (978) 988-7884
mySAP	SAP AG	Walldorf, Germany www.sap.com
OPEN4	Bonnecaze, McLeroy & Harrison, Inc.	Addison, TX www.open4.com (972) 702-0892
Oracle Human Resources	Oracle Corporation	Redwood Shores, CA www.oracle.com (650) 506-7000

Product	Company	Contact Information
People Manager	KnowledgePoint	Petaluma, CA www.knowledgepoint.com (707) 762-0333
PeopleSoft 8	PeopleSoft, Inc.	Pleasanton, CA www.peoplesoft.com (925) 225-3000
People-Trak	Technical Difference, Inc.	Bonsall, CA www.people-trak.com (800) 809-5731
Recruitsoft	Recruitsoft, Inc.	San Francisco, CA www.recruitsoft.com (888) 836-3669
reSource HR	Ceridian	Minneapolis, MN www.ceridian.com (952) 853-8100
Simpata	Simpata, Inc.	Folsom, CA www.simpata.com (877) 477-4675
SkillView	SkillView Technologies, Inc.	Plaistow, NH www.skillview.com (603) 382-9882
Solution Series/ST	Cyborg Systems, Inc.	Chicago, IL www.cyborg.com (312) 279-7000
The Safari Headhunting System	Safari Software Products, Inc.	Horicon, WI www.safarisoftproducts.com (920) 485-4100
!Trak-It HR	iTrak-It Solutions, Inc.	Citrus Heights, CA www.trak-it.com (916) 728-4880

Product	Company	Contact Information
UltiPro	Ultimate Software, Inc.	Weston, FL www.ultimatesoftware.com (954) 331-7000 (800) 432-1729
Visual 360	MindSolve Technologies, Inc.	Gainesville, FL www.mindsolve.com (352) 372-0000
Workforce Central Suite	Kronos Incorporated	Chelmsford, MA www.kronos.com (978) 250-9800
Workforce Management	J.D. Edwards	Denver, CO www.jdedwards.com (303) 334-4000
Workforce Vision	Criterion Incorporated	Irving, TX www.peopleclick.com (800) 782-1818

References

Fletcher, R. (2001). *The 7 habits of a highly effective negotiation team, project perspectives.* IHRIM.link

Fletcher, R., & Katavole, D. (2001, June). *Highly effective negotiation teams: How to make license negotiations pay off.* Paper presented at the IHRIM Spring Conference & Exposition, San Diego, California.

Fletcher, R., & Hanscome, R. (2002). *Sorting out e-recruitment: Assessing the vendor marketplace.* Presentation at IHRIM and Twin Cities Electronic Recruiters Joint meeting.

Fox, F.J. (1998, August). Do it yourself HRMS evaluations. *HR Magazine,* pp. 28–36.

Frantzreb, R. (1999). *The 1999 personnel software census: Vol. 1, departmental software.* Roseville, CA: Advanced Personnel Systems.

Frantzreb, R. (2000). *The 2000 personnel software census: Vol. 2, HR information systems.* Roseville, CA: Advanced Personnel Systems.

Greengard, S. (1999, June). HR technology trends: Beyond the millennium. *Workforce,* pp. 3–7

Hinojos, J.A., & Miller, M. (1998, July/August). Methodologies for selecting the right vendor. *Benefits & Compensation Solutions,* pp. 38–42.

Lokhandwala, S. (2001). MyHRIS: The HCM Implementation Tool for the Corporation, White Paper.

Loofbourrow, T., Kurzner, L., Ransom, P., et al. (2001). e-Benefits: An IHRIM go-to-guide (G2G). IHRIM.

Meade, J. (1999, May). Adapting to the shifting software market. *HR Magazine,* pp. 3–6.

Moore, K. (1999, August). Wire story. *HR News.*

Morgan, L. (1998, May). *The future of HR technology.* Paper presented to Madison Area SHRM Group, Madison, Wisconsin.

Morgan, L. (1999). *Human resources and the new technology.* Paper presented at ACA.

Roberts, B. (1999, June). Who's in charge of HRIS? *HR Magazine,* pp. 130–140.

Ryder, J., Schwarts, L., & Andrews, J. (1991, August). *18 steps to selecting a human resource information system.* SHRM White Paper. Arlington, VA: SHRM.

Spoor, J. (2000). *HR and the workplace: What will it be like in the year 2010? A vision of the future.* Presentation at IHRIM.

Spoor, J. (2000, September). *Analytics in HR.* White paper.

Spoor, J. (2001, December). *Fresh perspectives on evaluating and selecting an HR system for small and mid-sized organizations.* White paper from www.spectrumhr.com.

Witschger, J. (2000). *HRMS software—Myths and reality.* White paper from Technical Differences, Inc., Bonsall, California.

Witschger, J. (2000). *People, the ultimate technology.* White paper from Technical Differences, Inc., in Bonsall, California.

About the Author

James G. Meade, Ph.D., is an author, HR consultant, and magazine writer. He began writing software reviews for *HR Magazine* in 1989 and continued to write reviews there for over a decade . . . in recent years preparing one or more reviews every month. In preparing his reviews, he enjoyed the unusual opportunity to view a first-class "dog and pony" show from one vendor after another while, in addition, interviewing third-party users about their experiences with the product under scrutiny. As a consultant, he has advised companies of varying sizes and in varying industries as they approached the HR software market, evaluated products, and reached a decision.

Dr. Meade is the author of twenty-five books, most on computer and business topics, including several in the best-selling *Dummies* series. His own computer bestsellers have included *Ami Pro for Dummies* and *Using PowerPoint.*

Index

Human resources: benefits of software to, 189–191, 348–349, 351–352; complexity of, 24; cost of, 24–25; data modules for, 36; expertise of, 24; for human capital management, 27–28; legislation knowledge of, 24; management's view of, 23; needs assessment considerations for, 88–92; objectivity of, 67; pressures on, 23, 25; standard reporting of, 26–27; as strategic partner, 25–27, 191; technology knowledge of, 18–19, 28–29; trends in functioning of, 25–29; workforce management function of, 25–26

I

Icarian eWorkforce (Icarian, Inc.), 328, 329, 330, 331, 355

IdealHire (Pentawave, Inc.), 327, 328, 330, 355

iGreentree Employment System (Greentree Systems, Inc.), 315–316, 356

IHRIM. *See* International Association for Human Resource Management (IHRIM)

Implementation: and adaptation of business process, 202–203; consultants for planning of, 76–77, 198; critical software concerns in, 199–201; and customization of software, 205; and hardware, 199, 204–205; of high-end software, 344; key components of, 204–205; overview of, 197–198; project team in, 198, 204; and reports, 200; sample plan for, 203–205; schedule for, 199, 204; before signing contract, 185–186; testing software during, 203; training during, 201–202; vendors in, 198

interBiz. *See* Masterpiece/Net HRMS

International Association for Human Resource Management (IHRIM), 12, 57

International Data Group (IDC), 78

Internet: benefits of, 29–30; and employee self-service, 30; and management self-service, 30; trends in use of, 29–30

IT department, 182

iVantange (SPECTRUM Human Resources Systems Corporation): benefits of, 264–265, 266–267; company contact information for, 356; disadvantages of, 267–268; overview of, 264; primary capabilities of, 40, 41; summary of, 268

J

J. D. Edwards, 338–339, 358

K

Kadirir TotalComp (Kadiri Inc.): benefits of, 296; company contact information for, 356; disadvantages of, 297; overview of, 45, 46; summary of, 298

Kaplan, R. S., 27

Katavola, D., 181

Kile, B., 301

Kronos Time and Attendance Tracking, 45

L

Lane, E., 27

Lange, M., 27

Lawler, E., 25

Lawson Software, 330, 331–332, 339–340, 354

Legal department, 182

Legislation, 24

Lehman, J., 102–103

Link2HR (MBH Solutions), 308, 309, 311
Litigation, 191
Lokhandwala, S., 282
Low-end software. *See* Software, low-end

M

Management: buyoff of, 19, 75–76; consultants' interaction with, 75–76; needs assessment considerations of, 85–86; as negotiations participant, 181, 182; objectivity of, 67–68; PowerPoint presentation to, 188; presenting benefits of software to, 189; presenting research results to, 192; presenting return on investment to, 193–195; self-service of, 30; selling *versus* reporting software to, 188; view of human resources, 23

Manual records, 92
Masterpiece/Net HRMS (interBiz), 341–342, 356
Matheny, D., 236, 237
Mayo, L., 279
MBH Solutions. *See* Link2HR
Meade Ink, Inc., 79
Merritt, D., 336
META Group, 79
Microsoft, 18–19, 87, 121, 287, 288, 356
Mid-market software. *See* Software, mid-market
Miller, M., 60–61, 95, 106, 187
MindSolve Technologies. *See* Visual 360
Moe, J., 46
Moore, K., 25
Morgan, L., 23, 25, 31
Moxley, C., 248
Mueller, C., 299–300
Munini, L., 263–264, 269
Myers, K. D., 66
MyHRIS (NuView Systems), 280, 356

N

Needs assessments: of application service providers, 88; company background for, 85; consultants for, 68–70; data types identification for, 91–92; of databases, 87; examples of, 95–102; of hardware, 87; human resources considerations for, 88–92; identification of priorities in, 95; management considerations for, 85–86; of networking, 87; of operating systems, 87; overview of, 83–84; presenting to management, 192; of pricing, 93–94; of reports, 91; risk identification in, 94–95; of software, 88; of technology, 86–88; of telecommunications, 88; of training, 94

Negotiations: and emotions, 185, 186; key points in, 183–185; losing control of, 186; overview of, 179–180; participants in, 181–182; presenting to management, 192; and pricing, 184; problems in, 185–186

Networking, 87, 213
Norton, D. P., 27
NuView Systems. *See* MyHRIS

O

Objectives, defining of, 69–70
Occupational Safety and Health Administration, 24
Open4 (BMH, Inc.), 164, 285–287, 288, 289, 356
Operating systems, 87
Oracle, 87, 337, 356
Outsourcing, 23–25

P

Payroll department, 181–182, 214
Pentawave. *See* IdealHire